I WORE
BABE RUTH'S HAT

Sport and Society

Series Editors
Randy Roberts
Aram Goudsouzian

Founding Editors
Benjamin G. Rader
Randy Roberts

A list of books in the series appears at the end of this book.

I WORE
BABE RUTH'S HAT

FIELD NOTES FROM A LIFE IN SPORTS

DAVID W. ZANG

University of Illinois Press
Urbana, Chicago, and Springfield

Library of Congress Control Number: 2015935679

Not a word would ever make it to the page without the love and support of my wife, Joanie. She understands and takes seriously my serious love of sports, which is exceeded only by my love for her.

To Monk Howard, Steve Miller, Tommy Webb, Jimmy MacFadden, Denny Kubeck, Dave Noyes, Chalkhead, Sam and Walt, Dutchie, Les the Lip, Mike Colley, Pitt, Arte, John Michael, Duffer, Stultzie, "Scrapheap" Osterhoudt, the Three Daves, Big Strong Man, Geno Harris, Larry, Llary, Jon, and four late greats—Buzz Shank, Ira Nesbitt, Brian Farrar, and Tom "Ping" Young—in the vain hope that somebody will remember us all.

Note to Rhinee Yeung, who sat in front of me for three years of high school homeroom and wrote the following in my senior yearbook: "Dear David, Funny, comical, and always for the best things in the world. What do you do with that in life? But of course we all grow up eventually so the same should happen to you. Good luck after all." I'm getting there, Rhinee. Thanks for the inspiration.

Some names (though none of the above and not all the ones you may suspect) have been changed, either to protect people from further grief they don't deserve or to protect myself from the offended who might wish to visit future grief upon me.

Time is the most nostalgic of elements: time past, which determines who we are and how we got here; time present, which in its more poignant and pleasurable moments is quickly acquiring the patina of memory; and time still to come, that backdrop for the projection of both our fears and our hopes for the physical and spiritual Arcadia we ache to return to.

—Robert Eisner

CONTENTS

ACKNOWLEDGMENTS

A lifetime immersed in a subject means inevitably that some who are deserving will not get the thank-yous I owe them. There are, however, some people without whom the writing of this book would have been impossible. Friends and colleagues Elliott Gorn, Randy Roberts, Larry Malley, Dave Wiggins, Janice and Denny Kubeck, Susan Bandy, Sunny Cook, Steve Miller, Anne Romano, Robert Higgs, Mark Dyreson, and Bob Osterhoudt all read portions at one time or another, offering useful suggestions at times and encouragement always. Dick Crepeau, Don Mrozek, and Bob Osterhoudt had huge influences on the way I perceive and think about both sports and history. Don Steel, and my late father, Bill Zang, reinforced my belief in the value of play. Thanks to Steve Kralich, Jerry Wrenn, Walt McCulley, Sam Walton, John Eshleman, Tom Webb, Monk Howard, Dave Wottle, Claude Moore, and Greg Black for insights that became part of the narrative. I would also like to acknowledge Arnold Rampersad's fine 1997 biography of Jackie Robinson, from which I used many facts and quotes in my essay on Robinson, and the work of my late friend Jules Tygiel in his seminal *Baseball's Great Experiment*.

Thanks to Bill Stetka of the Baltimore Orioles and Paul Dzyak of the Penn State Sports Archives for help with photograph acquisition. I greatly appreciated the improvements suggested by Stephen Barnett and Jennifer Comeau during copyediting. Thank you to editor Bill Regier for his willingness to pursue this rather unconventional approach to sport history and to the series editors, Randy Roberts and Aram Goudsouzian, for their faith that it would turn out okay.

I WORE
BABE RUTH'S HAT

> An old letter coils up and explodes like a land-mine,
> an inscription in a book pronounces a life sentence,
> gramophone records screech from the grave ...
>
> *Cyril Connolly*

INTRODUCTION

I have sat in a parking lot outside my old high school, decades after graduation, so choked with nostalgia that I felt as if I could not move. I have gone to reunions—and skipped them—with a case of sentimental dread that hung over for me days, and in a few instances, weeks. Always I wondered whether all the others—those who went and those who stayed home—wrestled with the same sense of past that I did: torn between a desperate need to believe that revisiting the old days might make them better than they were and the tougher realization that it wouldn't—a rip in the fabric of life that I think must be behind Susan Stewart's contention in her book *On Longing* that nostalgia is a social disease.

Thankfully, in the last few years, for reasons I can attribute only to my grudging recognition that there are no perfect lives or loves, the disease went into remission, spurred perhaps by social media postings from former classmates turned philosopher kings that make it clear it could not have been the actual past I'd been yearning for, but merely a version of it that I'd never actually experienced. There are still old locations that send a shiver through me, but the association with specific events and people is fading.

The one area still vulnerable to unrelenting memory is the time I spent playing sports. Even there, I've made strides. I now see my time at play not as an unending streak of unfulfilled possibilities but rather as a constant running through my sense of time, of who I was and how I got here; they remain the most reliable source of poignant and gratifying moments; these

Author at Camp Chesapeake with YMCA Indian Guides, 1958.
Photo collection of author

memories of play are, in short, my Arcadia, or more accurately, my Neverland, a place where I am seldom asked to act like an adult. In my sports world, I am still younger than every major league baseball player. When I step on any playing field I still anticipate pleasure as sharp as I felt when I pedaled my bike—glove slung over handlebar—on the way to a neighborhood pickup game a half century ago. And when I look at old yearbook photos of my teams, I see a look as close to contentment as I've ever been able to manage. Even in the portrait of the wrestling team from my sophomore year in high school—a season that delivered the full catastrophe—I am wearing a smile. Of course, newfound insight hasn't entirely erased old fantasies. The late Jim Murray wrote famously of Muhammad Ali, "I'd like to borrow his body for just forty-eight hours. There are three guys I'd like to beat up and four women I'd like to make love to." I'm still with you there, Jim.

Though this is a collection of discrete stories and observations, not a chronological memoir, I figure in some way or another in each. Though I once shared a dinner table with Muhammad Ali, sat down for chats with boyhood heroes like Curt Simmons, and played racquetball with a star and future coach from the NHL, stargazing has not turned out to be my thing. So, while there are some pieces on well-known figures, I gleaned just as much from moments spent with Donnie Rose, Denny Kubeck, and Buzz Shank, none of whom will be familiar to anyone outside my hometown. This is not, then, the reminiscences of a former professional athlete, the diary of a championship season, or a how-to manual for players or coaches. It does not contain the "strength of a champion," "the soul of success," outrage, uplift, or more than a hint of scandal. It is a look at the ways in which sports insinuated themselves into and imparted meaning into the life of an ordinary athlete. If there is one theme common to every story it is the centrality of sport in my daily life and the critical need for play in all phases of any person's life.

The stories take the reader from my father's childhood in the thirties and forties, through my own adolescence in the fifties and sixties, and into observations drawn from my continuing interest in sport as an adult: into the often peripheral issues of mascots and media; into a search for the appeal of an athlete like Cal Ripken; and into the place where we'll all, at least metaphorically, finish—the graveyard. If the underlying metaphysic of sport is, as Michael Novak claimed in *The Joy of Sport* (1976), overcoming the fear of death, then this is where all these stories acquire their greatest meaning and then cease to mean much of anything at all.

In describing moments from more than half a century of sport, it is possible, I hope, to see how my own pattern of connection parallels the shift in sports from attachments that Americans once acquired through participation to those that sink their hooks in today's superhyped environment through spectatorship. While I once pretended to be Willie Mays, for example, fantasy league participants now pretend to be Brian Cashman. Some of the changes I note have been far-reaching, though I do not claim here that my recall of them should be confused with their meaning. I've noted in recent years that authors writing about sport are so defensive about their subjects that either they or their publishers have begun crafting titles they think make the topic more credible. Thus, we've had books about games, people, and times that "Changed the Landscape of College Hoops Forever," "Created Modern Sports," "Transformed the Sport and Changed the Course of Civil Rights," and signified "The End of America's Childhood."

As with any collection of stories filtered through personal remembrance, some of the facts in them may seem an improbable reach. Many of the tales center, in fact, around improbability: from half-court snuffs to police escorts following a 52–3 loss to my secret appearance as a professional mascot. I concede some seem unlikely stretches of the imagination, but then again, improbability has seemed both an unavoidable and fascinating phenomenon in my life: case in point, I once worked with a man named Hershey whose father had drowned in an industrial vat of molten chocolate.

A sufficient explanation for some of the seeming implausibility, I think, can be found in author William Maxwell's contention that "too many conflicting emotional interests are involved for life ever to be wholly acceptable, and possibly it is the work of the storyteller to rearrange things so that they conform to this end. In any case, in talking about the past we lie with every breath we draw." That is not to say that I have intentionally lied or rearranged, only that my memory may be as erratic as life itself.

My "photographic" memory has drawn enough attention over the years to make it feel like a parlor trick—useful for identifying every single member in a photo of my fourth grade class fifty years later, but not for much else. Sometimes it bewilders and angers others: in the midst of hearing a Three Dog Night tune, I tell an old roommate that it had once been a favorite of his. First I get a flat denial. But when I look at him again a few moments later and catch him tapping his feet, the look he now shoots me says it all: "Why the hell would you remember that—and what else do you know about me from those times?" Despite my inability to forget at that level of detail, there are no guarantees that I haven't rehearsed my recall inaccurately or reordered events incorrectly. For example, until two years ago, I swore that in the first major league baseball game I ever attended, on August 21, 1959 (this part I know to be correct because the trip was a gift on my ninth birthday), Richie Ashburn was ejected in the first inning after arguing a close call at first base. Box scores reveal this to be wholly delusional; where it sprang from is anybody's guess.

I've read some of the scientific literature on memory, and it seems inevitable that researchers will one day get much closer to figuring the whole thing out, but for now I am gratified by its mystery; in at least one case I have been spared by it. Twenty years ago I gave a college sophomore a B in a softball class. When he found me one day alone in the locker room he mentioned the grade and told me that he was going to burn down my house in retaliation. I waited for the "just kidding" laugh that should have followed. It never came—he was dead serious. Just a few years later, as I watched a game from the upper deck of Baltimore's Memorial Stadium, I hailed a beer vendor. It turned out to be the B student. I braced for the worst, but he looked me in the eye and sold me a beer without the slightest trace of recognition. When the Orioles moved to Camden Yards some years later, the vendor and I moved with them. I happily bought beers from him without his awareness for the next fifteen years. Then one night during a rain delay I found myself out on the concourse; the vendor had set up nearby. Suddenly, he looked at me and strode over. He cordially asked how I was doing and whether I was still teaching softball at the university. We chatted for a minute, then he was on his way. In the five years since, he has again failed to recognize me. How randomly must the neurons in his brain be firing? Maybe such distortions in our recall are just support for famed psychologist Albert Ellis's contention that "all humans are out of their fucking minds—every single one of them."

With regard to sport, most humans may not be insane, but they are deeply conflicted. Because of their inherent possibility for fun, what has always been demanded of sports—particularly in America—is that they prove they have some real-world value. For the century roughly from 1870 to 1970 the value was in the specious contention that sports promoted specific values like manliness, sacrificial effort, fair play, and submission to authority—in short, good character. After the cultural firestorm of the Vietnam era torched those already archaic attributes, it became more common for scholars to assert that sport merely revealed character, that it was, in essence, a reflection of society. Not much there of use, either, but it is what we are stuck with for the most part, meaning that a good portion of Americans currently believe that sports are inextricably entwined with the commercial interests prominent in much of modern life: entertainment, revenue, image, politics, and fitness. Which is to say we have allowed sports to become even more distant from being the fullest expression of human excellence and potential that mankind has ever devised—artificial contrivances that challenge us to do the impossible for no good reason other than to see if it can be done.

Though this is a book of stories about moments in sports that have touched me, they are not all stories about me. I was not a great athlete, but I was always good enough to be on fields with those who were great. The only field on which I was embarrassed was—and remains—a golf course (though golf is unique in enough ways as to render it useless as a yardstick for measuring athleticism)—and you could lump the dance floor in with the golf course if you consider dance to be any indication of physical competency. I can pick up a fiberglass pole and clear ten feet more easily than I can stand among friends at a wedding reception and move my hips in a way that does not call to mind a monkey romancing a football (imagery popularized by former U.S. Olympic hockey coach Herb Brooks). In my community, the jocks—at least the white ones—did not dance, and there's little I can do about the paralyzing effect of that now.

At their best I hope these stories reveal the ways in which sports are interwoven with more than money and status. I hope they speak to the ignominy and nobility of losing, the angst of adolescence, the transcendent power of team, the lure of dreamscapes, the sway of pop culture, the ideals of perfectibility, and the irrefutability of place. I tried to get at these things at the point where history and fiction intersect, as most people—myself included—lack self-awareness to a degree that leaves us living fictionalized lives anyway. Both the pretense of an objective past and the imagining of one are expressions about the human condition, not truths about it, since at times the only point worth pursuing is the denial of truth—"getting over on life," or death, whichever you prefer—while pretending there is meaning to it all. At any rate, I have nearly reached the point in life when all of it—the remembering and the forgetting, the fun and the misery—seems to be approaching absurdity, so in the end I hope primarily that the stories serve, in the words of novelist Don DeLillo, as chances "to encounter the crossing points of insight and memory that the act of writing allows."

LEARNING FUNDAMENTALS

A CHIP HILTON Sports Story

STRIKE THREE!

By CLAIR BEE

CHIP HILTON'S SPORTS CULT

My urge to take a whiz had begun in the second inning. I was nine years old, playing shortstop for the Loomis Brothers Braves in a game against the Elks Yankees. I was at Cooper's Field in West Chester, Pennsylvania, a county seat twenty-five miles west of Philadelphia. By the fifth inning, my dance from foot to foot had nothing to do with anticipating a batted ball and everything to do with the fact that in the absence of restrooms, the only place left for waste disposal was my blue jeans. I fought the possibility, but eventually control surrendered to relief. Tears followed in an empathetic stream. It was and still is the most shameful and unmanly moment of my life. As I retired to the family car to await the end of the game, I had just one lucid thought: this could never have happened to Chip Hilton.

I had become aware of Hilton two years earlier, in 1957, during a period in which it seemed that teachers and adults never tired of asking boys what we wanted to be when we grew up. They asked lightheartedly, as if the answers weren't cause for concern, or perhaps as if every choice was both fascinating and plausible, but their insistence made it seem an important consideration. So, believing a decision necessary, I gave thought to careers; most in America at that time boiled down to offshoots from the prototypes of the sedentary priest and the robust warrior. Though

Clair Bee's *Strike Three*: one of my Chip Hilton cult manuals.

I found the robes and pageantry of religion enthralling, I didn't really believe in a god, so that left warrior and its physical subsets: fireman, policeman, cowboy, athlete. Unfortunately, I was also smart and liked to read, so a third option emerged when my parents began speaking of 1956 Democratic presidential candidate Adlai Stevenson's similar qualities in admiring tones: I could grow up to be an egghead. I was spared this final possibility when I discovered the Chip Hilton series of sports novels. Reading literature that extolled athletic exploits allowed the egghead to find a respectable—even manly—bit of space in my developing identity, and every day, after darkness ended my neighborhood ball games, I jumped headfirst down the rabbit hole—headed not for Wonderland, but for Valley Falls, where every season Coach Henry Rockwell guided Chip Hilton and his teammates to clutch wins, clear-eyed thinking, and righteous behavior.

When I began reading the Hilton series (which eventually ran to twenty-four books), I had no idea that sport's place in American life had traversed a century of shifting terrain. Born under the sign of the 1950 Phillies' Whiz Kids, I did not sprout my sports antennae until after Jackie Robinson had been belittled by Phillies manager Ben Chapman, until after some of the best basketball collegians in the nation had tarnished their game by point fixing, until after West Point footballers cheated their way to academic expulsion, until after a Sanity Code signified the onset of insanity in college sports. In my world, Bob Richards, the pole-vaulting reverend, lived inside every box of Wheaties, Willie Mays always belonged alongside Mickey Mantle—and Chip Hilton, beset by problems book after book, always found a way to preserve the sanctity of sports and his beloved Valley Falls, an actual spot near author and coach Clair Bee's hometown.

In short, I came to the Hilton books during a twilight era of sport. Of course, childhood is itself a twilight time. You sense crippling adolescence the way you sense encroaching darkness, hoping the pressures of responsibility can be stalled with the same magic that allows a boy to evade the night—for one last inning, then one last at bat, and finally one last pitch. For me, the fifties were a good time to put time on hold. I know now, of course, that the decade was not just Disney, sock hops, and malt shops. I'm aware that it was also McCarthyism, the Korean War, game show fixes, nuclear dread, and racial segregation, cultural homogenization, suburban sprawl, and television pap.

What does one do, however, when the inner feeling of something righter—or better—won't pass? The depravity that runs through every period of American history is unavoidable. But line up all the things that are right about an era—a sense of safety, optimism, naïveté, and hope—and I think you might be able to argue that there are times when things just feel better to more people. Sometimes called the "Second Golden Age of Sport," those are the fifties that Chip Hilton trapped in amber for me. Those fifties were a fantasy, to be sure—but a compelling one for those who lived in or visited Valley Falls.

Valley Falls sat atop the illusionary world I built from fifties pop culture, a necessary respite from my real world. My childhood bred in me two conflicting perspectives: one, that life is basically a negative experience lacking in true joy, security, and esteem—this drawn from family life, and particularly life in a family dominated by the volatile moods of my mother—and, two, the comforting, idealistic possibilities for life that I drew from popular culture (particularly TV, movies, and song) to compensate for the first. These would not seem easily reconciled, but then again what is life but a constant resolution of dichotomy, the uncertainty it produces being so uncomfortable that we always make our selection of one thing or its opposite. For me, the deluded, artificial, but far happier world of pop culture was the only choice.

I was in this regard like many of my generation. To be part of the baby boom—the demographical "pig in a python"—left me predisposed to delusion—a tendency amplified by my family's middle-class standing, our suburban home, and the era's post–World War II prosperity that brought me new schools, playing fields, backboards, and bicycles. More important, it meant being part of the first cohort in history exposed from an early age to the influence of television. The long-term Annenberg studies on television's ability to implant insidious messages have still not been able to pinpoint anything concrete, but I know myself to have fallen under various spells of unreality. First came Neverland, home to Peter Pan, my generation's model for our most enduring myth, that of the eternal child.

Peter Pan was, of course, the nineteenth-century creation of Britain's J. M. Barrie, but it insinuated itself into America's "Happy Days" decade when it hit the Broadway stage in '54 and, more aggressively, the following year, when NBC aired it as a color TV spectacular that had me, my sister, and every kid I knew jumping off couches into simulated flight. Some believe the magic pixie dust necessary for takeoff later translated into the baby boom experimentation with hallucinogens, and the emphasis on never growing old contributed to the determination to "never trust anyone over thirty." Surely, my generation's adoption of Senior Olympics, regenerative skin creams, and stretch denim jeans are conceits born of our infatuation with staying forever young.

Only one TV masterpiece, despite my addiction to it, diverted me from pleasant imaginings. A recurring nightmare during my grade-school days had me held captive by African natives who would force me into a leopard-skin tunic and throw me into their jungle hut prison. The frequency with which I screamed myself into wakefulness from this led my mother to ban my daily viewing of *Ramar of the Jungle*, the television show that inspired it.

The happier messages from Neverland found support from Disney, which produced not only the wonders of Disneyland, complete with a seven-tenths-scale Main Street untouched by any hint of human nastiness, but also a series of dashing figures that mixed escape and delusion into aphorisms seductive enough to lure nearly any of us: Davy Crockett (decide what you think is right, then go ahead and do it), Zorro (slash your mark across the belly of anyone who challenges you—the Z being particularly alluring to me), Toby Tyler (if you don't like where you are, run away and join the circus), and Francis Marion ("nobody knows where the Swamp Fox is"). The annual appearance of Oz on TV screens joined Disney and Peter Pan in hinting for the first time in the post–World War II era that there might be places more pleasant to be than corporate America. For me, for a while, that place was the Tennessee wilderness in 1813. My mother made me a buckskin suit with plastic fringe, bought me a coonskin cap, and entered me in local contests, where I sang "The Ballad of Davy Crockett." But I was delusional, not insane, and by the time the Davy Crockett fad swept America, I was five and had missed the requirement for killing me a "b'ar" when I was only three.

As dreamscapes go, however, nothing topped Valley Falls. Though the place was obviously fictional, it seemed close enough to the reality of the sports world I knew to bring it within reach, certainly closer to realization than flight through pixie dust or a belief that I might one day become king of the wild frontier. My interest in Valley Falls and the Hilton books came naturally. I had begun watching sports at age five with my grandfather, always baseball or pro "rasslin." The latter I understood: large men would fight using techniques they'd gleaned from the Three Stooges until one would suddenly lie still beneath the other. I was already more sophisticated than my grandfather in recognizing that these dramas would wrap up in fifteen minutes and be followed by a string of commercials. My grandfather always seemed surprised by the sudden endings, which often occurred at just the point when he would be exhorting one of the rasslers "to rip his arm off and hit him over the head with the bloody stump," an outcome I still believed to be an anatomical possibility.

Baseball was a different matter. There was little taking place on the small black-and-white TV set that I could readily understand, but the tone of the announcers and my grandfather's silent absorption led me to believe that something mystical was unfolding. With few cameras in place, the view was a fixed gestalt of white lines, grass, and dirt, a landscape I felt compelled to reproduce. One Sunday morning my parents returned from a rare excursion to church to find that I had emptied a can of baby powder on the front lawn to create my own field: a magical mélange of on-deck circles, batters' boxes, and extended lines in no relation to one another. My father found this to be hopeful, a stance that quickly wilted in the face of my mother's denunciation of my waste of her "goddamn powder."

By the time I began reading the Hilton novels, then, I was aware that sports contained the ingredients for fantasy. Professional ballplayers, since I saw them usually once a year, at a distance, became, like Hilton, creatures of invention. I needed bubblegum cards, radio broadcasts, and lots of imagination to flesh them out. Only occasionally would I catch the Phillies on TV—exposure long enough to discern nothing beyond batting stances. Though the personal glimpses from the backs of Topps cards made some players seem little more than ordinary (catcher Valmy Thomas's 1959 card, for instance, revealed that "Valmy is a dedicated fisherman in off season"), just as often they came off as quirky, exotic, and sometimes even a little creepy. Stan Lopata's 1958 card informed me that "his hobby is decorating baseballs for his teammates." What the hell, I always wondered, did that mean? Was he gluing hair on them and painting them with red mouths?

Hanging around my hometown's West Chester State College, however, gave me a better feel for what sports at higher levels were like: the laughter, the salty language, the bench jockeying (which combined the first two), the nicknames, and the notion that there was nothing more fun than a life of play. Even being at practice seemed preferable to being anywhere else on earth. It struck me as very like Chip Hilton's State University.

When I couldn't be at West Chester State, I was often at an event at West Chester High School. My father took me to football, basketball, and baseball games as well as track and field meets. When the teams were on the road, I listened to radio broadcasts and kept score. For me, high-schoolers like Cliff Andrews, Randy Sweet, and Fred Sadler were characters so closely aligned with those I found in the Hilton books that it seemed possible that Valley Falls might turn up on next year's schedule. If you had asked me then whether I'd prefer to play for the Phillies or move to Valley Falls and play with Chip Hilton, it would have been no contest.

The Hilton books presented a Manichean world that was easy for a kid to understand, especially in the fifties, when the cleft between right and wrong echoed America's determination to see the Cold War as a struggle between good and evil—a fight that ignored the complexities and ethical muddles of real-world politics. Pop culture reinforced the split: whether it was Pan versus Hook, Bugs versus Fudd, Howdy versus Bluster, or Chip versus an unethical townsman, the white hats always triumphed. You might think a kid could wish for little more. But I did wish for more, and I found it in the promise that even episodes of profound moral wrangling could never overshadow what was most important in any life: that there was a game to play. Chip Hilton's days were an unending circus of sport. He and his teammates did not play meaningless contests; seldom was there a blowout. The regular season always led to the championship moment. Life was play; that was the promise beyond which I could envision nothing better.

Of course, what I didn't realize at the time was that my reading, my dreaming, and my playing were all of one piece—I was being inducted into a cult. Some years ago, an applicant for a faculty position in my university department presented her research on coaching behaviors. On a screen, she projected a list of behaviors associated with coaching: blaming, praising, bullying, voicing dissatisfaction, punishing, rewarding, withholding, scolding, and on and on. After each she asked for a show of hands from everyone who had ever experienced that behavior from a coach. Multiple hands went up item after item. She then asked how many had been on teams with a hierarchical pyramid of authority, on teams where designated leaders had ironclad control, on teams where any dissent was deemed disruptive and destructive, and on teams where an us-versus-them mentality prevailed. All hands went up. The researcher then revealed that all of the behaviors she had itemized and all the attitudes surrounding team consensus were taken from the literature on cults. Organized sport, she was saying, inducts its participants into a belief system by pulling the same levers as any other cult. Whether they are consciously aware of this or not, coaches intuitively know how to sort out and indoctrinate their novitiates.

I don't blame Clair Bee, or coaches generally, for this. Most coaches seem to be well-intentioned, if not particularly thoughtful. They were cult inductees themselves, after all. Still, you can't make what is false true simply by wishing it or saying it over and over again. And the most seductively false thing that athletes and coaches asserted then and continue to assert now is that sports build character. In other words, it wasn't enough that Chip was playing, he had to be playing for a good reason—one with real-world relevance. This was not why I played, but the more I read, the more inescapable the theme became.

The dust jacket from 1953's *Fence Busters* let me know up front that "there is a lot of wonderful baseball in this Chip Hilton story, and a lot of good sportsmanship and clean manhood besides." It is the "besides" that was most insidious—it carried the hint that good character somehow seeps into life through the sports experience. The bad things that threaten Chip always seem outside of the arena, yet his crises are always resolved through lessons that have somehow osmosed through the arena walls. Of course, I can see now that this sort of thinking smacked of the same illogic as faith in a deity: the good things become complicit evidence for what we wish to believe, and the bad are dismissed as something ungraspable to the nonbeliever. And I wanted to believe, sure that this was the entrance fee one paid to be admitted to a life of play.

As cult thinking goes, this is pretty benign—heck, maybe even desirable—stuff. It's not as if I were being asked to handle poisonous snakes or speak in tongues. Really, is allowing oneself to get trapped in an Arcadia of innocence and virtue underlined by daily ball games any worse than agreeing to live in any venue of suspended time—a monastery or college classroom, say? In many ways, I wish I were still trapped there.

Author Clair Bee aspired to make Valley Falls a place where adolescent choices and adult problems carried consequences. There was right and there was wrong, and a life lesson lurked in every crisis. In this way the books are both timeless and fraudulent. They embrace the broad inspirational themes that Michael Oriard traced in his book *Dreaming of Heroes* (1982), which mark Chip Hilton as interchangeable with other fictional sports heroes from earlier in the century. At points, Bee grounds his stories in Depression-era themes: exploited factory workers, a billiard parlor that is home to "shifty-eyed men," and the constant struggle to find work and get ahead. The books also carry the revelation of an anxious America. There is in *Hoop Crazy* a white town's reluctance to accept a black basketball player. *Tournament Crisis* revisits the theme with an Asian. *Ten Seconds to Play* involved a football player's psychosis. At other points, Bee foretells the future. There is a football stadium named for the pottery plant tycoon who has, in essence, bought the naming rights. There are broken rules, win-at-all-costs coaches, incessant griping about officials, clock management concerns, and endless advance strategizing.

Much of it traced to the real life experiences of one of America's most innovative, successful, rambunctious, and now largely unknown coaches. Bee was born in Grafton, West Virginia, in 1896—the date, like several other things in Bee's life, are open to speculation. There were no basketball courts or baseball fields in nearby Valley Falls State Park, but it is a place where Bee spent many boyhood hours nurturing his eventual manly strengths by swimming, running, and having rock fights with his friends. He spent part of his youth in a gang—the Hilltoppers—part of it as a waker, a boy employed to make sure that the men laboring in the coal mines got to work on time, and part of it reading the tales of Horatio Alger and Frank Merriwell. Nicknamed Buzzer and also Beezer, he became a regional three-sport high school letterman. Though the Army refused him as many as six times because of his small size, eventually World War I gave him escape from West Virginia. Local clippings and lore say that during his wartime days in France, he became an accomplished craps shooter, won a French hotel in a poker game, constructed the first basketball court in France, played baseball, and went AWOL. He also got into numerous scraps and claimed that he'd been "bombed, shelled, and gassed" without impairment.

After the end of the war in 1919, Bee spent a year at Davis & Elkins College and an undetermined period at Waynesburg College, where he coached and became a finance manager for the college president. He then coached high school sports in Mansfield, Ohio, before accepting a position at Rider College. Somewhere along the way he also may have played semiprofessional baseball in Maryland, broken both of his ankles in a college football game, and, as a 150-pounder, played semipro football for a Pennsylvania steel mill.

In five years at Rider as a coach and athletic director, Bee put together a championship football team, a basketball team that went 53–7 during one three-year stretch, and oversaw construction of a new gymnasium. His success—and the findings of the 1929 Carnegie Foundation report—led uneasy academics to deemphasize intercollegiate sport at Rider, and in 1931 Bee moved on to Long Island University, where, between 1933 and 1951, his basketball teams won 82.7 percent of their games (he still tops all college coaches in lifetime winning percentage), had two undefeated seasons, a 43-game winning streak, and helped establish Madison Square Garden's reputation as the nation's hotbed of college basketball. Among students, LIU became known as Bee College. Additionally, Bee developed the 1–3–1 zone defense, was influential in the development of the three-second rule, and later, in the pros, the idea of the twenty-four-second shot clock. He also authored nearly fifty books on basketball and coaching, and he initiated a number of youth sports camps, one of which led him to meet and mentor a young coach named Bobby Knight.

Not a single item from this biography, nor all of them added together, however, left an impression as large as the fallout from the 1951 season, when it was discovered that some of Bee's LIU players had been shaving points as part of the biggest scandal in college basketball history. The scandal cost Bee his job and sent him to Baltimore, where as coach of the 1954 Bullets he garnered one of the worst winning percentages in NBA history.

If fiction is, as John Updike has said, a "tissue of lies truer than anything that ever happened," there is nothing stranger than the coach of a disgraced team writing prolifically and persuasively for a juvenile audience about the most untested contention of all: that sports are innately good and powerful social agents. I have to think that Bee, like nearly every coach I knew in boyhood, became a coach because it was his only way of remaining tethered to those addictive days of unending games. Of course, to remain in the world of play, a coach has to pretend it is work, must adopt all the party lines about the goodness of sports—that it fosters community, builds character, promotes manliness, enhances fitness—and recite them until they feel authentic.

Bee dedicated each book to a former player or acquaintance, many of whom had served the country in World War II, had died, or in some other way deserved memorialization. Bee never dedicated one to Seton Hall basketball star Bob Davies, but decades later he revealed that Davies was the prototype for Hilton (unbeknownst to the model himself). Davies became an NBA All-Star and was, in point of fact, a virtuous man. But he was a strange choice for Hilton inasmuch as he had, even as a collegian, a dose of flash in him. Among the handful of possible innovators of the behind-the-back dribble, Davies' name stands out. Legend has it that he spent a year perfecting it, and his first use of it in a game caused a priest to faint.

How Davies married and fathered children is a mystery, however, because, as far as I was concerned, there was no sex in the fifties. Chip Hilton had a saintly mother, but the few females who appeared in the series were chaste trifles. Even after he made his way to State University, Chip was never romantically involved. He was the great asexual champion, a hero in tune with a culture that did not mind that Mary Martin played Peter Pan. My interest in sex involved ogling Jayne Mansfield, and thinking beyond that merely gummed up a world of obvious and perfect separation. When coaches warned us in high school that "dissipating oneself" through sex would lead to diminished performance, I didn't have a clue what they could be referring to. I could see that athletes and cheerleaders were linked through their popularity, but as far as I was concerned the attraction of one body to another ended with dates to sock hops and holding hands in the movies. How could that affect the ability to throw a forty-yard spiral?

I believed, like Chip, that manliness was distinct from sexuality, a naiveté born of an entire culture's juvenile embarrassment and its collective decision to whisper, giggle, and titillate rather than speak frankly. The simplistic denial sunk its roots deeply in me. When I see someone wearing a T-shirt with the saying, "Paddle faster, I hear banjo music" (paying homage to the 1972 film *Deliverance*), I still laugh; it is the unenlightened laughter of those baby boomers who went through junior high and high school with the most limited—and clichéd—notions of gay life. If you had asked me in senior high how many "queers" or "fruits" were in my class, I may have counted one (a number I know from class reunions to have been the most absurd conjecture in the history of the world), that solitary figure being a boy in my gym class who giggled delightedly when anyone held his feet for sit-ups or laid a steadying arm across his thighs during pull-ups.

As a kid, I saw only caricatures of gay men, a pronounced lisp or limp-wristed sashay performed by blue-collar workers in bars or by my father and friends in the basement during one of my parents' parties. The portrayals always accented weakness. I saw in them no hint of sexuality, just a lack of toughness—the one ingredient required of a man. The rules for being manly were simple: don't cry when you get hit by a baseball (getting hit in the crotch being an exception, one's eyes tearing up involuntarily); don't cry when a fullback twice your size runs over you; and, oh yes, don't piss in your pants while playing shortstop. Aside from that, there wasn't much. To be playing sports was enough. Wrestlers were no manlier than basketball players; football players no manlier than soccer players. The one exception may have been the runners on the cross-country team, an odd assortment of nonathletic types who seemed capable of little more than being able to run any of us down over very long distances—surely a useless skill inasmuch as there could be no benefit in running down people who would then kick your ass after you caught them.

Sports were a haven of belonging that encompassed exclusive locations, rituals, problems, and nicknames (there's that cult thing again). Chip and his gang hung out at the Sugar Bowl; we had the Eachus Dairy grill, the Foulks Pharmacy soda counter, and Gino's (a McDonald's clone founded by Baltimore Colt Gino Marchetti). The guys who decided sports weren't for them fell off my radar. A few of them I'd feared as a boy stopped trying to intimidate me once I'd made a team. They dropped, in the eyes of the community, a few rungs down the ladder. They were the guys who hung out at the bowling alley—not to bowl but to smoke cigarettes and shoot pool. The adults referred to them simply as "J.D.'s," juvenile delinquents. My neighborhood J.D. was Bobby Gus. He was a mean guy whose lack of athleticism drove him from our sandlots in junior high. Lacking other companions, he took up for a short time with Paul Schroeder, who similarly lacked friends, though he was not a bad guy. In fact, Paul was a bit of an egghead and loved scientific experiments. When he tired of being Bobby Gus's whipping boy, he got even by building a shack about three feet square, nailing Bobby inside, then setting it on fire. The experiment was to see whether a man could escape from a burning hut with no exits. Apparently, he can, but not by much, and not without losing his intimidating aura.

By late adolescence, the fields and courts had sorted the jocks from all others in my world. My days became littered with guys I loved to be around, and not one was named Thurston or Cadwalader. The cast of reappearing teammates at Valley Falls High School included Tuffy, Tippy, Taps, Soapy, Red, Biggie, Fats, Speed, Pop, Tug, Dink (a cheerleader, actually), Reb, Piggie, Jinx, and, of course, let's not forget Stinky. In West Chester we had Buzz, Monk, Lop, Dutchie, Bozo, Mule, Wood-Eye, Squeaky, Paco, Puddin', and, of course, a Chip (a boy decidedly unlike Hilton and, though I haven't seen him in nearly half a century, a guy I'm sure I still don't like). As diplomatically as I could, I tried to secure a nickname for myself. Of course, deliberately suggesting your own nickname is as taboo as campaigning for your own Oscar or Nobel Peace Prize. I could not mint my own, but I thankfully did not become Stinky (though for completely unwarranted reasons I was for a brief time known as Pinhead). Alas, the late fifties and early sixties turned out to be the twilight era for nicknames, for guys who played a different sport every season of the year, and for hours of play devoid of adult supervision.

It has never taken long—in any era—for a kid to surmise that most problems are either going to originate with or be exacerbated by an adult. Valley Falls, however, held out the possibility that sports might offer exceptions. Chip's legendary high school and college coach was Henry Rockwell, who made not a single misstep in the course of twenty-four books. He was stern but compassionate, wise but not intrusive, insistent but not dictatorial. He was, in many regards, like legendary UCLA basketball coach John Wooden—or at least the John Wooden we know by reputation.

He was not, then, like any of the coaches who dominate today's arenas. In the late sixties, when the nation, in the midst of a humiliating loss to tiny North Vietnam, sought desperately for winners, Vince Lombardi arose as the misinterpreted prototype for all future coaches.

Though my Little League and junior high days came on the cusp of this sea change, and while nearly all of my coaches were caring supervisors, not little Lombardis, I began to sense that both parents and coaches were heading in the wrong direction. They were in the process of substituting the cult of victory for the cult of character. My first awareness of this came from my matchups against a fireballing Little League southpaw, Stanley Shur. He threw hard enough and wildly enough to have once put a baseball-sized hole into the plastic-shelled helmet of a hitter. When you are twelve, you need no other tools. None of us ever wanted to step into the box against Stanley, and he might have gone on to achieve great things except for the fact that after every pitch he looked to the stands, where his portly, unathletic, but nonetheless ambitious and overbearing father, was giving him secret hand signals that resembled the gestures of a belly dancer. Stanley Shur would respond with a mix of pitches created by his father and thrown by no one else in the world. Nothing he threw was ever good enough, however, and after he peaked at age twelve, Stanley faded from baseball. Sadly, in the years afterward parents became unable to leave their kids alone. And, ironically, it was the baby boomers themselves, those who had advised one another to "never trust anyone over thirty," who became the most intrusive and problematic in the athletic lives of their children in the eighties and beyond, leaving me to wonder whether Stanley Shur, as a thirty-something father, sat in the stands and passed along his father's ancient code to Little League success.

Strangely enough, my eventual escape from both the cult of character building and the cult of victory came by way of my father. Because my brothers were five and seven years younger than I, for a long stretch of time I enjoyed the singular attention of my father when I believed he was at his best. He was my Little League coach from the time I was nine until I was twelve. This meant not only that I had round-the-clock access to the team equipment bag, but also that I had a de facto starring role on the team. On days I didn't pitch, I caught or played shortstop. From my undiscerning vantage point, there was nothing untoward about this.

I thought of myself as the team's best player, though I could not hit like my friend Monk. Though my dad rarely lifted me from the lineup, he also never mentioned my performances, either with praise or derision. In to-day's overheated youth sports culture, he would be regarded as a gem.

Our team always finished near the bottom, always lost the big games; still, we had fun, and always, win or lose, we enjoyed the reward of a post-game visit to the concession stand. There was no ranting or raving, no pregame pep talks, no recriminations for ill-timed errors. No evidence, in fact, that the losses bothered my father at all. In fact, when his beloved Phillies blew a six-and-a-half game lead with twelve to play in 1964, he framed his World Series tickets, now useless souvenirs, and hung them on the wall as if they were priceless Picassos. His major concern, in fact, seemed to be using his position as coach to impose some sort of soft-hearted justice. He enjoyed having black players on the team, particularly a fast-talking, animated pitcher named Joe Forman, who taught me how to throw a curveball and ruin my elbow in one easy lesson. He drafted kids who had no interests beyond the sno-cones at the concession stand; he was the only coach willing to draft Punchy Ford, a one-armed and seriously undernourished kid, and drive miles into the woods to pick up Punchy at his family's tiny, ramshackle cabin and return him there after practices and games.

My father's inattention to results led me to begin thinking of victory as extraneous, something apart from the real measure of quality. I found my satisfaction instead in daring moments that were detached from the game's outcome. I became a master of the delayed steal of home, a gam-bit that pitted an adrenaline-fueled sixty-foot dash against the pitcher's ability to remain composed and return the ball calmly to the catcher. Up 11–1 or down 11–1, the score meant nothing to my impulses. By the time I was nine, I could imitate the batting stance of every regular in the National League, which meant I really didn't have a stance of my own. I was always someone else, my bat, even in crucial moments of league games, sometimes hanging parallel to the ground as I crouched deeply in an attempt to replicate Wes Covington's unorthodox appearance at the plate, my ability to actually hit from this position being just a further exhilarating challenge.

When basketball season arrived, the damn-the-score approach translated to fall-away jumpers over players a foot taller, twelve-foot running hook shots, and a preference on defense for allowing my opponent to dribble by me just so that I could reach around and slap the ball away from behind. In my first few months on a tennis court at age eight I fell into a lifelong habit of standing fixed after my shots, waiting until the ball was on its way back to me before making a foolishly heroic crosscourt recovery run.

I thought that my affinity for athletic flamboyance (a Pete Maravich highlight reel can still transfix me) must have come to me in the same inexplicable way that knowledge of visits by Jesus to the Americas came to Joseph Smith or knowledge that an E-meter can identify unproductive thought patterns in Scientologists came to L. Ron Hubbard. It did not; it came from my father, and it furthered in me an obsessive, years-long search for the highs that sports provided.

Anything that didn't involve sports was a tough sell to me. I joined a Boy Scout troop—I'd been seduced by the uniform—but I quickly discovered that knot-tying, tent-pitching, and saluting my Scoutmaster dentist in his ridiculous khaki shorts and badge-bedecked shirt were not for me (perhaps I should admit that I was not predisposed to look favorably upon him under any circumstances: when I was eight, he'd filled eighteen cavities at one visit—without novocain). When the troop went to Camp Horseshoe for a weekend jamboree, I slipped away from the encampment each day for hours and hit rocks into Octorara Creek with a tree limb.

I did consent to join the YMCA Indian Guides, primarily because most of my fellow tribesmen were Little Leaguers. Other than entering a miniature boxwood race car (which my father built for me) in the Boxwood Derby and carving a block for the tribal totem pole (which my father also did for me), with a pictorial translation of my Indian name, Little Thunder Cloud, complete with lightning bolt, we spent Indian Guide meetings playing ball while the fathers smoked cigars, drank beer, and played poker—just like the real Cherokees had, I suppose.

Of course, I enjoyed my share of unorganized boyhood pursuits. For a brief time I joined a small band of neighborhood kids who spent long hours digging some elaborate—and ridiculously dangerous and deep—tunnels beneath a vacant lot (Make of that what you will—trying to slip into a world of invisibility? Looking for an escape route? Trying to do myself in?), but the fear was less exciting and more draining than any of the sports I liked, and they could not command absorption long enough to do me any real damage.

As my hand-eye skills improved from year to year, I became what I only later recognized as athletic. There were lots of things I could do well. I was a starting running back and All-Star for Benny's Pizza (though I gave up football at age twelve when I recognized my adversity to contact was increasing yearly). I was the catcher for the All-Star Little League team; I made the junior high teams in soccer, basketball, and baseball. Though I didn't know how to skate, I rifled slap shots across the basement floor using a straight stick and a furniture coaster. On days when weather kept me in, I forced my younger brothers to play endless games of ping pong, carom pool, paper football, and a tabletop basketball box game in which a ping pong ball settled into various hollows in the cardboard floor of the arena and were then sent hurtling toward a backboard and tiny wire rim by means of a lever and spring contraption.

Eventually, however, when my size lagged noticeably behind that of my classmates, the youth league all-star appearances and junior high triumphs that had come with talent shaded into bench roles, limited playing time, and, finally, a humiliating cut from the basketball team in ninth grade, made when the coach decided that a 6'3" amalgam of gangly, awkward ineptitude might be a greater asset to the team than my 5'4" worth of ball hawking, name calling, fall-away shooting and running hooks (did I mention that I would shoot them with either hand?). In my estimation, the coach had wrongly put his eggs in a 6'3" basket of crap, but he never asked for my view of things. The next year, exiled from basketball, I went out for wrestling, a four-year travail with few happy endings and fewer chances to exhibit any sort of athletic flair.

The resulting unhappiness left me in a brooding search for the people and events that had brought misery into my sanctuary. I never considered that in my substitution of unnecessary dash for competitive restraint, I was complicit in my own downfall. Instead, I reached up and pulled in this timeless story: the son lives in the shadow cast by his father, and, unless he can outrun it (which I clearly hadn't), the gloom would be a long time dissipating. I began thinking that I might find the sources of my increasingly sour sports life somewhere in my father's past. In short, I blamed my father for not preparing me for a world in which winning mattered. How, I wondered, could he have missed this point? Chip Hilton may have been wrong about the character building, but maybe the fact that he nearly always won the big one was the real point of all those games.

I could find nothing in my dad's past that foretold such a disastrous oversight. Bill Zang was the oldest son of a hare-lipped traveling preacher who gave his time generously to boring the pants off his parishioners but had nothing left for his six children. Because he took the family to live for an extended period in Lemont, Pennsylvania, during my father's formative years, both he and his younger brother Bob were able to counter their father's avoidance by immersing themselves in the nearby wonders of Penn State athletics. In the open fields by the campus's barns and silos they stuffed aviator helmets with rags and stockings and then reenacted the heroics of the Nittany Lions, playing a brutal version of tackle football— just the two of them. At night, they would move the action to the basement, staging boxing bouts that my uncle characterized as battle royals. In their backyard they built standards and imitated the high jumping and pole vaulting of their collegiate models.

Each summer, the family relocated to a spread near Carlisle known euphemistically as the farm. It had a broken down barn, but as far as I could tell, the only thing they ever raised there were great clouds of gnats that flew into and eventually encrusted one's eyes, making each step outside insufferable. The insularity of life on the farm led to more time spent at sport: games of volleyball played across a string, wrestling, and swimming in a pool that my grandfather had built of field stones deep in the woods. Hidden from the sun, fed by ice-cold spring water, and fancied by snakes, it nonetheless seemed to them as exclusive as a country club membership.

There are no photos from those days, but a few teenage visits to the farm during which the gnats nearly brought me to tears and a hike into the woods to see the stone outline of the old swimming hole make me trust family history. After that, I lose track of my father and his connections to sport. I don't see him again until he suddenly appears in an album of 2" × 3" black-and-whites as a skinny young adult in the forties, hamming it up with friends and his girl—my mother—on the beaches of the Jersey shore. I don't know how he has arrived there. From vague conversations overheard as a boy, I surmise that he first came to the Philadelphia area after my grandfather moved the family to accommodate his job as the disciplinarian at a reform school in nearby Glen Mills.

My father attended West Chester High School but played no sports and dropped out before graduating. He enlisted in the Marines, serving as a clerk in Camp Pendleton as World War II wound down. As evidence of his unpreparedness for military life he told me more than once that during his Marine physical, when asked to bend over and spread his cheeks, he bowed at the waist, grabbed the sides of his mouth and gave a tug. I later learned that this was a rather old joke among enlistees, but as far as I can remember he never told it for laughs, so who knows? Finding nothing to support my hypothesis that he'd intentionally left victory out of my training manual (in fact, my father loved to sing the Marine hymn, which is little more than a testament to a winning streak that stretched from the halls of Montezuma to the shores of Tripoli), I did the unkind—concluded I was right in the absence of evidence. And I did the hurtful—decided to visit my misery upon my father.

As I finished my high school days, what hurt him the most was my decision to stop playing sports. I took a job at Jimmy John's, a sandwich shop outside of town (owned by a local man actually named Jimmy John—a place not to be confused with the current national chain), where I worked alongside athletes from West Chester State College. One was the captain of the wrestling team. One was a punishing fullback who, upon arriving for his shift, would throw a dozen fish filets into the deep fryer and then wash them down with a couple of milkshakes. The other workers called him "Balloonhead" (though never to his face; even here I cannot risk naming him) because his head was so big that the helmet manufacturer was said to have had to piece together two helmets to make one that was large enough to accommodate his noggin. Nothing they told me about college sports seemed to shore up my eroding interest in play. I took the money I made and began spending it in deleterious ways. I could spend a week's wages in a night, hanging out at the drive-in, eating cheesesteaks, buying clothes. When the Goshen Fair began its annual one-week run, I'd go through a month's pay in a single night, eating from every booth, getting bilked by the barkers, and taking my turn at duping the ancient stage emcee into paging "Richard Head" and "Mike Hunt" over the loudspeaker.

Worst of all, I began to take an interest in horse racing, something my father thought would eventually leave anyone short of time, money, and integrity. Bud, the short order cook at Jimmy John's, began every morning with a half hour of poring over that day's racing forms. Eventually, he taught me how to decipher them. Because the Brandywine Raceway was just three miles down the road, many horseplayers, owners, and jockeys would stop by for hot dogs on their way to the track. In time, I decided it would be a prime spot to take Dianne Tenebruso on a date. Though I looked about fourteen, Bud told me that if I approached the window confidently, they'd be all too happy to take my money. Dianne and I arrived just minutes before post time for the first race; flustered, I lost all confidence in my ability to make sense of the racing program. So, I did what a six-year old kid would do—I picked the first name that struck me as interesting. Going nervously to the window, I found that Bud was right; my age was no issue in placing a bet. I put down two dollars on "I'm A Boot" to win. A 56–1 longshot, the return on my first bet was $114. I proceeded to pick the next five winners in a row. When I arrived home that night, I took the roll of cash from my pocket and began peeling off twenties and setting them down in front of my father on the dining room table. Each one came with an unspoken slap: "take that."

Soon enough, I left for college in Ohio. The wrestling coach there thought that inasmuch as I'd wrestled at 103 in high school, I might make a fine 118-pounder. That summer, however, I'd sprouted a few inches and I arrived on campus at 135 pounds, too heavy for the 118 class and not nearly good enough to challenge the 126-pounder, who would win a conference title in his freshman year. During the next four years, my belief about Bill and the shadow he'd cast solidified into a self-drawn portrait: I was the gifted child too small to be taken seriously, the quitter who never wins, the backyard imitator of the great who cannot bring himself to see himself as anybody other than someone else. I wanted back in the cult, but I had become an unwelcome outsider. I made half-hearted stabs at baseball and soccer, but I could not summon enough enthusiasm to overcome both my fear of failure (or success) and the even more regimented expectations of college coaches. I settled instead for hours of pickup basketball, mastering badminton in P.E. class, and for intramurals in every sport offered. There, my desire to play reemerged, as my teammates found my impulsive tendencies more amusing than debilitating.

Bill, meanwhile, gave up a thirty-year pension from the chemical plant, sold the family home, and moved with my mother back to central Pennsylvania to transform a broken-down biker bar at the top of a mountain into the Mt. Nittany Inn. He became again a fan of the Penn State Nittany Lions and developed, I thought, a sudden and excessive interest in winning. For the first ten years he was there, I became certain he'd gone home only to be near victory—a notion that troubled me so much that I'd damn Penn State athletes and teams in his presence. Hamlet twists the knife.

Suddenly, in 1995, when I was forty-five, I didn't need to twist it any longer. My father went into a hospital and never came out, felled by a common infection and the wonders of modern medicine. I think the last time he was conscious was when he was listening to a close Lady Lions NCAA playoff basketball game. As he lay in bed, equidistant from Lemont and Beaver Stadium, the nurse came over with the score tied and twenty-eight seconds remaining, and turned off the radio—and his life.

Having never bothered to talk to him about any of my assumptions, I was left with the same questions and aggravations I'd borne for forty-five years. Had he returned to central Pennsylvania to be near victory, or had he gone to live in the shadow of Penn State because it reminded him of how much more alive he'd felt there in his youth? Did he think winning was important and, if so, couldn't he have mentioned that to me at some point? It added up to another failure to me, and I saw his failures the way I saw my own—as shame, as a mark that anyone could discern in my posture's concession to gravity.

Unable to leave it alone, I turned more investigative. I started to look for the mysteries of sports in books and the academic world. There was no shortage of words there. It is no coincidence that the last Chip Hilton book was *Buzzer Basket*, published in 1962 (aside from the later revisions by Bee's daughter, "updates" whose absurd attempts to make Chip modern are compounded in their latest incarnation by Christian dogma insisted upon by their faith-based publishing house). Soon afterward, academics and a new wave of journalists would discover sociological themes in every corner of the sports world, and the recognition of sport's primary value as character building would be gone for good. From the all-black Texas Western versus all-white Kentucky national basketball championship game of 1966 to the creation of players' unions to Curt Flood's lawsuit to Woody

Hayes's dismissal from his Ohio State coaching position for punching an opposing player, the sports world became news fodder, reflections of the more important "real" world. I shouldn't complain. My career has been one of pinpointing some of those moments and writing about them.

Finally, from somewhere that was neither Valley Falls nor my father's Penn State, I found my own understanding of sport's meaning. Without intending it, Bill had passed along this: victory can't be as important as most people make it. Some of us are better able—and more willing—to absorb a defeat. It struck me that, having lived with my mother's constant beating on others, Bill may have come to regard victory—the beating of others—as its own form of cruelty. Maybe he even thought that I had an ego less fragile than those for whom loss threatened their very identities. This, I have come to hope, is the shadow my father cast over me: a fundamental decency of incalculable proportions.

If that is all a dodge to make myself feel better, it seems to be working. Maybe it is working in part because I also now understand that while winning may not be the only acceptable outcome, trying to win is the only acceptable approach once the scoreboard is turned on. How can one measure athletic excellence without keeping score and caring about it?

I could be wrong, but my gut tells me that this is what Clair Bee, Henry Rockwell, and Chip Hilton were getting at all along—the rest was just pixie dust sprinkled over a lifetime of endless play.

THE HALF-COURT
SNUFF OF
DONNIE ROSE

In the mid-nineties, driving from Cancún, Mexico, to the inland jungle
ruins of Chichén Itzá meant riding a long superhighway, made surreal
by its utter desertion and by an unannounced tollbooth that rose in the
midst of nowhere to shake down cars for twenty dollars and trucks for as
much as two hundred. Despite the road's dearth of travelers, the Mexican
government nonetheless had posted large signs every few miles that read:

No Maltrate
Las Señales

I had no idea what that meant. My poor grasp of foreign languages is
rooted in sibling rivalry. My sister has a PhD in Romance linguistics. As I
followed her example in secondary schools by just a year, I went out of
my way to sever myself from her egghead legacy, goofing on my French
teachers with hilarious things like, "Wee, wee, mon-sewer." This led me
to warn my Cancún travelmates, my fellow *señales*, to dump all of their
maltrates out the window in the event that we were being tailed by the

Witnesses to the half-court snuff: author kneeling fourth from left; Tommy Webb,
kneeling far right; Joe "Lop" Forman, standing sixth from left.
Photo collection of author

Mexican *federales*. Some months later my sister told me the signs translated to: "Don't deface the signs." Inasmuch as the only signs to deface were those that said "no maltrate las señales," I concluded that my sense of the signs was no more absurd than that of the Mexican government. And fitting, since my wish to see Chichén Itzá came from a determination to undermine a grander absurdity: that its famous Mayan ball court might be the birthplace of basketball. Though I like the idea of deep roots and suffer no jingoistic compulsion to honor James Naismith's peach basket origins, something didn't seem right in claiming that the Road to the Final Four began in Chichén Itzá.

The ball court there is a haunting sports arena. A large I-shaped field enclosed by high, deep stone walls that made boxed rats of the players, it is a gladiatorial dungeon—no place to hide from the thousands of bloodthirsty spectators who once massed themselves along its ridges. Lower down along the walls, carvings in full view of the players reminded them that the outcome would bring one team a ritual beheading. I read recently that some historians also believe that a loss in the ball court could earn players the torture of being bound up as a ball and then rolled down the steps of the nearby pyramid. The only description of the game played in the court comes from a Spanish priest in the sixteenth century, who made clear the physicality of the spectacle. Walking across the court I envisioned scenarios in which the crosspieces of the I at each end would leave anyone caught there in a terrible bind, looking to the stone deities in the temples for a timeout that would never come. More recently, I learned that the game was more likely a cross between tennis and soccer, with teams divided by a center line. At any rate, the attempt to knock balls through stone rings on the walls on either side at midcourt gave rise to the musings by some historians that it is a forerunner of basketball. Looking at the height of the rings and recognizing that the balls needed to be struck with the thighs and hips, however, made this a formidable and infrequent occurrence. In short, the game sounded like a version of hell, not basketball, and so I dismissed the possibility of meaningful connections and went my merry way.

In recent years, however, I have thought more about my own experiences with basketball, about peculiarities of the modern game, and have begun to allow that the ancient Mayan ball game was perhaps just a cross-continent skip pass away, a historical desperation heave that had landed closer than I would like to admit. An occurrence during eighth grade stands as a cruel scene that hints at a connection worthy of Mayan accolades.

Growing up in West Chester, Pennsylvania, a small town twenty-five miles west of Philadelphia, I was a talented but limited athlete, gifted with good reactions and hand-eye skills but stunted in size and self-esteem. I spent a great deal of time alone, but, because of sports, I was rarely lonely. In warm weather, I pitched complete games against a garage wall with a rubber-coated hardball. In cold weather, I played endless games of basketball in my driveway, taking the role of all ten players. I played one-on-one with friends when possible, but more often I shot alone, no one guarding me, free to swoop through the middle with no forearms nudging my skeletal frame off stride. Having been a 70-pound, twelve-year-old defensive back for Benny's Pizzeria—charged with bringing down Foulks' Pharmacy's 130-pound fullback (who got the call to carry the ball off tackle every single play)—I came to dread collisions of all sorts, and so grew up adoring Bob Cousy and shooters like Paul Arizin, players who seemed to elude the danger that sucked others into the whirlpool of contact: Cousy dribbling time off the clock as opponents chased him in futility and frustration at half-court; Arizin drifting quietly to the corners for jump shots that did not—could not—draw upon the assistance of the backboard. Nothing but net. A purist's game. My size and admiration for Cousy forced me to learn to dribble, but my heart urged me to shoot first.

My own shot was developed not just to go in the basket but, through excessive backspin and an unnecessarily high arc, to whip the net on the way through, causing a backwash of cotton cord to get hung up on the rim. To this day, I find it impossible to shoot at a basket without a net. In the brief periods between the times I had shot one net to shreds and the time my father could get a replacement up, I was profoundly unhappy and threw up only a few desultory shots at the bare metal rim each day. Making the shot was a penalty, the ball sailing untouched past the bottom of the backboard and rolling through fifty feet of backyard. No net, no basketball. Perhaps a starting point in my initial judgment that placed the Chichén Itzá contests at odds with the game I played.

The hours invested in solitary rehearsal paid off when I made the junior high school junior varsity in seventh grade. Unfortunately, my coach that year had been a local college football star, and he liked picks set with enough enthusiasm to send players crashing to the court. Each practice my second-string body absorbed the bruising lessons of interior linemen. This was in 1963, a time when I thought that there must have been many coaches who shared my vision of the game as a noncontact whirl of speed and finesse. Only later did I learn that the early professional game had in fact been a rough one, often played in a cage—hence, newspaper references to basketball players as "cagers," a term I mistakenly associated as a kid with the basket itself.

Though the game I was forced to practice each day was now the game found in a football playbook, I was careful to memorize the plays, run to the correct spots on the floor, and set the picks. Guards no longer looked skyward. They did not shoot in this schema of combat. They looked straight ahead as they ran, in fear of arriving an instant too late at their designated spot. Those who arrived late—or worse, at the wrong station—became a lesson to us all. Bruce Bohannon, a likable but distracted scrub guard, regularly forgot his patterns. The coach would approach Bohannon in a blistering rage, once bouncing the ball off his head with enough venom to send it on the fly all the way down to the varsity end of the gym. Bohannon's friend, Bob Benz, willfully disregarded the plays. His enthusiasm was for unleashed movement. His inability to rein it, and the humiliations suffered thereby, caused him to give up the sport for a time. I fit between Bohannon and Benz, smart enough and restrained enough to avoid wrath, but invisible to the coach's preferences. Near season's end, though we were loaded with talent in a school district that perennially produced great high school teams, my Stetson Junior High School Falcons were 2–10. We played just four-minute quarters, and our rigid offense was piling up morbid numbers, the ball and basket having become negligible accessories to our game plan of intricate and long-developing double and triple screens. We lost one game 9–4. My role was perhaps an accumulated three minutes of cameo appearances in lost causes.

And then one day . . . the coach got sick. Missed school. The only time I saw a band of junior high athletes more gleeful came the following spring, when a rifle throw from center field took one perfect hop into the crotch of our fungo-hitting baseball coach, disabling him for a week and altering his walk for the remainder of the school year. Of course, we were delighted at that in an abstract way, having no particular animosity toward the coach, but rather a general satisfaction in having witnessed a rare and random strike on all authority, a foreshadowing of attitudes that would mushroom in a few years to pay bigger dividends. We were gleeful at our basketball coach's illness in direct ways. We were playing that day our cross-town rival, Central Junior High. We reveled in the possibilities that arose from seeing all our talent finally unchained, released from the paralysis of the playbook. This surely would happen, since the varsity coach, Bernie Edwards, would sit in that day as our coach.

Bernie was a stern but kind man who had played college ball at nearby Cheyney State College, a historically black institution. On several occasions, Bernie took his junior high players to Cheyney games, where we'd sit like a nurdle of white toothpaste squeezed onto a piece of black construction paper. At the time, Cheyney was a small-college powerhouse. Its stands would fill up early, the student section swaying for more than two hours with gospel-tinged incantations, exhortations, and wailings that transformed the fieldhouse into the Baptist Church of Basketball, a place just barely big enough to contain all the emotion of a night's joys and miseries. When they swayed, we swayed, rocked from side to side, as unstoppable and rhythmic as a metronome.

It was rumored that Cheyney's big man, the slender, handsome Hal Booker (a first-team small-college All-American who would eventually be drafted by both the ABA and NBA), could pick a quarter off the top of the backboard. I accepted this as fact, never stopping to wonder how a quarter would get there in the first place or how anybody but Booker would know it was there. At away games, did he check the tops of backboards for spare change? I never saw him do his trick.

I did witness something just as miraculous. When the Cheyney team burst from the locker room for pregame warmups, it was led by an impossibly small guard in large, black-rimmed glasses, Urkel before there was an Urkel. He would never see game action, but he didn't need it. The trail of bigger men would follow him in a slow trot to midcourt. The crowd would rise in a buzz of anticipation. Then, half dribbling, half cradling the ball, he would flash to the basket, leap, and rise above all reality, finally throwing the ball down in a dunk that triggered full explosion.

My team at Stetson Junior High was mixed, and it is still hard for me to sort out what I made of color back then. While coaching my Little League team, my father had selected blacks and whites in equal measure.

He never mentioned race, and two of the black players, Joe Forman and Bobby Dorsey, were two of my favorite teammates. In basketball there was not yet a sense of black entitlement on the court—no belief that jumping was a black trait or that point guards should be white. In fact, the best player on our team (actually, on all our teams right through high school: soccer, basketball, and baseball) was Tommy Webb, a white athlete not significantly bigger than me who controlled every contest he played in. He was my secret idol, an athlete gifted with hand-eye coordination as good as any I've encountered in all the years since. There was nothing, in short, about abilities or styles of play that seemed foretold by skin color. Still, when Danny Brisbon and Glenn Norman, two black players with reputations for violence, tried out and made the squad, a jittery disquiet settled over the team—or at least over me—and stayed all year long. Neither made it through high school graduation. I lost track of Norman. Before he was twenty, Brisbon robbed a gas station, killing a West Chester baseball player who was working there. A few years later, a fellow prisoner stabbed him to death.

Whatever race may have been imprinting on our junior high team, it anchored somewhere beyond my consciousness. Amid the losing and the body checks, I had just one pleasure. I was the smallest player on the team, which meant I led the team out of the locker room and took the first layup before every game. That I could not replicate the Cheyney guard's dunk was a given, but one I never thought to associate with race.

With Bernie on our bench, we expected the Cheyney spirit to carry us along. It did not happen. Months of drills had driven the talent and spontaneity from our bodies. We responded with an ambiguous game plan, a mix of the usual bone-rattling picks set light-years from the ball and twenty-foot jumps shots taken simply because on this day they could be. With one quarter to play, we trailed 18–8, which was like a college team trailing by 40 with ten minutes left, or probably worse since there was no shot clock and no five-second count to aid the defense.

I got the call to start the last of our four-minute quarters. Most of what happened after is a blur. I only know that within two minutes I had hit three consecutive jump shots—nothing but net. It was suddenly 18–14. I stole an inbounds pass and fed Tommy Webb for a basket. A few seconds later our gawky, nervous center rattled in two free throws to tie the score.

A minute later it was all over—we had impossibly won. The one thing I remember clearly was Bernie patting me on the back over and over in the locker room. I thought my career had gotten a kick start. I saw in front of me a twenty-year ribbon of scripted glory. I forgot that we would be traveling the next week to Coatesville, our very own version of Chichén Itzá and the place where dreams went to die.

West Chester was a quaint town, complete with ornate movie theater, malt shops, and courthouse; it was a place where as a child I imagined that I might bump into one of the Mouseketeers or strike up a friendship with Spin and Marty. Coatesville, ten miles further west, had none of those things. What it had was a huge steel mill where much of the citizenry worked and which turned the atmosphere dark and gloomy. It also had streets pitched as steeply as those in San Francisco, so that when you entered town from certain directions, it was like rolling down into hell (when I went away to college in Ohio I met a fellow freshman named Coates. When he found out I was from eastern Pennsylvania, he told me that there was a town there named after his ancestors. He was intending a trip to see it one summer. I told him to spare himself a return drive that would be made interminable by bitter disenchantment).

Beyond its apparent physical limitations, Coatesville had—at least in West Chester—a reputation for meanness that frightened some of our folks, including my mother. My mother was often unkind. She turned misery into a spectator sport in my household, which bent everyone in it toward cruelty in one form or another. And what my mother feared she tried to diminish through insult. When my two brothers or my sister or I displeased her, my mother would threaten us with lifelong exile in one of three Coatesville institutions: the poor farm, the prison, or Embreeville State Hospital, a place my mother in her indelicate way always referred to as the nuthouse. As it turned out neither of the first two were even in Coatesville, though my mother had convinced us otherwise. Frankly, the poor farm held no fear for me. After all, what does poor mean to an eight-year-old who could find enough empty soda bottles roadside to keep himself in baseball cards six months of the year?

I also found the idea of prison less than daunting. I'd seen lots of television, and as far as I was concerned, if you had to spend time in jail, it meant that Opie would drop by for a morning chat, Aunt Bee would bring lunch every day, and Barney Fife would leave the keys hanging next to the cell in case there was anyplace else that you really needed to be. My younger brother was not as luckily naïve as that. One day, after he'd spilled jelly on his shirt or committed some other criminal affront to my mother, she angrily loaded him into the family station wagon and set off for prison. My brother, disbelieving the announced destination, rode along happily in the back until the car indeed pulled up at the prison gates, at which point he broke into frightened bawling—which my mother found hysterically funny as well as vindicating. It turned out that she was merely going to pick up a set of throw rugs woven by the prisoners, but it took my brother a long time to recover.

The prospect of the nuthouse actually worried me. My mother had convinced us all that a patrol wagon drove random routes throughout the county, searching for nuts. If they caught you on the streets acting like an idiot—a state my mother often proclaimed for us—men in white coats would jump out of the wagon, load you in, and take you to live in the nuthouse. Believing myself prone to involuntary bouts of idiocy, I kept my head on a swivel when outdoors and feeling happy.

I avoided my mother and the nuthouse by playing sports, not knowing that becoming capable and making teams was the one thing that would guarantee me several trips a year to Coatesville. The Red Raiders were our only real rival in the Ches-Mont League. At least in the sixties, contests against them had come to be marked by the era's violence. Maybe because I was already frightened of urban conflict, having been hassled on the way to and from street parking spots in black ghettos while attending games in West Philly's Connie Mack Stadium, I sensed there was some racial component involved. The Coatesville squads had more blacks than whites, but our teams were liberally integrated as well, so I may have had my finger on the wrong pulse.

Whatever the source, things were distinctly nasty in my day. Our wrestling coach had been beaten and stabbed while taking tickets at the West Chester–Coatesville football game. The Coatesville gang responsible carried its malice into the stadium, chasing one man across the track and to the field's edge while swinging chains. Two years later, after a Coatesville player stomped on the face of a fallen West Chester basketball player, the stands had emptied on both sides, creating the only melee I've been an eyewitness to. Visits to Coatesville, then, were fraught with anxiety. My first trip there was no exception.

We left school at midday for an afternoon game with Coatesville's Gordon Junior High. The bus rolled down into hell and stopped in front of an old brick building. When we entered, it seemed we'd arrived at the wrong spot. There was no one in the halls. As it turned out that was because they were all awaiting us at courtside—or in this case, poolside. The Gordon court was an old swimming pool drained of water, and basketball was played in it Mayan style.

The court had no sidelines or baselines—only concrete walls. The benches were up top. When you checked in the game you ran down a set of stairs—which were in play—to reach the playing surface. To throw the ball in, you were required to cock one foot flush against the wall. After a layup you got one step before you collided with concrete. The corners were instant death. The incline that had taken swimmers into deeper waters had been overcome by raising the floorboards in the deep end to a height level with those placed directly onto the surface at the shallower end. This meant that at one end there were great hollow expanses underneath that created dead spots in the flooring above. The Coatesville players, of course, knew each one by heart. For us, the situation was like the television show *Concentration* as we tried with each tentative dribble in the game to recall the map of solid spots our memories had drawn during warmups. When unsuccessful, the ball went to the floor but never came back up. Delighted Coatesville defenders swooped in to pick up the ball and begin a fast break in the opposite direction, passing often, putting the ball to the floor only in those places where they knew it would return to them.

That aspect of basketball in a pool was maddening but no real affront to our sporting sensibilities. Many gyms provided a home court advantage, from crooked rims to bad smells. What offended us most—humiliated and intimidated us, really—was that the spectators stood above us, leaning on a railing, hooting at our ineptitude, and then, to make sure we understood their hostility was genuine, by spitting down on our heads. We lost and got back on the bus as quickly as possible.

The following season's trip would end even more badly. The bus rolled down into hell, but instead of stopping at Gordon, it kept on going, straight out of town to a brand new junior high school built on a hill in the countryside. Having steeled ourselves for an encore performance in the swimming pool, we were relieved to come out of a new locker room onto a new gymnasium floor. We should not have taken the new surroundings as predictive of a more civil environment.

Coatesville's players had not left any of their meanness in the bottom of the Gordon pool. The overall experience was cleaner without the railing spitters, but the end result was not. We lost the junior varsity game, though I remember little of the details; they have been overwritten in my memory by an occurrence at the end of the varsity game. By the time we showered and took our seats in the bleachers to watch the varsity, Coatesville had already run out to a big lead. By the fourth quarter we trailed by dozens. The only number that keeps coming to mind—I don't know why—as a signifier of how bad it seemed that day is 56–12. Though that score is almost surely an exaggeration, the game was enough of a blowout for Bernie to turn to the bench as the final seconds wound down.

Both the first and second teams having already been pummeled, the choice was the third team, a choice almost as rare as a June snowstorm. Third teams existed back then because school systems were flush with money. They had enough uniforms to outfit fifteen, and it never hurt to please five new sets of parents when their sons came home and told them, "Guess what, I made the team." But in reality, there was no need for a third team. They weren't necessary for practices or scrimmages, and some of them were there because more talented players quit rather than suffer the humiliation of third team status.

At Stetson, the squad's fifteenth and last man was Donnie Rose. He was unremarkable in nearly every regard—size, appearance, ability—and so he seldom saw even those few meaningless end-of-game seconds when everyone but the refs stopped paying attention to the court. He did have one distinction: in an era when shorts rode up into one's crotch, Donnie Rose had gotten last pick of uniform parts. His green satin shorts billowed comically from waistline to mid-thigh. One door opening at the wrong time could cause an updraft that might carry Donnie Rose from the gym like a Macy's parade float.

Inserted with about thirty seconds left, Donnie Rose and his third team buddies chased frantically and ineffectually after the ball until Coatesville scored a final time. With the clock now at about 0:07, Donnie Rose moved swiftly to assure himself of receiving the inbounds pass. As he began dribbling up court, unguarded, he suddenly sped up. The light bulb had come on—Donnie Rose had realized that he might never again have the ball in a competitive, organized game. As he approached midcourt, something must have also told him that this would be the last time he would have both the ball and open space. If he risked trying to get to the top of the key, the very concept of taking a shot would become muddled.

So, with the reasoning and skills that had made him the fifteenth player on the squad, Donnie Rose suddenly pulled up at half court and prepared to take his shot. As his knees uncoiled from their deep bend and the ball reached his fingertips for release, only one other person in the gym was not surprised at Donnie Rose's audacity. A Coatesville defender had either seen the light bulb above Donnie Rose's head or had somehow smelled his desperation, and it drew from him a pitiless response. As Rose had neared midcourt, the defender had begun a running start from the foul line. His knees had gone into their own deep bend at the same time as Rose's, and now here he was, closing on Donnie Rose from far away, sailing in a long jump of uncontrolled malevolence. The ball arced only a few feet from Rose's right hand before it came ripping back at him, pounded with a closed fist and gleeful ferocity. It was so terrifying that Donnie Rose actually had to duck down to keep from being hit by the ball. It was the first and last time I've ever seen a shot blocked at half court. It was Donnie Rose's moment of Mayan torture—he may as well have been bound and rolled down the steps of the Gordon swimming pool. I've been watching basketball for the past forty years with eyes and ears tuned to a possible repeat—anywhere. As far as I know, Donnie Rose is the only player in the history of the sport to be snuffed at half court.

Watching from the sidelines, my first reaction was one of shame. We were all embarrassed by the rout, but the snuff was nothing short of deeply humiliating. So much so that it seems I'm the only one able to recall it. I've checked with other teammates—no remembrance. I asked Tommy Webb about it a few years ago; surely he would remember. No luck. The only evidence I have that it wasn't all a figment of my imagination is that three years later my friend Buzz Shank, who was on the varsity squad that day, signed my yearbook under Donnie Rose's photo with the fictitious entry:

Dave,

Remember that crazy game at Coatesville when my pants were hanging down to my toes.

"Rosebud"

I can only conclude that for most the memory was traumatic enough that it needed to be repressed; either that, or most of my teammates had already checked out from caring about the game once our J.V. game had ended. If I could find Bernie (when I last heard of him, he was the head of the Florida state lottery commission, but he's no longer there), I'd ask him. Reliable witnesses or not, it happened, and it struck in me a merciless chord. I responded as I imagine my mother would have. For years Donnie Rose was my King of Fools. I retold the story to hilarious effect at cocktail parties, perfecting the Donnie Rose cower as the ball shot back past him.

Then my mother died, and with her went some of the mean-spiritedness that she had fostered in all of her children. I married a kind woman who also muted my cruel streak. But the turning point in my regard for Donnie Rose came when I enrolled in graduate school at Arizona State. Part of my program in sport studies included making up undergraduate deficiencies that were the result of a political science degree. I took a history of sport class in which Dr. Bob Osterhoudt, a philosopher, Renaissance man, former decathlete, and the king of kindness, exposed me for the first time to thinking about the true wonders of sport. In the three decades since I left Arizona State I've become increasingly convinced of all that Bob asserted about our humanity and its connection to the purposes and meaning we bring to our participation in mankind's greatest institution, sport. It is, after all, the only institution that has at its core the pursuit, measurement, and celebration of excellence for its own sake.

When that finally settled into my psyche, the shame I felt was for my decades-long ridicule of Donnie Rose. When you love to play—as Donnie Rose did—the urge to extract pleasure from every instant is a given. The rules of basketball say that during the time allotted you try to put the ball in the basket as many times as possible, and in simple terms that is all Donnie Rose was trying to do.

The next year Donnie Rose moved on to high school, where he was promptly cut. But in a surprise that unnerves me to this day, back at Stetson Junior High, so was I. Following the obligatory tryout before my ninth grade season, I checked the locker room bulletin board with detachment, casually interested in knowing which unfortunate saps had been the latest to be pared from the varsity squad—surely Noble Johnson, who had played his two minutes of the tryout scrimmage with a limp balloon dangling from the waistband of his shorts, and Charlie Wilson, who was six feet three inches of sorry, undeniable ineptitude.

When I saw my own name on the list, I fled, flushed with the heat of shame and panicky to avoid the teammates I'd played with for two years on junior varsity, several times as a starter. The moment I got outside, my composure broke and tears poured down my face. By the time I reached the family car for the ride home, I was under control, having begun already to shield my shock and depression with a steely denial so deep that I could not confront it until thirty years later, penetrating it then only as a rented car headed into the jungle of Mexico's Yucatan peninsula. It goes without saying that I would not have made it in the Mayan ball court—and the cut would have been literal. But it turns out I wasn't tough enough to make it in Coatesville, either. The sport that I thought I saw when I watched the NBA's Warriors and Celtics, when I saw Arizin and Cousy, turned out to be part illusion—a willfully imagined dance in which Wilt Chamberlain and Bill Russell seemed to compete with a minimum of violence—and part historical anomaly. If they really were not shoving one another around in the paint, as has become the norm, they were an aberration, part of a brief period that seems lost forever, stomped to dust by the likes of giants who now carry the ball, at times run with it, and believe that laying hands on an opponent is the surest way of stopping him.

My exile from basketball was painful in many ways. I missed the game itself and the status that it had in West Chester. At seventy-five pounds I was always on the cusp of irrelevance anyway. My only cachet came from being on teams; being athletic alone did not help. In fact, when I had been the only seventh grader to win the presidential fitness badge, my tyrannical basketball coach—who happened to be my tyrannical PE teacher as well (he told us he did not expect anything from us in gym class that he could not do himself; he could do forty pull-ups)—required me to have my mother sew it on the front of my white gym shorts. For a year, it made me a boy marked for derisive comments and shoves from guys who thought I'd worn it there as an affectation of superiority.

When I reached high school, I became just one more fan in the crowded grandstands, forced to watch my former teammates in thrilling and agonizing contests with Coatesville. I would have melted into the crowd but for one thing. My old Little League pal, Joe Forman (nicknamed "Lop," because, owing to cranial shape, an unkind barber, or a combination of the two, his head appeared lopsided, a constant threat to his ability to remain upright) had learned how to lead a popular gospel-tinged cheer he'd seen at Cheyney. Mixing some set lines with some free-form riffing he'd begin, "I got the spirit," to which the crowd would respond, "Oh yeah." "I wanna hear it." "Oh yeah." "It's on the roof." "Oh yeah." One hundred proof." "Oh yeah." "It's in my locker." "Oh yeah." "I'm drinking vodka." "Oh yeah." It would continue until Lop's poetic capabilities descended into complete nonsense. Then, as the crowd chanted the ending, a rhythmic and muffled "team, team . . . teamteamteam," Buzz and his cousin Monk would grab me and lift me overhead until my head nearly scraped the gymnasium rafters. I hated it, but the alternative—not sitting with Buzz and Monk—would have been worse. In my yearbook, where senior photos are captioned by inside jokes, predictions of glowing futures, and clever sayings, mine reads simply: "C'mon, Monk, put me down."

So, as it turns out, it was I, right alongside Donnie Rose, who had taken his last shot in competitive, organized basketball. And, acting like a person who'd been left at the altar, I did the strangest thing of all. To cover my humiliation, I immediately went out for wrestling, a move that would for four years bury my love of play beneath a regular pounding handed out by 95-pound clots of muscle with oversized heads and a mean streak well beyond my own. This, not forearms knocking me off stride as I dribbled, was my hell. Only recently has it dawned on me that it's possible that for years I was the Donnie Rose of wrestling, the butt of jokes told by former opponents at cocktail parties of their own.

David Drew, in the *Lost Chronicles of the Mayan Kings*, asserts that Chichén Itzá and the other Mesoamerican ball courts scattered from Arizona to Guatemala served the Mayans as connectors between this world and the other world, between royal and common parts of the cities. I wish

I had recognized then that basketball was as close to a version of heaven, or another world, as I would ever find. The gym was a glorious refuge, one of the only entry points for a 75-pounder into the circle of people who mattered because we were doing something that connected us—even Donnie Rose—to the gods. So, it took me nearly half a century, but I finally learned my lesson from Donnie Rose: the next time I'm in Coatesville and the coach looks my way, I'm going in. I mean, what's the worst that could happen?

W. Wilson Pins Warriors, 52-3 In Dual Meet

It is our human need—to circle back to the stations of our sorrow.

Michael Hainey

DENNIS KUBECK RUINS IT FOR EVERYONE

If Charles Darwin could have gotten a glimpse of Dennis Kubeck and me as high school wrestlers, he'd have had no need for his voyages to the Galapagos. All the material he needed to settle his hunches about natural selection, the ravenous desires of our genes, and the pecking order that results from both would have been right in front of him, displayed convincingly in a slew of high school gyms; in fact, he could have studied the evidence in great detail thanks to my father's decision to memorialize a few of my inglorious efforts as a series of 35-mm color slides. Briefly a professional photographer (a vocation abandoned after he shot the wedding of one of his friends with the lens cap on), my dad once snapped a sequence so quickly that the match—all eighty seconds of it—is preserved in nearly the same painful detail as it would have been on 8-mm film. One moment both my opponent and I are standing. Five slides later I am caught on my back, cradled so securely that I could have been encased in quick-drying cement.

Victims of the 52–3 drubbing: author kneeling far left; Denny Kubeck kneeling second from right. *Photo collection of author*

For a brief spell I believed that a December day in ninth grade—when I looked in shock to see my name on the cut list for the basketball team—would be the most vivid memory of my life in sports. I was wrong. That would come two years later, when, thanks to Dennis Kubeck, my wrestling team required a police escort to our bus following a 52–3 loss. I'll tell you about that night later. For now it is enough for you to know that Dennis was my opposite in so many ways that it still hurts my head to think about it: confident, muscular, unconcerned, dedicated to and successful at quenching his many appetites. There are no 35-mm color slides of Dennis Kubeck flopping around on his back.

Me? I weighed seventy-five pounds on the December day—just a week after my basketball shock—when I reported to the junior high cafeteria and began a new career as a wrestler or, as the local paper frequently labeled practitioners of the sport, a grappler. There were only two 75-pounders out for the team; the other was Dutchie Huber, a tough little son of a bitch who had already mauled me in the two classes of phys ed set aside for wrestling. Dutchie was a natural little bully, fearless and uncorrupted by sentiment. One of his favorite ploys was to wait near the cafeteria cashier at lunchtime. When Dutchie saw somebody—anybody, size and gender not considerations—with a lunch that appealed to him, he would swoop in. With his prey handcuffed by the need to hold the tray, he would quickly pick up every item of food and lick it. At that point, the entire meal would simply be turned over to Dutchie, who never bought into the truism that there's no free lunch. Needless to say, structured practice and the opportunity to abuse the same target—me—day in and day out did not strike Dutchie as a good use of his time. Within a week he was gone, and so I ascended to varsity status without a rival and began four long years of competitive wrestling.

I've written elsewhere that wrestling "is as old and merciless as the human race," which made it, for me, devoid of fun. The ring is a line painted on a sea of compressed foam; it offers no escape; no ropes to slump against. "Matches feature barely dressed bodies entangled too intimately for some, and a pageant of disfigurement—crippled knees, crooked noses, and cauliflower ears—that mark it as coarse and vulgar to others. Indeed, wrestling's vocabulary is just a roll call of body parts and hints of what can be done to them: ankle picks, chicken wings, headlocks, arm bars, tight waists, high crotches, cradles, pancakes, and can openers."

There are no soaring flights as with basketball. Gravity, both as physical force and somber state, always wins, robbing the sport of playfulness. You may grab a friend to go play some hoops—you don't grab one to go play some grappling. Because it is deadly serious, you won't catch a wrestler high-fiving anyone midway through a match, spiking anything at its conclusion, or gloating over and taunting a beaten opponent: too much rides on every outcome to believe that victory in one match will spare you from humiliation in the next. I have seen wrestlers who looked invincible in one round of a tournament get demolished in the next.

In every realm of my senses, wrestling is a winter sport. It takes place indoors in artificially heated, often stifling wrestling rooms and in frigid basement locker rooms where one strips naked to stand on a cold scale next to that night's opponent. It conjures bus rides where the scenery is bare trees glimpsed in the headlights of a school bus lurching along in the dark January nights, heading toward or returning from another drubbing.

My own time spent on wrestling mats leaves me wounded til this day. I'd like to be humorous about this—and occasionally I am, describing for people how my undermuscled frame was shocked into submission by 95-pound clots of muscle topped by large heads—but there really is not much funny about the kind of humiliation that wrestling can bring. Even after a wrestling victory, then, along with pride I felt relief, not exultation at the sport itself.

Nonetheless, wrestling kept me in the varsity club, no small deal because outside of school I was invisible. Beginning in junior high I could see that weekend parties and dating were not to be my lot. I went to a few West Chester State football games with the in crowd, but I was terrified of girls. My lack of size fed my fears. Entering junior high school at less than seventy pounds I was perpetually, in the words of a slam book entry, "too small" to merit consideration. My mother had been a high school belle, and she found my reticence and lack of social presence unfathomable and worthy of persistent ridicule. I countered by playing sports and immersing myself in pop music, something that seemed to soften her a little and transport her somewhere closer in time to those high school days.

The music's effect on me was less heartening. At night I would stack six albums on my record player and lie awake long enough to flip them all over, a ritual of saturation that led me to believe that the music illuminated, encapsulated, and anticipated all my suffering. While most pop music crippled me, rhythm and blues was lethal. Though I knew R&B was black music and that the feelings it expressed were associated with the black condition, I wasn't listening for the echoes of slavery. For me it was simply about stunted possibilities. Ray Charles, in particular, seemed to understand what was ailing me: "afraid and shy," he let his "chance go by." Timid and socially awkward, I found this type of regret appealing: it was more heroically sorrowful than having a girl leave me; even worse than knowing that they were all going to leave me. This was the stab in the heart that came from knowing that I would never even meet them (of course, being human, once I'd finally gotten a girlfriend in high school, I promptly left her in a cruel and cowardly way that causes me pain even now to think of it). The exaltation of this misery in the Billboard Top 40 led to protracted and premature melancholy, and somewhere around the hundredth night of listening to Ray Charles, I had made up my mind "to live in memories of the lonesome times." I was fifteen.

Worse yet, while I was lying there steeping in R&B misery, I knew that somewhere Dennis Kubeck was out on the town, sometimes in the backseat of a car doing unspeakable things to a girl whose name and reputation I will protect, since she turned up at one of our recent class reunions.

Only in school sports was I a part of things. Having once played basketball and baseball with Buzz Shank, Monk Howard, Gary Woodward, Jimmy McFadden, and Tommy Webb, some of the school's movers and shakers, I still got by there—barely. Having been involuntarily removed from the competitive basketball world that I'd loved, I tried to take my fill of it in P.E. classes. I would leave a classroom on the run, get to the locker room ahead of everyone else, and be dressed in time to shoot baskets for five minutes before anyone else showed up. The only catch was that Buzz and Monk occasionally arrived to get dressed just as I was heading out to the floor. When that happened, they would strip me and throw my clothes around the room, and I would need to hustle into them a second time. Every once in awhile, they'd strip me down a second time, meaning I would arrive late for roll call. Once—thankfully, just once—they stripped me down and threw me out into the hallway just as the bell for class change-over rang. I can't be certain, but to this day I think a junior high crush of mine got an eyeful—or as much of an eyeful as an 89-pounder can provide. The resultant panic confirmed the authority of adrenaline. In shoving my way back to safety, I knocked Buzz and Monk, starters on the football team, nearly on their asses, and the madness in my eyes as I reentered the locker room sent them backpedaling.

My ninth grade wrestling season in the cafeteria ended after just a few unscored scrimmages, too quickly for me to understand that I was getting myself into something dangerous and debilitating. Getting cut from basketball meant that I had no shot at the high school team the next year when our junior high would merge with the other in the school district. My father, who liked basketball but thought wrestling was more ennobling, made it clear that my size made wrestling my best prospect for varsity letters and awards assemblies. I saw his point. Though wrestling was a marginal activity compared with basketball, being on the team meant that on match day I still wore my varsity blazer to school, still got invited to season-ending banquets, and still got counted in one of the ways that counted. What did I know?

Not much, as it turned out. When the first week of practice rolled around in November, all of us tenth graders reported unprepared for what lay ahead. The upperclassmen surely knew, but they never warned us, perhaps knowing that to do so would have shrunken our numbers before the first day. Our coach, Jack Stahl, was one of those gruff-exterior-hides-a-heart-of-gold characters. He was a frightening man to look at. He had a deep-ledged brow, and a broad nose, obviously broken in prior times, most likely by a woolly mammoth. He also had a mean streak that made it tough to find that heart of gold.

For our first week he had decided that rather than put down the mats and wrestle, we would instead spend each day running an obstacle course for an hour and a half. For the first five minutes we ran enthusiastically from station to station, clambering over parallel bars draped with mats, climbing ropes to the gym ceiling, doing squat thrusts, and bridging on our necks. For the final eighty-five minutes we slogged along, dragged ourselves over the bars, hung lifelessly on the rope a few feet off the ground, and tried to survive. Whenever Stahl's attention was not turned directly on us, we tried to do nothing, conserving energy for the moments when we were in his view. Unfortunately, we were seldom beyond his range for more than a few seconds. He camped out in the center of the stations, whirling around while swinging a six-foot length of bamboo pole; at the rope station, he waited for our upward progress to halt at the behest of trembling arms, at which point he would beat our asses with the bamboo until we found the strength to ascend a few more feet out of range or fall to the ground in exhaustion. This being the sixties, there were, of course, no water breaks. In fact, there were no breaks at all.

The experience inspired several wrestlers to call in sick a day or two, caused a good number of the uncommitted to quit, and gave me pause to think about how badly I wanted to wear a varsity blazer. Somehow, I was still there for week two when the wrestling began. Though most schools in our conference had new, compressed foam mats, we were not so lucky. Practice began each day with the chore of laying down our practice surface. About seventy-five 3' × 6' canvas mats stuffed with horsehair were hung on trucks like those the fashion industry uses to move clothes through Manhattan's streets. We had to take the mats off their hooks, align them in a large square, being careful to tuck in all the handles, then cover it all with a rubberized tarp that required the presence and strength of the entire team to be stretched tautly enough to wrestle on. It took about fifteen minutes. At the end of every practice, it took at least that long to fold the tarp and lift the mats back onto the hooks.

Once the mats were down, practice followed a set regimen: calisthenics for about fifteen minutes; demonstrations and drills for about forty-five minutes; live bouts of wrestling for another half hour. On the first day, Stahl summoned me from the pack to the center of the mat. We were going to learn double leg takedowns. Standing nonchalantly, still dressed in his teacher's white shirt and tie, he ordered me to shoot in on his legs. I slid to both knees straight on, but as I reached out to encircle his legs, he drove both of his knees together. My head became a clapper. He literally rang my bell. Woozy, I arose. Apparently, the double leg takedown session was over, ending with his growled instruction: "boys, the head goes on the outside."

Strange as it seemed, even at the time, I loved Stahl and his methods. For my first match, against a school that had just begun wrestling that year, he told me not to worry, assuring me that my opponent "looked like a pussy." I cradled and pinned him within a minute; I was 1–0. Before my next match, Stahl told me that when I locked up at the beginning of the match I should grind my forehead into my opponent's temple. I followed instructions. My opponent was shocked and outraged. As I ground my head, he began groaning, then let out a loud cry that pulled the ref in for a closer look. It was too late. Distracted and intimidated, another one bit the dust. I was 2–0. When my winning streak reached six, I began thinking that this was going to work out even better for me than basketball. It really wasn't so tough.

And then it happened: January arrived, and with it an allowance of two extra pounds for every weight class. Already giving away six pounds to my opponents, I would now be taking on guys who had once weighed as much as 120, but had decided to shed even more weight to enter the ranks at 105 and, occasionally, at my new 97-pound class.

Believing myself to be a genetic Lilliputian, it had never occurred to me that anyone small would want to voluntarily shrink themselves further, but wrestlers do so often, sometimes eagerly. Inescapably vulnerable, they choose a weight class based not on where the body feels best but where the ego perceives the least danger, and anyone who stays in the sport long becomes well versed in the ways of reducing. Pounds are sweated off in the timeless and ugly tradition that killed three college wrestlers in 1997—in rubber body suits, in steam rooms, and in the basement furnace rooms of buildings, where the heat pipes melt down fat, muscle, and sometimes the lifeblood and will of an athlete. I tried it myself for a few weeks my junior year. I slept under three layers of blankets in a rubber sweat suit, topped by a cotton sweat suit and a wool hat. When I would arise at 5 A.M., breathing in halting gasps, I could pull the elastic sleeves away from my arm and pour out enough liquid to fill a few glasses. Even so, I could not get down to the next weight class.

That year, when the scales at an away match declared nearly half of our squad to be over their limits, our coach turned on the hot water in the shower, sealed the overweight wrestlers in with a curtain and tape, and then had them run in place for the twenty minutes remaining to make weight. When they emerged from their thick prison of steam, I watched the coach towel down one wrestler, trying to remove every last milligram of sweat with such force that I truly believed he was going to draw blood from the pores. If they'd had five o'clock shadows, I'm sure he would have had them shave.

With many wrestlers, the preoccupation with weight grows to obsession. Some take jobs as cooks, learning to prepare intricate meals that their families, but not themselves, can enjoy. Shedding weight for an intramurals college tournament, I once bought a Sara Lee cheesecake and placed it in the refrigerator for three weeks, looking in on it obsessively like an anxious parent checking on a newborn baby.

Many of the guys on my team would walk to nearby Bevans Deli before a match, ordering a hoagie and filling a bag with Tastykakes and sodas or chocolate milk. If we were heading out of town, the aroma of cold cuts filled the bus. It was understood that the food was to be the payoff for delaying gratification, a reward that, win or lose, would be the deserved end to days or weeks of privation. Of course, the delay had to last until you had walked off the mat. Not everyone understood this. Joel Feldman, a J.V., once checked his weight on our home scales. Pleased to be a bit under his target, he congratulated himself by drinking a quart of water on the way to the match. When he stepped on the opponent's unforgiving scale, he was more than a pound over. When the coach asked him if he'd had anything to eat or drink, he said, "Just water, but there's no calories in that." I thought the coach was going to shoot him.

More entertaining was the case of Johnny Hayes, a round, likeable sort with a large appetite and unfocused competitive instincts. He was wrestling J.V. 145 at Owen J. Roberts, the league's best team, on a night when the school was rolling out a brand new, multi-thousand-dollar Resilite mat. Johnny ate his hoagie in the locker room after weighing in, but before wrestling. His opponent put a tight waist in and squeezed. Up came the partially digested hoagie all over the new mat. The O.J. Roberts wrestler was so disgusted that, keeping the tight waist in, he picked up one of Hayes's legs and proceeded to drive him back and forth through the slop, mopping up the vomit with the front of Hayes's singlet while irate parents, seeing their prized taxpayer purchase defiled, showered him with abuse. The concept of a "teachable moment" had not yet infiltrated society, so we were free to chalk this up not as a learning experience but simply as one of the dumbest things we'd ever seen.

The January weight allowance indeed brought a new caliber of opponents down to my 97-pound class, and from there on out, I struggled, outmuscled and outexperienced for the rest of the season by older, stronger athletes who had no interest in anything but winning. My memory turned out to be inaccurate, but I long had it set in my mind that the first of these oversized opponents was Walt McCulley from our hated rival, Coatesville. Though it turns out he was not in fact the first of my defeats, he dominated my thoughts for years, so in January 2012—forty-six years after we'd wrestled—I set out to find him. I was obsessed with discovering what had become of Walt and the others I'd wrestled. When his answering machine picked up my call, I knew immediately I had found the right person. Though I'd spent perhaps fifteen seconds talking to him after our only match in 1966, I recognized his voice instantly. A day later he returned my call. He knew my name and even remembered that I'd been taller than him. I made an appointment to visit.

Driving the back roads from Baltimore into the farmlands of southeastern Pennsylvania is like being in a time machine set on low speed: a trip backward via a landscape of two-lane roads, rolling pastureland, and the occasional four-horse plow team working an Amish farmer's fields. It seems, when your speed is just right, that you might even hit a sudden rise and dip in the road that will make your stomach sink. You won't, of course, because they've all been engineered out of our lives, a simple pleasure denied to anyone under the age of forty. Accompanied by music from the satellite radio's sixties station, I rode steadily backward, experiencing emotions as close as I'll ever get to those I'd had at age sixteen.

I rang the bell of Walt's nicely appointed suburban home and, if he was surprised by my six-foot, 180-pound frame, he didn't let on. While I wasn't surprised that he'd remained small—about six inches shorter and weighing no more than 130—I was surprised to learn that he'd been like me—not one of those who'd come down from the bigger weights, but an undersized 90-pounder wrestling in the 95-pound class. There were several other things that weren't what I had figured on. My assumptions about Coatesville—a frightening steel town ten miles away from West Chester—meant that I had penciled him in for a lifetime of blue-collar labor. But, though his father had worked for the town's wellspring, Lukens Steel, Walt had gone on to earn an engineering degree from Temple, where he'd been too light to even take a shot at college's lowest weight class, 118, and, fortuitously, too light as well for the Vietnam draft. What most subverted my expectations, however, was finding that he had entered tenth grade with no wrestling experience. Fingered by the wrestling coach for his size (the baseball coach took one look at him and told him not to bother), by his senior year he was 17–0–2, a sectional champion, and as tough as anyone I ever wrestled.

How, I wondered, had that happened? In his estimation, it boiled down to one word—desire—an answer that exposed my own effort as shameful. The winning had left him with esteem and a self-confidence that became apparent as he leafed through his scrapbook, pausing at the newspaper article recording our match. "I pinned you," he said, "in 1:18." He smiled as he said this, and while I didn't get the impression that his pleasure was at my expense, it clearly set us apart in ways that needed no further explanation. When he looked back at me, it was as if I were seeing him again at the weigh-in, a medieval affair at Coatesville conducted in a large open basement with cold concrete floors and a large platform meat scale. I had known when I had stepped off it that night that things were not going to end well for me.

So, there it was, suspended in my subconscious and Walt McCulley's scrapbook for nearly half a century: the seventy-eight seconds that broke the back of my season and ultimately of my competitive career. I had little zeal left for looking up the others. Why would the ones I'd beaten want to see me in light of how I felt after visiting Walt? I notified the Boyertown Bear that I'd pinned for my first win; he did not respond. The Phoenixville Phantom whose temple I had abraded with my forehead did. It turns out Sam Walton had a clear recollection, not only of "losing an inch of skin" to some "wire-haired" opponent (a remark that I both resent and resemble), but also of our follow-up match a year later. "I had you 5–0 in the first period with a seven-eighths Nelson . . . you rolled out of it; you reversed me in the second, cradled me and . . . we wound up with a 6–6 tie." It was comforting to know I'd fought back at least once, but how many more who'd beaten me did I need to visit to know that I'd feel the same after each? At least Walt had been a sectional champ and Sam had gone on to wrestle in the Marine Corps (where boot camp treated his 115-pound body to the delights of carrying a 65-pound backpack); how much worse would it get when I ran into those with less athletic talent?

McCulley had handed me one of my early losses. A month later, as my sophomore season neared the end, I'd had enough losses and enough wrestling. My final match came in the league tournament against a wrestler from Pottsgrove. When his team had come to West Chester early in the season my current opponent had been their J.V. 95-pounder. I'd pinned the varsity wrestler. Now, I got off to a bad start—taken down and ridden for awhile. Eventually I came back and led by a point with about thirty seconds to go. I planned to do nothing while making it look like I was working hard—the first tactic that all wrestlers learn. Suddenly, from my corner, I heard Coach Stahl bellowing: "Shoot!" He wanted me to shoot for a takedown. What, was he insane? Why would I shoot? As the clock wound down, I found it strange that my opponent, down a point, was aping my tactics—working hard at doing nothing. Stahl's shouting became louder and more urgent: "Shoot! Shoot! Shoot!" Sorry, no way, coach. The buzzer went off. I shook hands and waited for the ref to raise my right arm in victory. Instead he lifted that of the Pottsgrove wrestler. I was truly puzzled. I looked at Stahl. It appeared that his head was about to blow up. He was scarlet with anger; his teeth were clenched and bared; he was truly seething. As I walked off the mat he grabbed me by the arm and hustled me to the locker room, my toes barely tapping at the floor. He threw me down on the bench and yelled at me loudly for what seemed five minutes, though the rage was so intense that I doubt he actually sustained it for more than thirty seconds. The specifics of his constructive criticism were that my opponent had been sitting on two points riding time advantage, which gave him the one point win. The heart of his rage boiled down to this: "Always do what the coach tells you, no matter what your IQ is, smart guy."

After I had showered and dressed, I experienced the heart of gold. He put his arm around me and walked me out to his car. He took me to a diner to eat, telling me in soft tones that he knew I was one day going to dominate my weight class. At least I think that's what he was saying. Really, all I can remember is that someone had fed quarters into the jukebox, and while we ate, "These Boots Were Made for Walking" played what seemed like a dozen times. To this day, the instant I hear its first descending bass notes, I do not see what I should: Nancy Sinatra in go-go boots and a miniskirt that barely concealed the secret of life; I see instead the Neanderthal profile of Jack Stahl.

I'd let him down badly. A month or two later he announced that he was leaving our high school to work with special education students in Connecticut. Aside from thinking that was a curious fit—a nut in charge of the nuthouse—I also thought I'd miss him. For some reason he had a soft spot in his heart for me, and before he left he announced to the student body at assembly that I would not only be a 95-pounder for three years ("if we feed him," he quipped), but that he also saw little standing between me and a district championship. What did he know?

Our new coach my junior year was Harry Hoffman. He'd coached a state champ in the tough central Pennsylvania environs, and he brought with him the promise and prospect that wrestling was about to become something different. Unfortunately, he never made it clear to me that at the level we were at, strength and a willingness to bully (like rubbing your forehead into someone's temple) and to resist bullying trumped all other skills. He made it sound like the very things I possessed—quickness, stamina, smarts—were not just useful but were everything I needed. He was wrong.

Stahl was wrong, too. I wouldn't be wrestling 95 anymore. I'd bulked up to 100 and would now compete in the 103-pound class. I started off slow and stayed there. My interest waned; I thought often of basketball, sometimes lingering to watch the opening of the team's practice before trudging cheerlessly to the awaiting mats. In my match with Coatesville, I was pinned by Walt McCulley's brother, Andy. My Pottsgrove nemesis from the previous year's tournament didn't need riding time points this time around—he pinned me, too. I prayed for snow days and moved through practices listlessly. The worse it got, the more Hoffman tried to pump me up, praising me excessively to the local reporter after my few wins. Privately, he stressed my quickness and my smarts; there was no need, he implied, to be held down and tossed around by the slow-witted. I responded by trying flamboyant, showy moves: my way of turning wrestling into my own kind of something else. I was—in the great tradition of Dutchie Huber—looking for the free lunch, though there was none to be had.

The losing made me nasty everywhere except on the mats. There were only two guys in school smaller than me. One, Johnny McKee, came out for wrestling my senior year. Our 180-pounder, who was not a good wrestler but was an exceptionally cruel bully (and at the last reunion looked to be a 400-pound bully), imprisoned the 85-pound McKee in a locker for the duration of a practice. Understandably, when no one—myself included—came to his aid, McKee decided he did not need the prestige of being a grappler and promptly quit the team.

I selected the other small man—John Eshleman, the 90-pound statistician for the football team—as the scapegoat for my laziness and frustration. I had stopped doing homework somewhere around the eighth grade (which means I have yet to read the *Red Badge of Courage* or *Moby Dick*, though I did eventually get around to Huck Finn on my own), but I enjoyed algebra, at least while the solutions were being teased out in the classroom. I just didn't want to do any of the teasing on my own; instead I spent my evenings being educated by *My Mother, the Car* and *Gomer Pyle, USMC*. This meant that whenever called upon by Mr. Fielding to put a homework problem on the blackboard, I had nothing to show.

I solved this by walking past Eshleman's desk on the way to the board, lifting his completed and usually correct homework, copying it onto the board, then returning it on my way back. By winter, he'd had all he could take. As I snatched up his work one day and strode to the board, he rose from his seat and hurled all of his books at me while screaming obscenities. I did not turn around. Instead, I nonchalantly erased the work of a previous student and posted Eshleman's work again as my own. Returning to my seat, and still holding the used eraser, I launched a furious stealth attack, clapping it across the top of his burr-cut melon. A great cloud of dust arose and when it had settled, John Eshleman's head was a bright yellow. For the rest of his high school days, he was known as "Chalkhead." Adding further indignity, the dusting so overjoyed Buzz and another football player that they swept Eshleman onto their shoulders and marched him down the hallway. As I lost sight of them, the last sound I heard was that of Chalkhead's pants ripping open at the crotch. (At my fortieth reunion I bumped into a bearded, six-foot, 180-pound teacher from Detroit. He asked if I remembered him. It was, of course, Chalkhead. He recalled the origins of his nickname with good humor—or at least without animosity—and I was pleased to know I had not scarred him for life.)

The incident marked a rare victory for me. My junior season congealed into an unvaried glob of defeat, each final slide in my father's portfolio looking identical—me, helpless beneath a faceless opponent with his ass in the air as he brought his full weight to bear on me. I was aware that my father, though he remained patient, was increasingly disappointed. He never missed a match, sitting with the other parents, where he and teammate Steve Miller's dad, Harold, would bellow at the officials. If I won, he took me out for a beef sandwich at my favorite spot, the Farmer in the Dell. At one point he asked Coach Hoffman to have a private word with me. It was a variation on the "you've got too much athleticism and intelligence to be losing" speech he'd already delivered at practice. I was unmoved. Not to put too fine a spin on it, but I was in some way paying my dad back for his passivity at home, which had allowed my unrelentingly critical mother to steamroll all of her kids too many times at all the wrong times.

With just a few weeks before the season-ending league tourney, we set out for an away match at Woodrow Wilson High School, a school I now know to be located northeast of Philadelphia near Bristol. At the time I'd never heard of it; I was just grateful that it was not conference rivals Coatesville, Owen J. Roberts, or Downingtown. As we dressed in the locker room, I noticed a sign titled "Rams Rip List" on the wall. It was a tally of opponents who'd lost to Wilson that season, but to us it was just a list of more schools we'd never heard of, and when our J.V.s—Billy Hayes, Joel Feldman, Smokey Stover, and the rest of our ne'er-do-wells—returned joyously to the locker room celebrating a rare win, we all breathed easy. It was going to be our night.

We ran out to the mat, circled around our co-captains and moved in unison through the mindless warmups that all wrestling teams did back then: jumping jacks, pushups, neck bridges, squat thrusts, and then some spin drills, and some half-speed single and double leg takedowns. We took our seats on the sideline and waited for Woodrow Wilson to go through their own mindless routines. Suddenly, however, the gymnasium shook with a roar. I hadn't been paying any attention to the bleachers, but I knew a crowd of fifty fans could not make the sound I was hearing.

I looked to the stands and fell into shock. There were hundreds of spectators, filling every seat on both sides of the mat. A moment later, the loudspeaker took over for the crowd. The theme song from *The Bridge on the River Kwai* blared out, and as the crowd whistled along, the Woodrow Wilson wrestlers burst from their locker room. They were not jogging. They were running. One of the bigger ones, a swarthy, hairy dynamo who looked to be about twenty-five, seemed to be nearly frothing from the mouth. The smallest, their 95-pounder, was carrying a small stuffed gorilla. Mouth set in an open bellow and grasping at the air with stubby arms, it was outfitted in a tiny Woodrow Wilson singlet. This, it would turn out, was the team's talisman, to be awarded at night's end to the outstanding Ram wrestler.

It was the damnedest thing any of us had ever been a part of. The next hour floated by, shrouded in paralyzing disbelief. We forfeited the 97-pound match, which put me on the mat first. Perhaps because the crowd was so large and I was so numb, I wrestled better than most nights, scoring the first takedown and leading into the second period. Surprised at my good fortune, I began moving without plan or reason and in the third period found myself fighting once again from my back. When the ref slapped the mat with just twenty-eight seconds left, we were down 12–0.

My friend Steve Miller went next at 112. I wasn't paying attention to his match, being focused instead on the crowd, the little gorilla sitting matside in front of the Wilson bench, and the complimentary orange slices that I ate guiltily as an undeserved reward for losing. Steve was a lot tougher than I was, and losses bothered him a lot more (after being pinned by a Downingtown wrestler, he hadn't slept that night), but he only lasted fifteen seconds longer than I had. The next day's paper quoted Coach Hoffman as saying, "I'm still pleased with our boys even though they did lose by a big score. A number of the boys were doing a fine job, but this club just put us on our backs and pinned us like crazy." Well, that's sort of the point, isn't it?

And so it went, one of our guys getting pinned in twenty-seven seconds. As we headed to the penultimate match, we trailed 46–0 and fully expected to leave on the short end of a 58–0 score. At 180 pounds, Denny Kubeck and his opponent traded shoves and stares for the first two minutes, and the period ended 0–0. The wrestlers in the upper weights tended to do a lot of that sort of non-wrestling, and Denny was particularly inclined to spend as little energy as possible, on the wrestling mat as elsewhere.

I have no idea what attracted Dennis Kubeck to wrestling. I knew little about him when he'd come out for the team that year. I knew he smoked— a surefire killer for a wrestler. And I knew he'd been off to military school somewhere for a few years before being allowed to resume the life he was destined for. Though he shared my lack of intensity, he was nonetheless a good wrestler. For some reason, it seemed that every time he took the mat, something out of the ordinary happened. Against the Haverford School, the local paper reported that he'd "suffered a pinched nerve that shut off blood circulation in his head and made him dizzy." Somehow, it is always seemed like he was wrestling with no blood circulating in his head. Not that he wasn't smart; you just couldn't tell if he was thinking about anything out there.

He began period two on top of the Wilson wrestler. His opponent escaped for a 1–0 lead, but Denny took him down to go up 2–1. Thereafter followed a series of events as riveting and dumbfounding as any I've seen in the sport. Denny ran out of gas, but he still had three minutes—half the match—to go. Instead of throwing in the towel, he continued to wrestle— and score—but did so in ten-second segments that he struggled through as if he were on the Bataan death march. The whistle would blow, he'd head directly for the out-of-bounds line, and upon reaching it, would flop down, then lay unmoving until prodded and threatened by the referee with stalling points that would lead to disqualification. He would then slowly drag himself back to the center of the mat and, upon hearing the whistle, do it all over again.

The ten-second mini-shows meant the match was going to last forever, but it was a pleasant forever, sustained by drama that rose to unbearable proportions. Every time Denny would get reversed or give up an escape, he'd come back to score despite looking as if he was incapable of standing or walking, much less wrestling. As the time ticked slowly toward the match's conclusion, Denny's act got richer. He looked like a beginner in an introductory mime class: prostrate, gasping, crawling, moving at times as if he were walking on the seabed, at times stumbling like a drunken Foster Brooks. As he made it to the safety of the mat's edge with only a minute to go, both the Wilson fans and his opponent were frustrated beyond their capacities to endure.

It turned out that his opponent was the guy who looked twenty-five and was frothing at the mouth during warm-ups. I later found out he was Joe Landman, Wilson's undefeated district champion. He was so distraught with Denny's dead man act in the final period that he asked for a time-out. There are no time-outs in wrestling, except for obvious injury, but Landman got one anyway, and he used it to dash out of the gymnasium and into his locker room. Everyone sat in surprised and speculative silence: where had he gone, and why, and for how long? After about a minute he came charging back out, nearly unhinging the doors. His roaring and intensity fanned the crowd into its own frenzy, but he'd made a grave mistake. His time away meant great gasps of oxygen for Denny. The whistle blew, and ten seconds later it blew again. Denny had gotten out of bounds once more, and the cycle began anew.

When the final buzzer sounded, Denny had won, 8–5. As far as I was concerned, Denny deserved to take the little gorilla home, but Landman was apoplectic and many in the crowd were now frothing at the mouth. Our heavyweight wrestled amid a storm of bloodlust. He led into the third period before being pinned, bringing the final team score to 52–3. The crowd remained inconsolable, screaming at us (well, mostly at Denny) as we left the mat. I didn't look into the stands; I didn't want to know if my father and Harold Miller were going to be taking on a pack of three hundred.

My father could never have captured Denny's victory with his slides. Too bad it came before the era of videocams and smartphones—I would love to see it again. Then again, it's probably best I can't. The most lasting memories seem to be those that, because we can't get them back and are forced to rehearse them over and over in our minds, are the most textured of all. In the end, Dennis Kubeck's display—all the better for his oblivious-ness to its impact on every other single person in that gymnasium—was one for the ages. When we left the locker room half an hour later, the crowd was still loitering outside. They were waiting for us (well, mostly for Denny), and we needed the local police to board the bus without injury.

On the ride home, I thought about the overhyped spectacle of Denny's match, savoring Joe Landman's manic misery as if I'd been the one who had beaten him. It should have stuck in my mind as a pleasant memory, but it didn't. Instead, the Kubeck win has haunted me until now because of this: though a smoker, a drinker, and an athlete not given to abstinence,

Denny was a winner. Had he lost that night, not a soul would have held it against him or remembered it for more than a few days. But he didn't lose—and his win sparked in me the questions that have dogged me for decades: why did he keep getting up? And why couldn't I keep getting up, too?

Famed football coach Bill Parcells once remarked that "losing may take a little from your credibility, but quitting will destroy it." Doing research for this recounting, I rolled through spools of newspaper microfilm, loss after loss creeping across the reader's screen, while I searched for clues as to whether I had been losing or quitting all those years ago. In some odd ways I was more welcoming to the latter possibility: if I had quit, it meant I may have had talent and simply chosen—for reasons I could later justify and defend—not to use it. It is an odd consideration, but not an uncommon one. It has been said that the first black heavyweight boxing champion, Jack Johnson, claiming to have taken a dive after going down in the twenty-seventh round of a championship fight in heat exceeding 105 degrees, would rather have had people think that he threw the fight than lost it.

I have joked in recent years to students that I spent my final season of wrestling hoping to impress Dianne Tenebruso with my potential as a prom date. In reality, although I never missed a practice, I was a has-been by my senior year. I had bloated to 113 pounds but chose to wrestle in the 120 class, where I had an easier time meeting my objective in wrestle-offs, which was to make certain I always fell just short of landing on a varsity mat again. As it turned out, Dianne knew nothing of wrestling and never came to a match anyway. This is probably one of the reasons I ended up with the prom date.

Though I went on to win an intramural championship in college and once placed second in an over twenty-five tourney in the Lehigh Valley, I was never pressed to go very deep into my reservoir of moves or my resolve to win at those places. The truth of my high school career is that I did not lose because I lost heart; I had none for wrestling to begin with. It was inevitable, then, that I would cheat the sport. I have for fifty years carried a heart that is, in the words of songwriter Leonard Cohen, "torn by what we've done and can't undo." That inability to undo is why my head hurts when I think of Dennis Kubeck.

I recently tracked down the Woodrow Wilson heavyweight, Nelson Plunto. As it turned out, his brother Ken had been my 103-pound opponent that night (he too has become a 180-pounder in adulthood), but Nelson's name had stuck in my mind because he'd gone on to become a district champ. He remembers Wilson's halcyon days but retains none of the details from the match on January 31, 1967. I asked if he could put me in touch with Joe Landman. No, he said; not possible. Joe Landman, who to this day holds the all-time Woodrow Wilson record for pins, had been in the fencing business but died a few years ago of causes unknown to Nelson. The news brought me up sharply, and for the first time I tried to put myself in Landman's shoes. At the end, did he ever think back to that night—did he wonder if he had quit the match or lost it? Dennis Kubeck is still quenching his appetite for fun—he made a lot of money, married one of the prettiest girls in Chester County (a cheerleader, of course), and, when I see him at reunions, he seems a happy man. There is little, in short, to undo. When he goes to sleep at night, he doesn't need to wonder about that match at all. We should all be so lucky.

DARK EDGES

There can be given no sound reason against race separation. All experience and every deduction from the known laws and principles of human nature and human conduct are against the attempt to harmonize two alien races under the same government.

Moses Fleetwood Walker

FAILING TO MEET JACKIE ROBINSON

I was in Jackie Robinson's presence in the summer of 1962. I had traveled that August with my father a few hundred miles from our home outside Philadelphia to the Little League World Series in Williamsport. Robinson was there as an invited guest, and I found myself before one of the games standing nearby as he stood momentarily alone near a dugout full of pint-sized Japanese players. My Dad said, "There's Jackie Robinson—go talk to him." I asked who he played for and was told he had been a Brooklyn Dodger. Well, I was a Phillies fan, and though I had no knowledge of the history of bad blood that had passed between Jackie Robinson and the Phillies, I had no interest in meeting a Dodger. And this was an old one—he had silver hair and, in his blazer and tie, he didn't look much like a ballplayer to me. Still, my father gave me a nudge, so I trudged toward Robinson. But as I got close, an alternative to shaking hands with a Dodger presented itself when I saw three of the Japanese players coming out of the dugout to warm up. Taking advantage of their smiling faces, I waved my program at them, and they immediately came over to decorate it with the exotic Japanese characters I took to

Jackie Robinson in a scene from *The Jackie Robinson Story.*
Library of Congress

be autographs (I still have the program's innards, but, alas, have lost the treasured cover—how does that happen?). When I turned back, I saw the exasperation on my father's face. Robinson was now being shepherded elsewhere by his official hosts—adults who were clearly enjoying the chance to be around a famous man. "Why," I asked my father, "are you so worried about Jackie Robinson?" "He's famous," he told me. "He's the first black man to play major league baseball" (in actuality, it is much more likely that he told me he had been the first Negro). I returned a look of genuine incomprehension. In the fifteen years between the time Jackie Robinson had first put on his Dodger uniform and his appearance at that Little League World Series, baseball had been integrated to a degree that left a boy growing up in the in-between years (the fifties)—like me—with no understanding of what that had required—or what it had meant to millions of Americans. In following the Phillies for just a few years, I had seen what seemed to be a hundred black men playing major league baseball. My Little League experience had also borne the fruit of Jackie Robinson's pioneering—I shared a uniform with a handful of black team-mates and thought nothing of it.

What, I thought as a kid, could possibly be important about a Negro playing baseball? Why wouldn't they? Who in their right mind didn't want to play baseball for a living?

The answers crashed down on me several years later. In 1968—now a senior in high school—I was riding home when my bus was bombarded with bricks thrown by local blacks—at least one of them a former Little League teammate—enraged by the assassination of Martin Luther King. It was the first time that I truly understood what an American quicksand the issue of color was, and it was the first time that I could be said to be awakening to its meaning in the life of Jackie Robinson and the many black players who'd come before and after him in high level sports.

I've thought often about my experience with him at that Little League World Series, and I'm coming to see it more as revealing not just something about my perceptions of the world but also revealing a great deal about Jackie Robinson. I've wondered why I hadn't rushed up to him the way a young kid would run up to, say, Derek Jeter now; I've wondered why there was not a crush of cameras and microphones trailing him.

True, a great deal of that hinges on the big changes in the ways that we now perceive—and then plague—celebrities. No one has enough distance from public scrutiny anymore to grow into a hero's role. But there was something more: Jackie Robinson was, by all accounts, at least in public, a rather shy and quiet man, a very improbable man to be at the center of one of the most tumultuous storms in American history. And because he was quiet and private, what has come down to us about Robinson is his symbolism—we have, over the past half century, been unable to probe into his private life past the boundaries that he, and then his wife Rachel, set, a barrier that the 2013 film *42* respected. Nothing unseemly or scandalous has been discovered, as current biography seems to demand, and so he has become to us increasingly an abstraction, a title, a name, a cultural totem: he has become just "the first black major league baseball player."

In trying to pull together stories that bring Robinson back to life for a presentation to teachers at the Georgia State Historical Society, I looked for moments that made him flesh and blood rather than a retired number hanging on outfield fences. What constantly struck me was the ironic extent to which this isolated and private man's story always seemed to be told through his connection to someone else: Rickey and Robinson; Robeson and Robinson; Reese and Robinson; Chapman and Robinson; Rachel and Robinson; and even, in my case, Japanese Little Leaguers and Robinson. It is a story also told through his connections, not so much to the way he played the game of baseball as much as to the way he played the game of life.

This real-world connection, of course, is often said to be the best possible outcome from a lifetime of athletic participation—a balanced perspective that recognizes that sports are just games, mere trivialities not to be confused with something that is actually significant. In that sense, athletes are deemed most important when fulfilling their missions as role models. Robinson himself bought into this, claiming at one time that "a life is only important in its impact upon other lives."

That claim is a crying shame. If he meant that his impact as a player—the verve and nerve with which he played—was important in shaping the way others played the game, now that would be valuable. But I sense he meant it in the way that everyone else does: that the value of sports is in their ability to shape character. I have for decades now been entreating students to give me one specific act, one off-field moment of behavior linked to good character that they have seen a child enact as a result of an athlete's influence. I am still waiting for the first concrete example.

Sports, of course, don't build character—they reveal it. At some intuitive level, we know this—and if we don't, we could stop for a moment and think about it. We could look at Mark McGwire or Mike Tyson or Aaron Hernandez or O. J. Simpson and see that people who have been in sport for a long time—the people who should present our best evidence of its character-building properties—often have questionable behavior. So, why do we as a nation keep proclaiming this? Because we want to be able to explain our love of sports, to justify the time we spend immersed in it. So we say that sports teach lessons for real life. Of course, we say lots of things.

Why, then, do sports matter enough so that Jackie Robinson becomes just as compelling to know as a sports figure as he is as a civil rights figure? Because sport is the only institution devoted to the human potential for excellence—something done well for the sake of doing it well. Many people dismiss sports and play as the toy department of life, but play is what we do when we hear only our own voices urging us to do something well in and for itself. It is this intrinsic motivation and voluntary effort that make sports heroic. Who would applaud a mile covered so swiftly that a runner's lungs threaten to catch fire if it were run at gunpoint? No one, but the whole world applauded in 1954 when Roger Bannister accomplished what physiologists claimed at the time was humanly impossible—the four-minute mile. "I had a moment of mixed joy and anguish, when my mind took over," Bannister said. "It raced well ahead of my body and drew my body compellingly forward. I felt that the moment of a lifetime had come. There was no pain, only a great unity of movement and aim. The world seemed to stand still, or did not exist. The only reality was the next two hundred yards of track under my feet. The tape meant finality—extinction perhaps. I felt at that moment that it was my chance to do one thing supremely well." Sport, more than any other institution, in valuing play, honoring excellence, demanding integration of our physical, emotional, and mental selves while demanding no real-world payoff in return, turns us into human beings. That is what sport is about, and it is impossible to watch old newsreels of Jackie Robinson and not be struck by his intensity—at how much he loved playing baseball well.

Robinson had some advantages in his reach for excellence. Though poverty and war certainly played a role in his life, he gained enough distance from those things to allow him to invest great amounts of time in playing sports. Color may have limited him, but his time at UCLA marked him as a very exceptional man among blacks. It gave him choices in career paths that most could never dream of—and yet he chose baseball. This is important. He didn't have to choose this very visible and publicly scrutinized arena. He didn't have to have millions of eyes upon him every day, a million amateurs passing judgment on whether he—regardless of skin color—belonged in the company of elite athletes.

By participating in sports, an institution divorced, for most of us, from survival—a blank slate upon which we can write our hopes, fears, and aspirations—Robinson should have been testing nothing more than his athletic abilities. Instead, owing to the stature and symbolic significance of baseball in America, he ended up testing the limits of American tolerance and goodwill. It is one thing for the owner of an industrial plant to hire blacks to work alongside whites in the quest for profits—it is quite another to hire a black to play with and alongside reluctant whites in a game whose daily enactment reinforced national racial ideology.

In doing this testing, it is both unfortunate and understandable that Robinson could not outrun his status as a race hero to the rest of the nation—and ultimately to himself. One might say he became a slave to his role. Race is what we use as a society to take the visible—skin color, bone structure, hair texture, and maybe even speed of foot—and turn them into indexes to the invisible: intellect, temperament, sexuality—things that we supposedly carry in the blood but that aren't immediately evident. Of course, it is wrong—scientifically and ethically—to do this, has been wrong for centuries, and yet we, as a society, persist in doing it. And when Jackie Robinson played, we were still publicly advertising and endorsing our belief in this false science of racial typing, a development that made his appearance in baseball extremely meaningful. In fact, sports were knee-deep in the process of assigning value and meaning to skin color and had been for at least fifty years. Why, then, did Jackie Robinson enter a world in which his very entry would seem like an earth-shattering commentary on American life?

Robinson knew he was not the first black major league player; he knew that nearly seventy years before him, Moses Fleetwood Walker had been the first. Robinson knew of Walker, though how much is unclear. In the late nineteenth century, when Walker played, many whites believed that character was an elusive and unreliable quality among blacks; they contended that African heritage imparted even to economically and socially well-off blacks a predisposition for bad behavior, something that lurked as a genetic menace in the blood, undetected and ready to spring forth at unpredictable moments. When the dapper, intelligent Walker, who had attended Oberlin College and the University of Michigan's law school, pulled a loaded revolver on fans in Toronto, the incident spurred questions about the importance of skin color as compared with life experiences—experiences like college and participation in sports—in determining character.

For whites, the issue was settled on the side of genetics and bloodlines. And the place where those bloodlines (Walker was a mulatto—a designation thought to imbue him with both white and Negro qualities) could be most easily seen and confirmed or challenged was on the playing fields. That is, it became important to bar blacks from competition because sports offered a visible disproving ground—a place where blacks could show in concrete ways—in numbers tallied on a scoreboard—that they were the equal of whites.

The ban on black-white athletic contests was a highly effective way for whites to reinforce the notion of white superiority—and their claims of black inferiority. Indeed, before the color line was drawn, thirteen of the first eighteen winning Kentucky Derby jockeys had been black, cycling and pedestrianism had black stars, and baseball had, beside Fleet Walker, several black players performing at high levels.

There are some eerie parallels between Robinson and Walker. There was the fact of college—an unusual thing for blacks in either man's era. There were the taunts that accompanied both as they played as the only blacks in the major leagues. There were the threats of physical harm; and there were the hair-trigger tempers that left both men seething.

In one of his final seasons, Walker decided not to turn the other cheek, electing instead to brandish the revolver in Toronto. Eventually, just a few years out of baseball, Walker stabbed a man to death after an exchange of insults and some flying rocks. When Jackie Robinson was eight years old, living on Pepper Street in Pasadena, California, a poor neighborhood girl addressed him as "nigger." When he responded with insults of his own, the girl's father emerged, and Jackie and the man began throwing rocks at one another. What's interesting is that in Walker's case, he became increasingly bitter and hostile, even after acquittal in his murder trial. He went on to invent a guaranteed-to-explode artillery shell and wrote a book advocating the removal—forcible if necessary—of all American blacks to Africa. He saw it as the only solution to the race problem. But Robinson headed the other way—possessed of a temper and increasingly encouraged to display it—he learned to hold it, and, despite receptions as hostile and vicious as any black in America was enduring, he embraced the hope of integration. What was that, beyond a fundamental decency, except the knowledge that there was more at stake than just his own success?

Surely he knew something of the damaging effects of allowing temper to erupt in violent behavior. And surely, too, he knew at least indirectly of the damaging effects of arrogance on race relations. These he learned through the example of boxer Jack Johnson.

The color line drawn for Moses Fleetwood Walker and other black athletes had held for nearly two decades before Jack Johnson burned through it in 1908, becoming the first black heavyweight champion in history. Johnson was famous for his arrogance and his insistence on rubbing his superiority in the faces of white society. His victories over white men, and his insistence on doing what he wanted to do—which included marrying white women—infuriated white society to the point of violence. Films of his wins set off race riots in which white mobs set upon blacks.

Following the loss of his title, whites again refused to fight blacks, and it was not until Joe Louis came along in the thirties that another black ascended to the heavyweight throne. And what Joe Louis was told was this: do not be Jack Johnson—do not be arrogant, do not be seen or photographed with white women, do not stand smiling over your beaten white foes. It was a strategy that, along with his victory over the Nazi symbol Max Schmeling, worked to make Joe Louis as popular among whites as Olympic star Jesse Owens.

What Louis and Owens did was provide an example to Robinson of the benefits that came to all blacks when famous individuals comported themselves publicly with humility. But while Robinson would use their examples to good effect later on, he was in some respects always more daring, always a bit more courageous in defense of his rights.

Here's an example. Joe Louis, already established as the Nazi-slayer, the heavyweight champion, and a "good Negro," stood up for black soldiers in World War II and helped to integrate the armed forces. But Jackie Robinson also served in the military, and he created waves before he had a big-league career or a celebrity's reputation to protect him. He was barred from cashing a check at a white officers' club, had endured outhouses on federal property marked "White," "Colored," and "Mexican," and was assigned to a black unit, all without incident. But when he boarded a bus headed to Fort Hood and was ordered by a white driver to move to the back of the bus from a seat he had taken next to a female acquaintance, he refused. During the ensuing involvement of officers, police, and witnesses, Robinson fought for his rights, reportedly bowed facetiously and offered sloppy salutes, and, in essence, risked his military career (and whatever might come after it) to fight unjust social convention. The incident resulted in his court-martial. He was found not guilty of all charges, in part because of the eloquent testimony that he delivered when asked the meaning of the word "nigger." "I looked it up once," he said, "but my grandmother gave me a good definition, she was a slave, and she said the definition of the word was a low, uncouth person . . . but I don't consider that I am low and uncouth . . . When I made this statement that I did not like to be called nigger, I told the Captain, I said, 'If you call me a nigger, I might have to say the same thing to you.'"

And where did Jackie get this judicious mix of humility and assertiveness? Probably in no small degree from his idol—his older brother, Mack Robinson. Jules Tygiel, who wrote one of the first and still finest scholarly books on Robinson, *Baseball's Great Experiment* (1983) mentions Mack just once, but he was a huge influence. When Jackie was seventeen, Mack was a one-time world record holder at 200 meters and the silver medalist (behind only Jesse Owens) in 1936 in Berlin at the "Nazi Olympics." After returning to Pasadena from Berlin, Mack Robinson applied for a job. The city rewarded him with "a pushcart, a broom, and the night shift as a street sweeper." He repaid the city by sweeping those streets while wearing his leather U.S.A. Olympic jacket. Officials thought he was being provocative and ungrateful; he coyly maintained that it was simply the warmest thing he owned. In their early years, Mack saw his younger brother as competition to be crushed. Likely he passed this attitude on to Jackie because a friend of Jackie's remembers that in high school days, "Jackie wasn't a very likable person, because his whole thing was just win, win, win, and beat everybody." Mack's inability to win at everything later turned him sour on life. Jackie took note, saying, "I sort of look back at my brother's experience every once in a while—and resolve to make the best of things."

This is exactly the trait that Dodger executive Branch Rickey wanted to see in Jackie and one of the traits that make Robinson truly significant: the resolve to make the best of things. It was the trait that is now most often mentioned as the thing that allowed him to get through his baseball career and his later conflicts with others. Nowadays we might cynically regard this "looking on the bright side" approach as spin. But I've never heard of anyone who thought that Jackie Robinson was ever calculating or false in this—he simply had resolved to make the best of things. When he was hit as often in the first half of his first season as any player had been in the entire preceding season, he often joked about his reflexes, and, indeed, many thought that except for his quickness he would have been hit more. After being hit twice during a slump, he said, "Since I can't buy a hit these days, they're doing me a favor." Witty, but also simply making the best of things.

Making the best of things is what earned Jackie Robinson a good and meaningful baseball career. It allowed him to respond early on to situations that could have done him in. My favorite photo of Robinson is one taken with Ben Chapman. Who could tell, without knowing the whole story, that each of these smiling men despised the other? Or that the bat is more than a prop—it is the means by which Chapman was able to avoid actually having to touch the black hand of Robinson. Chapman, the Phillies manager, was from Alabama and had, in the thirties, been reprimanded for making anti-Semitic remarks. When the Phillies came to Brooklyn in April

1947, Chapman led the torrent of abuse that Phillies players showered on Robinson. This is how Jackie described it in Rampersad's biography:

> Starting to the plate in the first inning, I could scarcely believe my ears. Almost as if it had been synchronized by some master conductor, hate poured forth from the Phillies dugout.
>
> "Hey, nigger, why don't you go back to the cotton field where you belong?"
>
> "They're waiting for you in the jungles, black boy!"
>
> "Hey, snowflake, which one of those white boys' wives are you dating tonight?"

According to a writer, "Chapman mentioned everything from thick lips to the supposedly extra-thick Negro skull" and the "repulsive sores and diseases" he said Robinson's "teammates would be infected with if they touched the towels or combs he used."

And this fewer than ten years before I became a Phillies fan. Even now I am distressed by Chapman and the fact that the Phillies were the last National League team to integrate and distressed to know that racial animosity persisted on the team well into the sixties. But to hear these taunts now is not the same as hearing—really hearing—them at the time, a time when they held real venom and, more, the promise of fulfillment. It was nothing less than heroic, then, when, amid this as well as death threats to himself and his wife, Rachel, and threats to kidnap his son, Jackie Jr.—Jackie went out and played baseball. And it was the furthest stretch possible of the term "making the best of things" when Robinson made the effort a few weeks later to cross the field before a game and have that photo taken with Chapman, when what he was feeling inside was that he wanted to "stride over to that Phillies dugout, grab one of those white sons of bitches and smash his teeth with my despised black fist."

How genuine and sincere was Robinson's determination to make the best of things? We know it was authentic because in the years after he left baseball, as the climate for race relations vacillated and the participation of blacks in fulfilling an American mission shifted from one position to another, Jackie Robinson persisted in spite of highly personal consequences to remain steadfast, to make the best of things as he understood what that meant not just for himself but for all blacks.

In particular, remaining steadfast meant that, as a public figure, Robinson was constantly called on to articulate positions for all blacks—a very awkward and unfair situation. In 1949, when his career had scarcely begun, he was called before a hearing of the House Committee on Un-American Activities regarding communist infiltration of minority groups. There he supported the unconditional service of blacks to any U.S. military efforts that might be needed to combat the spread of communism. In doing so, he directly opposed the views of one of America's most famous and accomplished blacks, Paul Robeson. Robeson, a former All-American football star and a renowned singer and actor had, in front of the Paris World Peace Conference, reportedly said, "It is unthinkable that American Negroes would go to war on behalf of those who have oppressed us for generations against a country [the USSR] which in one generation has raised our people to the full dignity of mankind."

In supporting the military, Jackie Robinson not only disagreed with Robeson, he referred to the actor's testimony as "a siren song sung in bass." The press praised Robinson, but as Tygiel has noted, the incident "contributed to the pillorying and banishment of one of the most talented figures in American history," which led Robinson in later years to have regrets. Shortly before his death, he proclaimed a new respect for Robeson and added that "I have grown wiser and closer to the painful truth about America's destructiveness." Still, he defended the content of his 1949 testimony—in his mind he had been clearly and honestly making the best of things.

Perhaps the most painful part of this honesty hit Robinson in the sixties when he found himself berated and scorned by black militants, including Malcolm X and Muhammad Ali. In a controversy involving a steakhouse in Harlem, a group of blacks called Robinson "Old Black Joe." One of the group labeled Jackie a "so-called Negro," "Negro" having become a pejorative euphemism for "Uncle Tom." In this, Robinson was not the sole target. Harry Edwards, a black sociologist who led a proposed boycott of the 1968 Olympics by black athletes, hung a picture in his office of Jesse Owens, with the caption "Negro Traitor of the Week." Robinson was more than hurt by these developments—he was genuinely baffled. He defended

Ali's right to be a Muslim, but he did not understand the appeal of associating with Malcolm X. "Malcolm has big audiences," he said, "but no constructive program. He has big words, but no record of deeds in civil rights. He is terribly militant on soapboxes, on street corners of Negro ghettoes. Yet, he has not faced Southern police dogs in Birmingham...nor gone to jail for freedom."

It may be that late in life, Robinson was feeling overlooked and obsolete. As Rampersad noted, at an Oakland A's game, where he was being honored for the twenty-fifth anniversary of his signing with the Dodgers, Robinson went into the Oakland dugout. To at least one observer, columnist Dick Young, few players had any interest in Robinson. "I was surprised," Young wrote, "by their indifference, especially the blacks. There seems to be a feeling among the current black players that they owe Jackie nothing."

They were wrong, of course; we all owe him something.

First, for playing. We'll never know whether it was better to have one stellar player—the right player—integrating a huge institution all on his own, or whether it would have been better to have an entire team of blacks integrating major league baseball collectively—as was Bill Veeck's plan for the Phillies. We just know that under pressure that none of us could really imagine surviving, Jackie Robinson flourished. Herman Hesse asked, "Are ideals attainable? Do we live to abolish death? No—we live to fear it and then again to love it, and just for death's sake it is that our spark of life glows for an hour now and then so brightly." And, I would add, nowhere are we more alive, and yet walking so precariously near metaphorical death, than in sports, and nowhere does the spark burn more brightly. The playing field is where we truly live not for the moment but in the moment. And Jackie Robinson's baseball career was nothing short of one electric moment after another, strung together across 1,382 big-league games. Whatever problems were presenting themselves to him, he never let them get in the way of playing well and joyfully. After Jackie's funeral in 1972, Red Smith wrote, "The word for Jackie Robinson is 'unconquerable'... He would not be defeated. Not by the other team and not by life."

As a former baseball player, I am in awe of his on-field electricity. But as an adult living in a world constantly confounded by the strange behavior of human beings, I am in much greater awe of Jackie Robinson's ability to make the best of things. To make the best of things is not to give into whatever, it is not to dismiss grievances or pretend that things are all right. It is simply to take what is—and make the best of it. In this sense, Jackie Robinson had a bit of the Zen master or mindful Buddha in him. If you want to know how tough it is to make the best of things, you need only consider the toll it took on Robinson. In his 1972 autobiography, *I Never Had It Made*, he had grown weary of the effort. "There was a time I deeply believed in America," he wrote. "I have become bitterly disillusioned." In echoing Fleet Walker, Robinson was reflecting more than the public abuse he took on baseball diamonds and in political arenas. He had, the year before, endured the arrest of his son, Jackie Jr., for drug and weapons possession following his return from the Vietnam War and then his death at age twenty-four.

Of course, growing tired of the fight doesn't mean you've abandoned it. In the year before his death, he saved a white man who was being assaulted by a group of young blacks; when a white police officer tried to stop him from entering the Apollo Theater, he protested his manhandling. The policeman drew a gun and backed off only after others told him who Robinson was.

Perhaps Robinson's biggest contribution to my life was my lack of interest when my father told me who he was in Williamsport that day in 1961. And it may not have been a wholly good contribution. My disinterest in matters of color during the important years of my youth was positive. My mother's racial views, which could become at times publicly inflammatory, counted less with me because I had black teammates I liked and respected. Additionally, I had Phillies like Tony Curry and Pancho Herrera who were the equal of any other Phillie in my esteem for them (okay, maybe not to Richie Ashburn). I had no fear of attending basketball games at all-black Cheyney State College. I had those things because of Jackie Robinson.

These things were good, at least for a boy, but they added up to racial indifference, which is not the same thing as color blindness. I knew which of my teammates were "colored," and I knew what many in the town thought of coloreds. I knew that my mother's vitriol represented something more than just her maladjustment to life. I believed that because there was a game to play, and because my teammates were on the same side, the issue of color was unimportant on the ball field. And if it was unimportant on the ball field, the most important place of all to me, then just how important could it be anywhere else?

Jackie Robinson allowed me and others of my generation to live as if that question did not need to be answered. Not having an answer left me unprepared during high school, when the basketball coach cut every white player in my senior year, when my bus was bricked following King's killing, when trips to North Philadelphia's Connie Mack Stadium became fraught with anxiety about parking in the surrounding ghetto and walking six blocks to the game, when a black came out for wrestling in eleventh grade and quickly established that there was no one on the squad—regardless of weight class—who could hold him down. And it left me unprepared to think about issues of race and genetics that now command attention in the community of sports scientists. In my junior year of high school I wrestled Winston Still, a light-skinned black from nearby Great Valley High School. We were mirror versions of one another in terms of somatotype, temperament, and ability. When I beat him 6–5, it did not feel like a triumph having anything to do with race. Again, if the victory might today raise questions about the relative athletic capabilities of whites and blacks, it didn't raise any in my mind at the time.

Not having an answer to the question of color's importance in sport freed me from trying to weave all those strands of experience into a pattern I could discern. Of course, had I decided to make something from those threads, they would have had to be untangled first because they were all tied together in a knot that had been four centuries of American life in the making, a knot so densely and tightly pulled that even Houdini would have surrendered to it. But we all need to keep trying—for another four centuries if necessary.

So now—a half century too late, I know who Jackie Robinson was. I wish to this day that I'd shaken his hand at that Little League World Series—not only to negate Ben Chapman's refusal years earlier, not because he was a pioneer, and not just because taking account of him then might have made me less indifferent years later. I wished I had shaken his hand because he was a human like all the rest of us—and because we all need to have our hands shaken, our lives confirmed, and our souls valued. It's probably just my delusion, but I think if I'd gone up to him that day, when he was alone and thinking who knows what, and extended a hand—from a Dodger-hating white kid to the first black Dodger—he would have appreciated it. If not, I'd have never known, because you can bet he would have made the best of it.

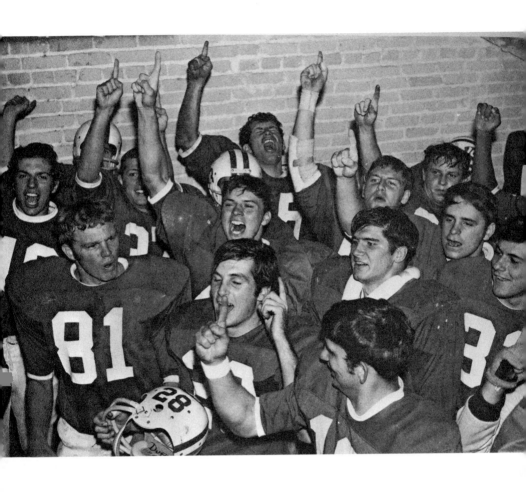

> I will not permit thirty men to travel four hundred miles merely to agitate a bag of wind.
>
> *Edward D. White, President, Cornell College, 1873*

> You don't have 87,000 people at a spelling bee.
>
> *John Mummey, Assistant Football Coach, Ohio State, 1974*

BEWARE!! DANGEROUS JOCKS AHEAD

1968 was a riotous year—literally, with fires burning through Newark, Baltimore, Washington, and Cincinnati, and figuratively, with the murder of a Kennedy and a King, all accented by thousands of smaller events that seemed foreboding omens of an unsettled—and for me, unsettling—future. In the fall of that year I enrolled at Wittenberg University in Springfield, Ohio, a place that I believed still might belong to the fifties, and so a place that promised to deliver a version of the past that I was desperate to reclaim and hold. The school had first caught my eye when the *Sports Illustrated* preseason football issue a year earlier spoke little of linebackers and tight ends at this small-college powerhouse but a great deal about freshmen noses painted green and a campus kissing bridge.

The possibilities that I read into those things did not hold against the cultural firestorm burning across America. By the time I arrived on campus, the flames had reached even this hidden Midwestern outpost. No one painted my nose green, and no coeds ambushed me on the kissing bridge. A kid in my freshman dorm, however, was busted for receiving a package of pot from his hometown, the campus cops shot a frat boy to

Gary Duff, #28 in center, helps Wittenberg celebrate a 9–0 season.
Photo collection of author

death for climbing onto a dorm balcony to filch a few more minutes with his girlfriend, and by my sophomore year the campus was awash with racial tension, anti-Vietnam rallies, a sexual revolution (which no one took the time to alert me to), and guys who were indistinguishable from girls when viewed from the rear. I retreated into the only area resistant to the future: jock culture. I joined the jock frat, where football players from western Pennsylvania mingled with tough guys from all over Ohio to cast a Dionysian light on life in which a toga party, a phenomenon obsolete for a decade or more—a literal step back in time—became one of the greatest nights in many of our lives. Even in this insular pocket, however, change and challenge were present, which made my four years in its clutches a great time in which to observe incidents that continue to guide my assessments of the century-and-a-half-long experiment by American colleges of trying to integrate balls and books.

What I learned from living nearly exclusively among jocks was that sports have nothing to do with education, though both sports and jocks sure can make campus life more fun. Perhaps that is overreaching, for obviously not everyone likes jocks, not every jock deserves liking, and fun is in the eye of the beholder. Let's just say, then, that they make things more engaging and spirited. Jocks had—before the sixties changed everything—a playful (again, not everyone deemed it to be playful) side that grew from their initial status as intellectual outcasts and prodded them to overindulge in the physical splendors of life.

In the nineteenth century, sports were one of the activities that college students used to escape both restrictive curricula and restrictive social environments. Administrators generally disliked sports and considered them a scar on the campus body. Students, of course, dismissed faculty objections and played when and where they wished. Unable to eradicate sports, college administrators eventually co-opted them, angling for a say in their conduct. This required concocting a rationale for their existence, and so the ruse of the amateur scholar-athlete was born. The problem with the concept of the scholar-athlete was that many athletes were—justifiably—much more interested in the athlete half of it; in fact, many college teams fielded players who were not students at all, and legitimate students sometimes stopped attending classes

once under the sway of playing sports. And once the faculty had institutionalized them, sports became powerful symbols of a school's identity,
meaning colleges needed their athletes, whether they were scholars or
not.

It did not take long for this reality to produce four durable paradoxes.
First, institutions for the cultivation of the mind achieved status through
the prowess of their athletic teams. (What is Notre Dame to most of the
nation's public other than a football team? How many care where its
chemistry department stacks up in the Big East?) Second, institutions
devoted to professional careerism became the leading proponents of
amateurism. Third, institutions devoted to amateurism created large professional infrastructures to support their amateurs. And fourth, by dint of
the first three, athletes became the most glorified and vilified students
on campus.

Universities learned to accommodate the hypocrisy associated with
these paradoxes in two ways: first, by claiming that having intercollegiate teams contributes immeasurable intangibles to a campus, such as
pride in community, alumni loyalty, general public-relations benefits, and
leadership through the character-building process supposedly integral to
the concept of the scholar-athlete. The idea that students attend a college based on school spirit does not hold much water. For example, the
institution where I teach, Towson University, saw its enrollment explode
during one of the worst competitive periods for football and basketball
any school has ever had (culminating in a record-setting 1–31 basketball
season). Besides, a student might want to go to Duke to watch basketball,
but if he doesn't gain admission, he doesn't declare "well, to hell with
college, then." He simply goes somewhere else, dragging his spirit with
him. So, a good number of students may want to go to Notre Dame, but
only a sliver will get in; the rejected will adapt to campus life elsewhere.
Similarly, no school can argue empirically (in some schools, even an anecdotal case can scarcely be made) in support of character building and
the other emotionally laden concepts pushed on the public by the NCAA,
its member schools, and their financial beneficiaries: the media and mer-
chandisers. Police blotters, campus judicial boards, and NCAA sanctions
offer persuasive arguments that college athletes are no better than the

rest of the student body at demonstrating traits of leadership and good character.

The second justification propounded by administrators is that successful intercollegiate programs provide revenue to their schools. But only a dozen or so Division I universities—and not the same ones every year—can rightly claim that they turn a profit (and then primarily because capital expenditures on new stadiums and arenas are left off the books or amortized like mortgages). Everyone else loses money year in and year out, yet the public seems to have been sold on this false proposition despite decades of evidence to the contrary. Further, successful teams do not enhance alumni contributions, which have historically been shown to react more sensitively to economic conditions than to winning percentages, and when contributions do go up, they tend to be earmarked for specific athletic teams—they don't put even a small ding in the budget for a university's overall operating expenses. Alas, this is what happens when those with power (ESPN, the NFL, NBA, and Division I universities) control the dissemination of what passes for "knowledge" among the nation's sports fans.

The fact that the American public chooses to believe that sports build character and that college sports are revenue producing would be understandable, but for this: the public also generally believes that intellectual prowess is more important than physical talent, that sports are the toy department of life, that the very notion of "physical" education is laughable, and that highly paid professional athletes are undeserving—regardless of a market economy run by the sacred principle of supply and demand—of their salaries because in the end sports are just "kids' games."

The funny thing is that these are the same people who wear purple wigs on Sunday, drive six hundred miles to park amid other fans on Saturday, watch *Sportscenter* five times daily, get into fistfights with one another over team loyalties, defend the right of Ray Lewis to be unaccountable in a murder despite tossing out his bloody suit in the aftermath, and spend more than a billion dollars a year on sport-related merchandise. They may spend thousands more hours in a bleacher seat than on an operating table, but they still claim that brain surgeons merit greater pay than quarterbacks, that "serious" careers and the money that accrues to them are marks of a society with its priorities in order, and that education is for bettering one's prospects in a real world full of people who believe likewise. In short, the people who believe these things are willfully ignorant.

We are a nation that prizes physicality, and the evidence is everywhere around us. We not only value our academic institutions according to athletic prowess, we also hold ourselves—despite relatively mediocre international rankings in science and math—to be the world's most formidable power because of our military, unhesitant to throw our physical might into countless wars. We crown Miss America on the basis of her physical attributes, favor film and television solutions that rest on physical retribution, and seem to think it clever to exhibit bumper stickers that say things like "My kid can beat up your honor student." In a world that claims it values stockbrokers and lawyers more highly than pro rasslers, we are still awaiting the first Wall Street action figure.

But in life at large, we are uncomfortable in being explicit or even observant about this reality. On campuses, this goes double, because, despite—again—great mounds of evidence to the contrary, people still like to pretend that American campuses are where bright students go to swallow vast oceans of intellectual—and, thus, important—knowledge that will one day transform into collective wisdom. The NCAA, of course, is willfully complicit in promoting this falsity. Their recent insidious ad campaign claiming that "there are over six hundred thousand student-athletes, and nearly all of us will be going pro in something other than sports," is false assurance to the public that athletes themselves take academics more seriously than athletics.

In the ongoing standoff, then, between mind and body—a Western dichotomy without many prospects for reconciliation—colleges like to pretend that they are about the mind. Preeminent athletic teams are a direct assault to this pretension. Unlike the other physical arts (and what is sculpting, playing a cello, miming in the theater, or ballet other than physical art?), which receive academic credit by virtue of their connection with high culture (band members may receive academic credit for playing in the halftime show, but football players may not receive credit for their competition), sports have always existed well outside university mission statements because of their status as low culture. Universities thus tell athletes to keep their aspirations to professional sports careers to themselves, make backup plans, and never forget that they exist as extracurricular adjuncts to campus community life. I have never heard a faculty member tell a theater major that their chances of landing on Broadway are slim to none and that they ought to get a degree in criminal justice as a backup, nor have I ever heard any faculty imply—as they do in the case of athletes—that perhaps music majors, sculptors, and actors don't really belong in college. The fact is that now that most colleges have become advanced high schools with an emphasis on career prep rather than learning to think broadly and well, a great many students don't really belong in the ideal version of college that many professors still profess to value.

College professors, for the most part, take offense at the canard that they are nothing more than ivory tower dwellers. They like to think that their big ideas can pay off in the real world, and, some of them no doubt do. But if you want lessons about what life in the real world will be like, the dynamics of college life away from professors is more reliable, and the dynamics of living among college jocks was, at least for me, particularly instructive. They were constantly at play, which meant that when they weren't on a field or court, they were out of their element and thus in serious opposition to stated administration values. Even then, I had little confidence in the self-serving ideologies of administrators of any stripe (I served as one for four years, long enough to realize that the further I got from students, the more the university paid me), so I suspected that if they misunderstood and feared athletes, these were the very people who could teach me things more useful than what I was getting in the classroom. College athletes exist in their own sphere, having been exiled there by administrators and faculty too near-sighted to understand what the jocks knew intuitively from a young age: that the mind must inhabit a body, that the body is the source not only of sensual pleasure but also the fulfillment of great human possibilities, and that if you wanted to insist on their separation and mutual exclusivity—if you wanted, that is, to treat athletes like dumb jocks—your payback would be constant torment. During my undergraduate years, I had neither the time, ability, nor inclination to wonder about all of this, but in retrospect it became easy to see that Big Al, Jake, Camel, Root Hog, Ping, Sloopy, Duffer, Pitt, Blackjack, and the other jocks of my acquaintance pursued the physical with what appeared to be, at select moments, mindless determination. They were not, in most matters, mindless. In fact, some of them were very sharp. But they resented the mindlessness of supposedly smarter people who looked at their achievements with disdain and condescension—and they knew how to get even for it.

Let me apprise you of some of the episodes in my life among the jocks at Wittenberg and tell you what I learned from them. Let me begin with a central premise of campus life: that athletes are dumb jocks, the constant bane of intellectuals who would prefer to regard their campuses as descendants of the classical Greek academies. Unfortunately, this foundational notion begins the whole downhill slide for lofty-thinking academicians, since American colleges were, in their nineteenth-century beginnings at least, sectarian, religious-based places that took a dim view of pleasures of the flesh. From the outset, then, American colleges were at odds with the traditions of the *palestra* and *didascaloi*, the primary agencies of Greek education, one devoted to the physical, the other to the intellectual, both of crucial importance. Famed Hellenist Edith Hamilton wrote that "the Greeks were the first intellectualists," but her most riveting contention is that "the Greeks were the first people in the world to play, and they played on a great scale." Of course, if play is an omnipresent impulse, which it appears to be, we don't really need to teach people to play. I think what Hamilton meant was that the Greeks taught the world to appreciate play, an observation dismissed as irrelevant by most American faculty; at Towson, students are required to take zero credits of play. It would solve our intercollegiate athletic conundrum if schools promoted acceptance of play on its own terms—acknowledging why sports matter, why play is an acceptable adult urge, how valuing something for its own sake is a necessary part of liberating the soul, and how it is every bit as much of a cultural necessity as theater, music, or sculpture. When this occurs, look carefully before going outside, for there will be flying pigs crashing into the streets all around you. Let's move on, then, to what I've learned as a college student and teacher.

Lesson 1: Even good and respectable colleges are filled with lots of people every bit as dumb or dumber than jocks.

I offer as counterargument to the "dumb jock syndrome" the case of the recently deceased Chris "Twit" Smith. Twit—not a jock—joined my fraternity a year after I had. He gained notoriety for throwing a wooden bowling ball through a dry cleaner's window, for being chased through the streets of Mexico City by knife-wielding locals after using a gesture he had been warned not to use (one implying very bad things about one's mother), and, above all, for an incident involving a card game and lack of good judgment.

The surest way to win at a card game named double euchre, our fraternity favorite, was to "shoot the moon," a feat requiring that one player take all ten possible tricks from his opponents without help from his partner. It happened about once a semester, so when Bill Stultz announced his intention one day to shoot the moon, he drew the expected ridicule. But Stultz succeeded. The very next hand he declared that he would attempt it again, odds against him now jumping to at least a million to one. He succeeded again, which inspired an opponent, John Cogan, to announce that if Stultz did it again on the next hand, he would run naked through the student union. As the cards were being shuffled, Stinky Stoddard, a varsity wrestler and relentless gadfly, came up behind Cogan and clamped a half-nelson on the back of his neck. Within seconds, Cogan and Stinky were tussling on the ground, and as they did so the other three card players quickly fixed the deck in Stultz's favor. Cogan returned to his seat unaware of the fix. Stultz, with the cards stacked, shot the moon for the third consecutive time. We spent the next half hour drawing up plans for Cogan's run through the Union: who would hold the doors open, who would run interference, who would drive the getaway car, etc. No detail was too small. Plans complete, Cogan decided that he just couldn't bring himself to carry them out, a reluctance we all understood. At that moment Twit walked by. Overhearing the to-do, he said that as long as the plans were all prepared, he would be happy to do the naked running.

My assignment was to pull the coat off of Twit in the alley across the street. Watching his fat ass in full flight was not a pleasant view, but, from the girlish screams I heard coming from the Union, it was a better one than those inside were getting. The caper went off without a hitch. Back home ten minutes later, we were cheering our daring victory when campus security arrived looking for "a Christopher Smith." It seems that the ski mask Twit wore had been insufficient disguise inasmuch as he had—in an era when only sailors had tattoos—taken a pen in high school and, jabbing it repeatedly into his calf, self-branded himself with the word "SEX." There was not a co-ed on campus who didn't know about it.

Lesson 2: Some jocks are indeed as dumb as anyone else.

It would take many pages to list all the things that the jocks did that matched Twit for lack of good sense, so one example will have to do. Damian DeMal was a wrestler who wormed out of writing his seventy-five-page senior thesis by convincing his advising professor that a broken wrist would prevent him from typing it up (I know—what does buying that excuse say about the intelligence of college profs? Why is there no "dumb prof" syndrome?) DeMal's wrist was, of course, fine, which meant that every afternoon before class he had to have John Leshinski, a pre-med major, put a plaster cast on the arm. When Damian would return from class, they'd saw it off, necessitating a new one the next day. Sometimes the cast would run to his biceps, some days it would barely cover his wrist; one day, they put it on the wrong arm (I know—what does that say about the prof's powers of observation? See: "dumb prof" syndrome cited above). But that incident is not my example of dumb. In fact, you might even find it clever, and DeMal did one day end up as a successful attorney. What he did that was dumb was to tee up and take a full swing at a golf ball in a living room where ten to fifteen people were sitting. The fact that the caroming missile avoided every eye, forehead, and temple in the room I regard to this day as a modern miracle. Were I so inclined, I'd say that there was a god on someone's side.

The bottom line: few males between the ages of eighteen and twenty-one—jock or nerd—are incapable of acts of great stupidity. If you want to claim that males are more inclined to such acts by virtue of being jocks, I will not argue, but I think it has more to do with living down to the low expectations created by society's trivialization of their expertise than it does with the essence of sport. I never read a tale in Herodotus, for example, of a young Greek athlete bouncing a discus off the walls of Socrates's crowded palestra (or streaking tattooed through the agora), though it doesn't mean it never happened.

A corollary:

Sometimes jocks live up to their stereotype in full public view. Former Wittenberg All-American guard Tom "Ping" Young told me that in the year before I arrived on campus, a lineman whose nickname was a term for all members of the rat family led the team onto the field. Mistaking a slogan-bedecked cotton bedsheet for the tissue paper sign he was supposed to crash through, he ran headlong into the sheet, became helplessly swaddled in it on the ground, and took out as well the two girls who had been holding it.

Lesson 3: Grades and learning have less to do with one another than do sports and education.

Big Al, a barrel-chested linebacker, was, when drinking, a 5'8", 240-pound terror. In his first term, his many nights in the bars left him with little time or ability to study. A history professor with the most mind-numbing style of delivery I've ever encountered anywhere advised him that he would need a near-perfect score on his final exam to overcome his F standing. Back then, profs typed their tests, ran off copies on a mimeograph machine, then threw out the stencil. After nightfall, Big Al made a visit to the dumpster outside the prof's office, found the stencil, and spent the night before the test looking up the answers to the thirty-two multiple choice questions (a task that took him all night). He wrote the answers down the side of his pencil, took five minutes to copy them onto his exam sheet, and strode out of the classroom to the open-mouthed disbelief of the professor, his eligibility assured. I can only imagine the distraught prof that evening as he graded Big Al's perfect—he decided not to miss a single question—exam, now powerless to catch him at his ruse.

After graduation, with his drinking under control, Big Al earned a PhD, worked with the mentally challenged, then died young—in his fifties. While I don't applaud his dishonesty on the test, I am convinced that he learned more from looking up those answers than he would have had he taken notes and then tried to memorize them. Colleagues of mine find my stance appalling, but I was in that class with Big Al, I remember the zombied presentations of the professor, and I am convinced, both by Big Al's experience and my own years of teaching collegians, that students tend to cheat primarily when there hasn't been a convincing case made for the material's worth.

A related observation:

You can actually learn more in many areas of life—sometimes even the classroom—while taking shortcuts and detours around the required route. Sports, on the other hand, are the only endeavor in which there is a guarantee that cheating the system will also short-circuit any advance toward excellence—just one more point undermining the idea that the lessons of sport and education share any sort of pedagogical foundation.

Lesson 4: Don't judge a book by its cover.

I know, they told me this in grade school, but I never believed it until I met another squat, barrel-chested linebacker. Root Hog defied description. He was funny, quirky, tough on the football field, and prone to doing things like stripping down to his white briefs for sumo wrestling matches during parties. He was also incredibly sensitive and wrote poems for some of his teammates for poetry class. Meeting Root Hog on all levels allowed me to see, in a way that the jocks themselves did not, that there was actually great diversity in the jock community, despite its disdain for the nonconforming look and behavior of the era's hippies.

Lesson 5: Athletes can be effective problem solvers, providing that we admit that sports can present problems every bit as challenging as anything we find in math class.

While Root Hog has me thinking about jock intellect and diversity, let me mention Dale Pittenger. Pitt was one of small college football's best linebackers, one of the world's kindest men, and a jock uninterested in much of the content being offered in many of his classrooms. He majored in physical education, doing what was required so that he could one day coach (which he did, after one detour as a Stanley Steemer owner and another as proprietor of a sporting goods store). Eventually he wound up back in his hometown of Tipp City, Ohio. He has the best intuitive sense of a game's flow of anyone I've ever known. His play calling is extraordinary. A few years back I was asked to be the honorary football coach at Towson. The head coach laughingly insinuated that he might let me call a play, so I phoned Pitt to get a suggestion. He told me to run a "fake fake punt," a play whose particulars still escape me, though he's explained it to me numerous times. On game day I was not, of course, asked to call a play. Midway through the second quarter, we were down 36–0 (on our way to finishing the season 1–10). We dropped back to punt and I know—I just know—that the fake fake punt would have gone for our only score of the day. It could have gone down as the only D-IAA touchdown ever engineered by a high school coach five hundred miles away. On a related note, a friend and classmate Art Meyer was asked to be Wittenberg's honorary coach for a day a few years ago, a position that offered him the chance to call the game's first play. In Division III they honor such crazy promises, and Art called a play that went for a ninety-six yard touchdown.

A corollary:

Wittenberg had a starting offensive tackle who arrived on campus for his senior season a few hours too late to participate in class registration. Panicked, he decided to go through the semester as if he had in fact registered. He bought books, walked them under his arm across campus, and sat in on more classes than he doubtless would have otherwise. The team finished 9–0, a triumphant season that ended in ashes when a chance occurrence revealed his lack of registration (this could not happen today owing to the tyranny of computers). The discovery disqualified Wittenberg for that season's title playoffs (they would win the national championship a year later), gained the school notoriety in Time *magazine, and left head coach Davey Maurer (who, despite being at a small school, held such a revered status in the coaching ranks that he was elected the president of the national coaches' association) apoplectic. Four decades later, as Maurer's health declined, the player asked a former assistant coach to escort him for a visit. Ducking his head in, the*

assistant told the wheelchair-bound Maurer, "I've got someone here to see you."
Asked who it was, the assistant gave him the name of the offending player.
"Well, Coach, you better get my gun," Maurer replied. A moment later, he invited
the tackle in, shook his hand, then gave him a big hug. The takeaway: not
all athletes are effective problem solvers; also, time heals all wounds, except
when it doesn't, and rarely does it heal them quickly.

Since I mentioned Pitt's physical education degree, let me take a brief
detour to address the place of PE in college. A former chair of my kinesiology department (PE wearing a new name as a disguise) once
asked the university president where he thought we stood among
the many other departments on campus. "How many departments are
there?" the president asked. "Thirty-two," he was told. "Well," the prez
replied without any hesitation, "then you're thirty-second." That lowly
status, confirmable, I'm sure, by surveys that could be done on any
college campus, was induced and reinforced by the discipline's own
professionals. Just as Einstein once noted that the difference between
genius and stupidity "is that genius has its limits," the ignorance of
physical educators is, like stupidity, unbounded. For a century they—
and their jobs—were linked inextricably to sports. The PE teacher
was invariably an ex-college jock turned coach. In the gym each day,
he or she had the impossible task of pretending that everyone could
learn difficult physical skills equally (imagine if we thought everyone could get calculus or quantum physics equally—but of course
they can't, and academia has no problem in dividing the academic
population into an intellectual hierarchy). When frustration inevitably
overcame them, they stopped the pretending and with great joy and
relief rolled out the balls so the varsity athletes could have at it while
the others sat in the bleachers or along the wall picking at their nails
or reading their physics texts. If those along the wall were wearing
the required uniform and reported on time they would, naturally, receive the same grade as those running up and down the court (again,
imagine if all you had to do to get an A in chemistry was turn up on
time wearing the proper lab apron). At the college level, the same

attitude applied, except that students were required to take only a class or two for a year or two before their debt to a healthy lifestyle was paid in full (at Wittenberg and the universities where I've taught, you could pay that debt by shooting pool, leisurely paddling a canoe, or dancing aerobically—and I defy you to specify for me how that last one holds any potential for movement excellence). Even at that, you could spend three hours a week in that class and receive only one credit while getting three credits for spending the same amount of time sketching nudes in art class (I once took a drawing class and was punished for attempting to broaden my interests by the presence of a nude male model, sixty-five years old, who needed, thankfully, to come down off his perch every fifteen minutes to go outside for a smoke. Exposure to his body alone should have doubled my credits). Physical educators should have—a century ago—advocated for equal credits for equal time, for a grading system that rewarded progress in skill development, and for a division of classes according to skill level. Why didn't they?

The short answer is that they were afraid, I suppose, that they might find themselves with no place on campus if they pushed such issues, which I guess they thought would be even worse than being thirty-second out of thirty-two departments. But the deeper reason is that they themselves were and are complicit in undervaluing physical excellence for its own sake. So duped have they been by society's dismissal of them and so under siege by society's demand that they produce real-world relevance that they readily acceded to the idea that the primary value of physical education was not in progressing and actually learning an athletic skill but in fitting activity into some box that would allow them to claim that what they did served a greater purpose—like making somebody's kid less obese or keeping them more alert for their "real" classes, or providing instruction that would pay off in some way beyond movement excellence or exhilaration (and exhilaration rarely accompanies anything short of excellence). Why, they might even learn something about character.

If you are not convinced of this need to dress up sports with some sort of real-world relevance, take a look at a portion of a syllabus distributed to a badminton class some years back at Towson (italicizing by me):

Course Objectives

Upon satisfactory completion of this course, the student will be able to:

1. Demonstrate the forehand and backhand grip. (*Academic Outcome: personal and self management skills*)
2. List the rules of play for both singles and doubles competition. (*Academic Outcome: communication*)

If you're like me, you'd like to laugh, but you're afraid that you might end up crying. I could go on forever about the ways modern physical education fails to be any sort of education at all, but shooting fish in a barrel gets boring after awhile, especially when everyone around you keeps eating the fish as if they were caught in a respectable and defensible manner. So, let me return to Wittenberg for a final lesson.

Lesson 6: Jocks and their unending contests carry the burden for this nation's fear of fun.

Unbeknownst to me during my days of undergraduate matriculation, my most effective mentor would turn out to be Gary Duff. Now a dentist in Cambridge, Ohio, and still a friend, Duffer took an irrepressible delight in competition that at times hurt me dearly: he leaped on me from an overhanging tree branch during a tube ride down the nearby Mad River, an assault that stripped me of a ring, a hat, and a shirt, all of which I watched ride the current downstream on its way to a confluence with the Miami River in downtown Dayton. During a snowball fight, he hit me in the eye from a few feet away—while on my team. (I recently played on Duffer's team in a Wittenberg golf tournament, where I discovered that his competitive enthusiasm has not abated in older age. He swung at balls in the rough as if a rattlesnake were at his feet and attacked tee shots as if the ball was "Mr. Tooth Decay" himself.) A second-team halfback on the football team, his most noted feat came the day he caught a pass in the flat. With eighty yards of open field in front of him, he fell down untouched. Those of us who witnessed it swear he tripped over the chalk of the twenty-yard line.

He trumped all previous moments of infamy, however, the day Art Meyer, working part-time at a stationery store, called the frat house to say that he had secured two large cardboard boxes used to ship filing cabinets; Art believed that the boxes would make fine outfits for pledges to wear while racing down the street. We cut small openings in the front of each, cordoned off the avenue between our house and the student union, set the cartons over the heads of pledges, then watched them struggle up and down the street in 200-yard races that drew the interest of a sizable portion of the student body.

Though he was a junior, not a pledge, Duff could not bear watching. He needed to be inside one of those boxes doing the racing. He challenged Doug Jones, a pledge who happened to be a sprinter on the track team and the fastest man we knew at the time. Fearing defeat and amped by adrenaline, Duff ran the race as if the box were on fire. He made the turn at the Union a good thirty yards ahead of Jones. He, of course, did not know this, and, hearing the screams of the crowd, decided it was time to really pour it on. He dropped his arms inside the box, which made the eye slot a useless, bobbling trifle. Completely unsighted, Duffer, yard by yard, began drifting to starboard, his furious pace finally stopped dead by the rear end of a parked car in the street. His box teetered on the edge of the trunk momentarily before he fell to the asphalt. Inside his cardboard uniform, Duff, knocked nearly unconscious, lay still. We dragged him out and found that his most crippling injury—other than the one to his pride—came because he had hit the car at groin level, badly cutting the manliest piece of his anatomy. As the crowd rushed to laugh at, ridicule, and profess feigned care for Duffer, Doug Jones continued on to victory, reaching the finish line only to discover no one there.

To most of those watching, Duffer's collision carried the message that competition dressed as mere fun was a silly pursuit at best and a dangerous one at worst, and it was always bound to cost you something. Competition without a serious by-product of real-world relevance (good character, community, health, money) has become unthinkable to most

Americans by the time they reach high school. Fun settles to the bottom of the real-world barrel, becoming the sludge in society's cogs. To most, jocks are the cover boys and girls for this dangerous impulse (it is why we have a problem with a baseball player making twenty million dollars a year but have nothing derisive to say when Robert De Niro gets the same for a turn in *Meet The Fockers*). Across a century and a half, American athletes have learned to deal with this by turning clannish and defensive, gathering themselves into a cult that fears outside judgment, makes enemies of those who can't understand the appeal of high-level play, and shrinks from most aspects of change. The resistance to change means that politically there is seldom any group on campus more conservative than the jocks.

In 1968 Columbia University's athletes ringed the buildings that had been occupied by protesters in an attempt to keep food from reaching the "pukes" inside. At about the same time, Towson University's lacrosse players were reporting early every morning to the student union to prevent hippies from trying to pull down and burn the flag. At Wittenberg, athletes generally disdained hippies and protests; one football player spent hours removing, in the wee hours of the morning, hundreds of tiny crosses placed on a campus lawn in opposition to the American bombing of Cambodia.

I have often wondered why this is so, and I can only trace it to the fearful and superstitious armor that life in the cult of fun requires. With only an extracurricular role in any university's mission and armed with a desire to play beyond high school, college jocks are destined to remain outsiders. There is no cure for this. So long as the NBA and NFL—with the complicity of universities—continue to use college athletics as free minor leagues for the development of their future stars, athletes with no interest in the classroom will be forced to continue to sit in them; they are the only seats available that allow for participation in sport at that level of competition. Colleges, of course, could decide collectively and conclusively that physical learning and excellence are as important to human life as teaching nursing students how to give injections or business majors how to depreciate office furniture.

This is all unfortunate because there's nothing wrong—other than our Puritan paranoia—with the fact that sports can be fun. I had my own final turn at high-level athletics my sophomore year at Wittenberg. Having outgrown any shot I had at wrestling, I decided to return to baseball, the thing that had been more fun to me than anything else in life. So I showed up for the first practice at fall ball only to find that I was the only catcher there; the first- and second-stringers had been excused from fall practice. The coach, who was in his seventies, was clearly in the late winter of his career; he was going through the motions without meaning to or even knowing he was. Not knowing what to do with just a single catcher, he decided that what I should do was catch batting practice for two hours each day. Because batting practice was being thrown by freshmen pitchers trying to prove they belonged, it meant that I spent two hours digging curve balls and hard sliders out of the dirt while batters flailed away. Okay, that's just a learning experience. But the coach, who stood behind the mound throughout, began calling out to me, "Throw one down to second." He did this every third or fourth pitch. By the end of the second day my arm was so sore that I could not lift the dinner fork to my mouth with my violently trembling right hand. At the end of the week, I could barely carry the arm at my side. I told the coach I would not be out for the second week of practice. He looked at me in puzzlement. He did not know who I was. He certainly did not care that he wouldn't be seeing me the following week. Knowing now what I didn't know then, I should have gone back out. I should have taped my arm to my side and hid in the outfield for enough days to make it onto the spring squad. Though I'd have been a third-string catcher at best, it would have been fun to be on a team again. I regret to this day that I wasn't.

I would give back a small part of my salary each year if my classrooms could be filled only with students absolutely enthralled by and engaged with the topic of the day. I don't expect it to happen. In all my years I've seen only one activity with the power to absorb students intellectually, physically, and emotionally—that is, humanly. That is sports, and those who govern our educational institutions (including the NCAA) treat athletes—except on game day—like unwanted stepchildren or like thirteen-year-olds sewing clothes in a factory for a few dollars a day. The simple fact is that athletes are exhilarated by competition—and since when do we find enthusiasm and immersion in any activity so fully human a bad thing? Why didn't we all learn this in college? Yet even the jocks I know

are little more conscious of sport's beauty than the pukes. They go through
their athletic careers as part of a club in which they've been taught to in-
ternalize the initiation rites that inculcate submission to the coach, loyalty
to trite claims to good character, and slavish attention to victory rather
than excellence. Hard to believe, because sport's lessons can be learned
simply by deciding to get inside a box, drop your arms, and run like the
wind.

> In arcs of … passionate pursuit … affiliations might be found with people, places, and events far removed from ourselves; bonds formed with strangers we've never met, sorrow felt for losses we never suffered, pride taken in victories we never abetted.
>
> *Devin McKinney*

I WORE BABE RUTH'S HAT (AND POE'S HEAD)

Greg Black, in his years with the Baltimore Ravens, was regularly kicked in the shins, pounded in the head, verbally taunted and abused, and threatened with arrest on more than one occasion. He was tough enough to survive the assaults and talented enough to garner two invitations to the year-end all-star bash, the Pro Bowl.

Of course, in a technical sense, Greg was not a Raven. Rather, he was one of a trio whose contracts called for somewhat more distinctive and conspicuous uniforms. Alongside his compatriots Edgar and Allan, Greg played Poe, the shortest, orneriest, and most lovable of Baltimore's pro football mascots.

Having had an affinity in my youth for the guys dressed as apples and grapes in Fruit of the Loom underwear commercials (something I've kept under wraps until now), having spent a number of recess periods dressed as Davy Crockett and Zorro, and recognizing that uniforms of all stripes are part of our way of making sense of social strata and status, I can't say that I was immune to the appeal of dressing in a costume and performing. Still, while I found Poe, the Phillie Phanatic, and mascot fights amusing, I

My turn as Poe, the shortest, most lovable Baltimore Ravens mascot. *Photo collection of author* was also somehow put off by their ascendancy in the world of organized sport. I'd gotten to know Greg when he was the tiger mascot at Towson University and a student in my classes, and one lovely fall day I decided to leverage that relationship into an opportunity to find out firsthand what it was that was making me so uncharitable.

I accompanied Greg on his rounds before a home game with the Kansas City Chiefs. Roaming the tailgate parties and walkways more than an hour before kickoff, I could see that being Poe was a risky and arduous task. Every kid wanted a wingshake, a picture, or a peck on the head from his big foam rubber beak. Every man who'd had a beer wanted to slap him on the back, shout loudly into his eyeholes, or sneak up behind him for some simulated sex that would set his friends to roaring (how the mascot rather than the mascot-humper is the larger butt of this gag is unclear to me; apparently beer goggles alone aid comprehension). The day was hot, and I knew Greg was sweating in the heavy suit. Still, once we entered the bowels of the stadium, Greg became a celebrity with an all-access pass. Security guards waved, midlevel executives nodded politely, and the few players moving between locker room and training exam rooms high-fived him and called him by name ("Greg," not "Poe"). Best of all, in the eyes of my colleague Vince Angotti, who was also tagging along, Poe had his own dressing room, which, when the right doors were left open, provided a view of the adjacent cheerleaders' dressing area. The volume of cosmetics on their tables led me to believe each would be taking to the sidelines about five pounds heavier than when they'd arrived.

Once the game started, we followed Poe through the tunnel into the sunlight. Being on the field for a professional football game is nothing like being on the sidelines for a high school or even college game. It is madness—more people than you can comprehend, all taking enough space to create a minefield of human clutter. There are cheerleaders, dancers, policemen, security minions, management personnel, VIPs and close friends of VIPs, ex-players, ballboys, athletic trainers, emergency workers in golf carts, the chain gang, and people who surprisingly seem to have no reason to be there—like me and Vince. Though sideline passes hung from lanyards around our necks, we drew lots of disapproving glares from security. We stuck close enough to Greg so that we were never in one spot for more than a few seconds, with one exception: after a touchdown we were behind the end zone to watch the extra point. Two security guards

yelled loudly and urgently at Vince to get the hell out of there. Seconds
after he moved, the net that keeps kicked balls out of the stands was
hoisted sixty feet into the air. Vince had been standing on top of it, and
had he tarried another two seconds he would have been carried upside
down by his feet right to the top. It's too bad he moved—he could have
been on ESPN highlight reels for decades.

As we moved around the floor of the stadium, I saw that Poe was just
one star, albeit a highly visible one, in an overcrowded firmament. Fans
in the first rows sometimes shouted at him as he went past, but by and
large Poe was just a clown in one of the circus's outer rings. Following
him was interesting but not what I'd come for. Greg had made a promise
I knew he was growing reluctant to keep, but sometimes you can't take
back promises. So, between the first and second quarters, we went back
to Greg's dressing room, where he quickly peeled out of his fur suit and
helped me into it—no easy feat since I'm about five inches taller than
Greg and my shins and ankles extended below the costume fabric that
was meant to hide them. The switch happened quickly enough so that I
didn't have much time to get nervous before we headed back to the field
where I emerged in front of sixty-five thousand fans who had no clue that
they were looking at an ersatz Poe.

I did what I could. I waved, strutted, and stopped every twenty yards or
so to flap my wings in slow motion and lift my head skyward as if I were
taking off. Within a minute I was out of material. Greg told me to go over
to the sidelines and kick over a few of the cheerleaders' megaphones, assuring me that they'd think it was funny and that I would appear lovably
mischievous. The cheerleaders did not think it was the least bit funny; in
fact, a few of the male cheerleaders (and don't get me going on that) got
pretty testy about it. I didn't care; one way or another Greg would get the
blame for it. The suit was hot, the head was heavy, the need to perform
relentless. In short, I was having no fun. I was sure this was not like being
on set as a Fruit of the Loom apple at all. As I trudged back through the
tunnel at halftime to swap outfits and let Greg carry on, it dawned on me
that I had absolutely no sense of what was happening in the football game.

And I knew then what was making me so uncharitable—this was a
sports event, and I was not an athlete or even someone charting the
game's ins and outs. No, I was an entertainment auxiliary, and while that
role may help sell tickets and goodwill to those who don't need football

to enjoy the experience at M&T Bank Stadium, it was a betrayal of all that I believe about sports and their place in our society.

In fact, as we moved around the various levels of the stadium later in the game, I could see that Poe, like beer vendors, cheerleaders, and zealous fans, was not just an auxiliary but at times an impediment to any real appreciation of the game itself. An illustration: in Greg's very first game, he'd had an experience that had inadvertently made him the center of attention for nearly fifteen minutes, stealing the thunder from the field. Moving along a concourse during the game against Pittsburgh, he'd paused behind a row of Steelers fans and begun pecking one of them on the head—in good humor, he thought. While Ravens fans laughed, however, the fan—not with any sign of humor—feigned a heart attack; his friends flagged down police and security to report in hysterical overkill Greg's malicious act. It took nearly fifteen minutes to calm the scene. Greg the rookie mascot was shaken and headed for an exit as quickly as he could; thus, he missed the arrival just a few seconds later of Edgar, who, with absolutely no knowledge of what had just transpired, walked up behind the same fan and began pecking him on the head. The hubbub began anew. Police, now believing Poe and Edgar to be in cahoots, threatened both with arrest. Eventually, the Steelers fan ended up with some free tickets, and Greg, though not carted off to a holding cell (M&T Bank was the first stadium built in America with permanent cells drawn right into the blueprints), was chastened by his superiors.

Whatever humiliation he endured paled next to that of sport's earliest human mascots, a group that included Clarence DuVal, a midget and mascot of the Chicago White Stockings in the 1880s. Sox team captain Cap Anson referred publicly to DuVal as a "little darkey," a slight indignity compared to being dragged through the streets of Cairo, Egypt, by a touring big league All-Star team, which did permit DuVal the luxury of wearing a catcher's mask (pretty much what passed for a mascot costume back then), though it's easy to believe that this was offered as affectation rather than protection.

Of course, DuVal was a mascot in its original, demeaning sense. He was a good luck talisman, and thus somebody who could expect blame whenever luck ran out. Through the early decades of professional baseball this was the plight of the physically slight, impaired, or unusual. Babe

Ruth had his own personal mascot with the Yankees, and many clubs kept someone like DuVal around as scapegoat and gopher. In Philadelphia, young Louis VanZelst, transformed by an accident as an eight-year-old into an undersized hunchback, spent several seasons as mascot for Connie Mack's Athletics. Players rubbed his hump for good luck, laughed at his spot-on impressions of opposing managers, and took up collections at season's end to get a few hundred dollars into VanZelst's hands. Mascots, in short, were kept around for the benefit of players, not for the seduction of spectators.

Many teams, professional and college alike, selected nicknames beginning in the late nineteenth century that did not lend themselves to much in the way of mascots. What does a Phillie, a Mutual, a Hilltopper, or a Redleg look like? Beginning as early as 1889, however, college teams, lacking, I suppose, the insensitivity to drag hunchbacks around with them, began adopting real animals—a bulldog at Yale, a goat at Navy, a war eagle at Auburn—as substitute rabbits' feet. By the twenties, or possibly earlier (mascot history can be hazy), students began dressing up as mascots, eventually becoming entertainers. Sometimes they were terrible ones, such as my high school's warrior, my college's moth-eaten tiger, and a wildcat I once saw that was pure chipmunk both in appearance and manner, but they became an accepted, and eventually, an esteemed part of the sporting landscape. It is reported that competition to become Stanford's Tree is intense enough to have caused applicants to allow themselves to be shot and set on fire in a bid to get the job.

It's hard not to admire that kind of devotion, especially when it comes to the status of a mascot like the hawk from St. Joseph's University in Philadelphia. I began making trips to the Palestra on the campus of the University of Pennsylvania in the mid-sixties. By then, the hawk, created in the mid-fifties, had already established himself in the lore of the bloodlust that surrounded basketball games among the city's Big Five: Penn, Villanova, Temple, St. Joe's, and LaSalle. The hawk never wore a particularly well-crafted costume; even in this day and age, he (I say he, but there have been two women who have served as the hawk) has not been reworked into a Disneyesque design as with so many other mascots. But the hawk had a singular distinction right from the start. From the time he took the floor before tipoff until the time he returned to the locker room after the game, he never stopped flapping his wings. Estimates are that the hawk flaps them about thirty-five hundred times a night. In the early sixties, St. Joe's nationally ranked team drew the envy and ire of the other Big Five fans in the direction of the hawk. When a rival got an insurmountable lead in the final minute or so of a game, half of the Palestra would shake with the chant "The hawk is dead." Even then, however, the hawk would go on flapping those wings as rhythmically as a metronome.

I spoke with one of the former hawks, Steve Klarich, who was inside the suit from 2001 to 2003 (his younger brother would later also become the hawk). The conversation revealed just how deeply the hawk had burrowed into the tradition and competitive temper of St. Joe's basketball (the school does not have a football team, so basketball sits atop its athletic program). First, the hawk is on scholarship. He has a locker alongside the team members, is required to attend all practices (and, though Klarich didn't have to attend conditioning sessions, he trained by flapping his arms for two hours at a time while watching television), and, most important, because of the mascot's long tradition, enjoys a unique grandfathered privilege as the only Division I mascot permitted to travel to away games. It is this final point that, accompanied by the wing flapping, has put the hawk in the middle of numerous scraps across the decades. The most notorious one came in 1998 when Rhode Island's mascot, Rhody the ram, tried to slip an inner tube over the hawk's wings to stop the flapping. This ended in the only way possible: a fistfight. The hawk's head came off, though he did not stop flapping, and Rhody the ram was ejected. Klarich told me that attempts to stop the flapping were persistent and known to all the hawks. He'd been in a fight with the Temple owl, had fended off a rabid Villanova fan at midcourt, and had been escorted from the floor at St. Bonaventure, when police feared for his safety as the seconds wound down in a tense contest.

The hawk has proven his worth over the course of sixty years. The team and coaches regard him as vital, the fans regard him as nearly sacrosanct, and, Lord knows, when those chants and scraps break out, it is impossible to look away. Who in this world doesn't like amusing entertainment, especially those of us incapable of partaking in the showtime presentation of religion? The problem with the flapping and the fights, the hot dog-launching cannon of the Phillie Phanatic, the foot-races of the Washington Nationals' big-head presidents, and the other capers of mascots is that they make me smile at and like what I don't want to like. They are the first step in what has become a parade of distractions. (I know, many will say I'm taking this all too seriously, like the enraged paranoiacs who swear all drug addiction commences with the first puff of marijuana.) There is no hope for me other than to admit to base hypocrisy. I love college sports, though I know they have nothing to do with education, and I love St. Joe's hawk, even as it distracts me from the game. In fact, if you told me there would be no hawk flapping his wings along the baseline, I don't know if I'd go to another St. Joe's game at the Palestra. As it is, I try to get to one every year.

I suppose, in looking for a way out, I'm just going to have to pretend that mascots as deeply entrenched in team activities as the hawk are not, in fact, a first step toward ruin. I will save that for others who have found side doors into the spectacle of sports—have, in fact, become nothing more than spectacle. Cheerleaders, for one, do not actually lead cheers anymore. They do gymnastics routines (I saw one of them take a hard fall at the Palestra a few years ago, requiring medical emergency workers to strap her head in place and remove her on a board—talk about a showstopper) that draw attention, and they think of themselves as athletes, but they do not lead cheers.

Cheerleaders are at least preferable to the other auxiliary sideshows in our sports world. There are novelty entertainments at minor league baseball games between every half inning: people who blow themselves up in boxes with explosives at home plate, kids racing in opposite directions tethered by a bungee cord, and dogs that catch Frisbees. All of them deliver the same message: the game is not enough.

Even more bothersome are the fans who now insist on active roles during the games. Not content to let other spectators decide on their own level of involvement, they turn their backs on the field to exhort all those nearby to share their fervor by standing and making noise, an insistence that usurps the job of the scoreboard operator, who also is now required to command crowd clamor via the Jumbotron's electronic clapping hands. Worse are the fans who also now insist that their neighbors, strangers though they may be, exchange high fives in celebration of something or other. The feeling I get is that these fans actually think that whatever has transpired on the field is an achievement in which they share. Recognizing the trend, advertisers have capitalized. Bud Light presents fans turning bottle labels in one direction to help a field goal attempt and eating unappetizing quinoa burgers during the tailgate party because "it's only weird if it doesn't work."

The strangest incident of fan involvement I witnessed came in an empty arena. While at the University of Maryland in the eighties, I occasionally played racquetball with the spouse of one of my fellow grad students. The spouse happened to be Doug Jarvis, a star of the Washington Capitals, and a few times he gave me game tickets. Once, I had no way to the arena except with him, which meant I had to arrive many hours early. Sitting alone in the empty arena and killing time, I was surprised to see two Toronto Maple Leafs take the ice for a very early warmup skate. One of them was one of the league's most feared fighters, Tiger Williams. As Williams and his teammate skated leisurely and gracefully, they were suddenly verbally assaulted by two fans across the ice from me. I have no idea how they got in, but they were shouting obscenities at the Leafs, one through a curled up program. As Williams skated past them, he smiled and playfully lifted the puck over the glass toward his antagonists. A nice gesture, I thought. Despite their enmity, they'd be getting a souvenir. The fan who caught the puck, instead of gratefully tucking it in his pocket, waited for Williams's next time around. When Williams neared, the fan threw the puck at him as hard as he could. Within seconds, Williams and teammate were in the stands, trading blows with the two fans. This was surreal; was I on *Candid Camera*? No, there was absolutely no one else in the arena—no security, no vendors, no ushers—just three fans and two fighting hockey players. I'm only guessing, but I imagine those fans, despite their lack of uniforms and locker-room access, felt themselves part of the ice hockey world that night.

Perhaps they should be forgiven this misperception inasmuch as many fans have been consuming for many days, weeks, and years the attitudes of ESPN Sportscenter anchors who likewise insinuate themselves into our sports as icons on a par with athletes. Both in the smug laughter that sometimes accompanies their narrative of gaffes and errors committed by multimillionaire players and also in the show's clever ads that show those players performing menial tasks around the ESPN offices, the message is that "we're all equal here." Some of the ads go further, depicting on-air personalities as athletes in their own right, delivering a show so exhausting that they need cornermen to come in and resuscitate them during the commercial breaks. I have been told by what I regard as a reliable source (though I've never been able to confirm) that one of the anchors showed up at major league baseball's All-Star game in the nineties and was livid when officials had the temerity to keep him from getting in the cage with All-Stars and taking some practice cuts.

Yet more troublesome are fantasy leagues. Fantasy leagues take athletes who aspire to human greatness and turn them into commodities, mere number suppliers for those who never have to leave their couches or computers to pretend that they share in some common quest. This substitution of numbers for flesh has a parallel in the way that fans now know things useful only to a spectator. Where fans once knew something of technique and strategy learned while actually playing a game, they now know the height, weight, weaknesses, and strengths of an offensive tackle from Utah State, which will be useful to them as they watch the NFL draft for two full days. It still defies my senses that the draft is regarded as television programming. It is akin to watching stockbrokers select stocks for two days. Fantasy league players are not far removed from the horseplayers I see beneath the grandstand at Pimlico racetrack, bettors who don't care if they ever see a horse. They are attuned to the numbers coming in from tracks around the nation, hooked on the myriad video screens that let them know whether to fling their tickets on the floor or take them to a window for cash. The only difference, in all honesty, is that fantasy leagues are perhaps more dehumanizing, replacing the horses with men. Teddy Roosevelt's famous scolding of "those cold and timid souls who neither know victory nor defeat" certainly applies to fantasy league participants. These pseudo–general managers render the whole enterprise of a team and victory as secondary to the stats piled up by an individual. If you think I'm making too much of this, consider that a book was published in 2013, a fantasy league player's insider look at a world presented as a thrilling, topsy-turvy adventure. Are we to take this seriously? A pox on them all.

Worst of all, of course, are the athletes themselves who buy into the culture that views them not as volunteers in a great human pursuit but as mere entertainers. Why should we expect it to be otherwise? Sports have been trivialized for so long and celebrity glamorized for so long that it is not hard to see why athletes would think that the worlds of business, personality, and performance art are better paths to recognition and acceptance. This perspective has yielded end-zone dances, sack celebrations, in-your-face jams, and other incivilities that collide in a muddled world of disrespect, fun, solipsism, and ignorance. To challenge any part of that muddled world is to invite scorn. If you don't like these things, then, in the minds of the collective fan nation, you just don't understand sports and their appeal. You are a cranky stick-in-the-mud, out of touch with the times. In short, the cranky, stick-in-the-mud, out-of-touch view of twenty-first-century American sports is that the further they drift from athleticism in service of performance to athleticism in service of entertainment, the closer they drift to the debased attitudes surrounding the Roman Colosseum.

At a deeper level, my dissatisfaction with things as they are can be viewed as nothing less than hypocritical, coming as it does from someone who makes a living doing history—what is that but vicarious attachment? Besides, I've got my own side door into sports: the fetishistic connection to collectibles.

In the forty years I've known my wife, there has been only one chore from which she recoils. She refuses to dust my office. This owes to my accumulation of decades' worth of what she refers to as tchotchkes but what I regard as treasures: cartoon Beatle figurines; a dancing, screaming James Brown statuette who always feels good; bobbleheads; my grandfather's baseball glove from the twenties, my first pair of rubbers (size two, I believe); three-inch white plastic statues of all the presidents from Washington through Eisenhower (premium enticements from the Mr. Softee truck), and medals, plaques, and a can of Muhammad Ali shoe polish—white, of course.

My university office contains spillover: three seats from Connie Mack Stadium; a piece of chain-link fence from Baltimore's Memorial Stadium; a wooden javelin suspended invisibly from the ceiling by fishing wire; a sawed-off piece of a fiberglass vaulting pole I borrowed for keeps in my senior year of high school; and, most improbably, the hand-wrought wooden hash pipe of America's only elite hippie athlete, the now-deceased Rick Sanders, 1968 and 1972 Olympic silver medalist in freestyle wrestling. Why do I keep them all?

Because they are private portals into sports memories I wish to hold on to. Sportswriter Heywood Hale Broun once remarked that watching Babe Ruth gave you the sense of being in the presence of greatness, and, if you're in the presence of greatness, "then some tiny fleck of it is attached to you." By that reckoning, I was able to acquire much more than a fleck of Ruth. When I first moved to Baltimore, I was invited to be on the advisory board of the Babe Ruth Birthplace Museum, at that time a collection of artifacts housed in the tiny row house where he'd been born. Seeking to expand and modernize, the museum decided to produce an advertising poster that highlighted some of its holdings. They'd arranged all of them on a table in the museum's basement, where they awaited a photographer. Happening to be in the building one day, I wandered downstairs in search of one of the curators. Perusing the artifacts, I noticed that hanging from a hat rack behind the table was a hat Ruth wore as a member of the Boston Red Sox. I could not resist. I put that enormous hat on my head and was looking for a mirror when the museum director came down the stairs. He shot me a withering glare, and I quickly put the hat back. It did not seem the appropriate moment to ask him if he'd take my picture in it. The hat's magic, however, was already in me. I never hit a home run in all my years of youth baseball; I just had no power. But I've taken up one of the Babe's favorite pastimes, golf, in my advanced years, and I can hit a golf ball a long way. My instructor would like me to believe that it comes from my ability to turn my hips beyond the point that most players my age can reach. But I think it is from the flecks of greatness that were attached to Babe Ruth's hat.

Owning pieces of the past is one of the ways we reach for connections, completing our arcs of affiliations with "people, places, and events far removed from ourselves." Artifacts have that power. Though they can serve the same function, I should point out a distinction between artifacts—actual remnants of another time and place—and souvenirs, which are mass-produced, commercial products meant to artificially gag the nostalgia reflex in the name of profit. People—or Americans, at least—know the difference. When the Phillies played their final game in 1970 in decrepit Connie Mack Stadium, the club, in anticipation of vandalism, passed out fake seat slats to all entering customers. These were souvenirs; the fans were there for artifacts, and by the early innings the fake slats were being used to hammer apart the real seats. The rhythmic clack of wood on wood persisted long enough to induce headaches, according to one sports scribe. Four of the real slats, brought home by my father, now frame a photo of me on the field at Connie Mack, at age eleven, with four members of the woeful Phils. It served the team right.

Autographs seem to exist in an in-between niche. When they are collected in person from a willing athlete, are they an artifact? If I buy them from an online site and assemble them into a collection, does the lack of personal connection rob them of meaning? There is a funny, oft-told autograph story in which a waitress, upon seeing golfer Lee Trevino at one of her tables, beseeches him for an autograph: he is her favorite golfer; she is, after all, his biggest fan. Lacking a piece of paper, Trevino graciously signs a five-dollar bill to "my biggest fan." An hour later, while paying the bill, he notices among the change returned to him a five-dollar bill signed by himself to "my biggest fan." For most fans, the importance of autographs is that ephemeral. When they are nothing more than commerce—easy money for past stars at signing shows—they lose the sinews of connection that can make them more.

As a kid in elementary school, I spent afternoons writing letters to ballplayers and politicians, asking for autographs. In archival-quality envelopes, I still keep—and more often than I'd like to admit—pull out and look at black-and-white glossies of JFK, Nelson Rockefeller, Richard Nixon (complete with a letter wishing my Little League team a season of success), Don Drysdale, Ernie Banks, Johnny Callison, Robin Roberts, Stan Musial, Chuck Bednarik, and others. Later in life I learned that the presidential signings were likely done by auto-pen machines, and the baseball signatures were likely forged by clubhouse attendants. They are artifacts to me, however, remnants of a time during which a ten-year-old boy's letters would get personal responses from famous men and reminders of the active process I undertook to get them.

I also think of my baseball card collection in the same light. About ten years ago, I was in a shopping mall where collectible card sellers had set up tables to sell their goods. A man in his sixties approached one of the vendors and asked about buying a complete set of cards for the year in which his young grandson had been born. Wouldn't this make a perfect gift, he thought, to share when the child first became absorbed in the glories of baseball? When he asked to see the cards, however, the salesman told him that he could not unwrap the set from its cellophane—to do so would depreciate the mint condition of the cards. It is hard to describe the look of puzzlement and then disgust that passed over the grandfather's face as he left empty-handed. Cards are now monetary tokens, collections are investments, and collectors are passive speculators.

My own absorption with cards in the fifties and early sixties was active. In my mind, the cards were almost living things that could have been improved upon only if they could talk. A blend of artifact and document, they offered a heady mix of bubblegum smells, textures, graphic styles, and esoteric value. We flipped them, pinned them to our bicycle spokes as noisemakers, wrote across them, and, as was the case with one of my friends, inexplicably typed the name of the player across his photo. They became records of batting stances, of ballpark ambiance you could identify from the background, and of catchers' mitts that looked like big leather doughnuts. I still have every Phillie card I ever owned; I never traded a Phillie, never sold one, and never mistook the stats on the back for a truer index of worth than the face on the front.

I am more conflicted about the worth of foul balls or home-run balls, maybe because in over a half century of going to ballgames, I've never gotten one. I've seen them rattle around the seats next to me, and I've been as close as you can imagine, but still failed. I took a faculty colleague, Paul Rardin, a music professor, up to Veterans Stadium in Philly the year it closed. We sat in the first deck under the overhang of the seats above. Noticing that there was about three feet of clear space available for a batted ball to reach us—and then only as a line shot—I told Paul, "no foul balls today." Paul, however, had already told me about the many foul balls that had come his way over the years; he fancied himself a sort of foul ball magnet. In the third inning, to my surprise, a left-handed hitter lined a screaming shot that landed about five rows in front of us, hitting a small boy. Well, I thought, that was pretty close. On the very next pitch another rocket came whistling our way. I ducked to the side; it was hit that hard. I heard the crowd roar and turned to see Mr. Foul Ball Magnet beside me triumphantly waving the ball he'd just caught. I'm either snakebitten or smart.

I'll go with smart. My instinct to duck seems to me a good one. I once saw a father of a teammate pay the price for lacking those instincts. He was sitting among a group of women in the bleachers, and as the ball began its descent upon them, they scrambled and screamed. The dad, wanting to appear nonchalant and manly, did not look up—the attitude was "I've got this one judged." The ball hit him square on the head and bounced straight up. He didn't quite lose consciousness, but none of the women ever wanted to sit near him again.

I don't know that foul balls are worth such a risky investment of body and pride. I wonder what Paul did with the ball he caught. I've been in homes where I've seen autographed balls on display, but never a foul ball. After shoving people aside, scrambling madly over seats, falling onto the field, and injuring ungloved hands, you'd think fans would exhibit their prizes as special artifacts. At Camden Yards I sat in front of an Oriole fan who had secured a foul ball by shoving the lady next to him to the ground, where she lay like an overturned turtle, wedged on her back between seats and unable—despite a streak of blue language like I've never heard before or since from a woman—to right herself. The explanation from the Oriole fan was succinct: "Fuck her—she's a Yankee fan." I am guessing, however, that foul balls are only fleeting signs of a moment in which fans feel themselves to be part of the action. Perhaps I never got a ball because I knew it was some hitter's wasted opportunity, and because I knew better than many that those of us in the stands are not players: we are all auxiliaries.

Recognizing that, it is strange, then, that I have for decades been obsessed with a relic that was always an auxiliary and that now exists in my mind only: Philadelphia's Connie Mack Stadium. Maybe it's because we were allowed as spectators to exit the ballpark by walking along the warning track to an outfield gate, maybe because I was photographed as a kid on the field with four Phillies, or maybe it's something deeply entrenched in my psyche tied to that first walk up the ramp at age nine when I was hit by the burst of green, brown, and blue that has enraptured so many of my generation. Whatever the cause, I am still seeing the now extinct structure fairly regularly in my dreams. I walk around a bend and there it is, not in west Philly at all, but wherever I happen to be dream walking. Some nights, it looms in the distance and I never quite reach it. Other nights, I am in the stands, watching a game that has no detail other than the features of the stadium itself. It was Churchill who said, "We shape our buildings and then our buildings shape us." Amen.

Connie Mack Stadium has been so inescapable and so integral to my sense of sports that I have for many years been attempting to build a scale model of it. I have been to the Library of Congress to trace its outline in detail from the old Sanborn Company fire insurance maps drawn in every city nearly a century ago. I have purchased all the craft supplies and tools necessary to do the job. Still, the model is barely underway. My urge to build is, I know, my chance to recapture it, control it, have it always available. My stronger urge to procrastinate is because I am afraid to reduce the verve and energy of what to me is still a living place. I think, in fact, that its nonexistence reinforces its power. Would I be so mesmerized by what was, in the end, a decrepit, rat-infested dive if it were still there? Will the power of Fenway Park and Wrigley Field be amplified when they one day meet the wrecking ball? Something about the disposability of American buildings lend them great nostalgic power. As Alexander Stille has written about eloquently in *The Future of the Past*, American culture takes disposability as a given. In China, buildings that have been replaced board by board over time until no remnant of the original is left are nonetheless treated as ancient artifacts: exact copies as highly regarded as the originals. In the United States, we reject that type of veneration. When George Steinbrenner allowed Yankee Stadium to be renovated in the seventies, Yankee fans knew it was no longer the "House That Ruth Built." And when the organization built a facsimile next door to it in the new millennium, even though the outfield dimensions and certain elements were retained, Yankee fans knew it was the "new Yankee Stadium," a copy not to be revered with the same sense of awe as the original.

I am not sure, then, whether my model will ever get done, but I am encouraged to keep trying by Susan Stewart's assessment of the power of miniatures. In *On Longing*, she wrote that because they occupy "a space within an enclosed space, the (miniature)'s aptest analogy is the locket or the secret recesses of the heart: center within center, within within within." As the most seductive of all sports sites I ever encountered, that is where I want Connie Mack Stadium; if a model helps me keep it captive within within within, I really ought to get cracking on it.

Maybe the autographs, the foul balls, the artifacts, the models, and the tradition of mascots are, in the end, all of one piece. Maybe they all possess the power to do what Stille says all artifacts from the past do: "change your sense of time and your place in the world, making the ups and downs of the present seem smaller, while also making you feel a part of a much larger continuum." That's not something to be easily dismissed.

> Fans don't come to watch you play. They come to watch you win.
>
> *Lou Holtz, former coach, Notre Dame*

LOOK AWAY, LOOK AWAY

The sports corollary of Voltaire's declaration that some people are hammers and some are nails holds that some are born winners and others are destined to lose. It is a cruel and succinct summary of the athletic experience, and if it is true, then on the morning of November 7, 1961, as the football team from tiny Aurelian Springs High School in rural North Carolina approached the end of a winless autumn, they resembled little more than a bag of nails. It was that depressing thought that must have been with the Aurelian Springs coach when he arose early that morning and turned over in his mind a strategy that might that evening keep larger Franklinton High—forty miles up the road—from becoming the season's ninth and final hammer. It was a strategy he had considered but was forced to abandon the previous week, for while it held out the possibility of victory, it clearly insulted the sense of honor of the school's principal, Claude Moore, who caught wind of it and—despite the winless season— explicitly forbade its use.

Twenty years old and ambitious, however, the coach had grown frustrated and desperate. It was game day in North Carolina, and the eight losses, including an 8–7 heartbreaker two weeks before, marked a trail leading away from the dreams he'd nurtured upon accepting the job four

Robert E. Lee: "Let the past be but the past."
Library of Congress

months earlier. So, when Principal Moore awoke with a recurring bout of hoarseness, he decided not to ride the bus to Franklinton. Hamstrung by the fact that the school had only forty-six boys, and only nineteen of them played football, the coach decided that in Moore's absence, the time had come to supplement the squad's meager numbers. To meet the challenge at Franklinton, he unveiled four new players—all of them ineligible as it turned out—including an impressive halfback, who ran for a touchdown in Aurelian Springs's ensuing 19–7 upset win. A local sportswriter watching

This is not the Aurelian Springs locker room—but it could have been. *Library of Congress*

the touchdown run is rumored to have leaped from his seat, exulting, "I don't know who that guy is, but he's got my vote for all-state." Who was that guy? It was the coach himself. He and three townsmen had suited up and played the entire game. Only afterward, when a former college acquaintance refereeing the game recognized him, did the coach's plan backfire, leading to a forfeit, the season's ninth loss, the termination of his job, and the disbanding of the school's football program.

The incident, so improbable that when I first heard it from a faculty colleague during a game of lunch-hour hoops I thought it must be an apocryphal bit of folklore, posed a simple question: how far would one go for victory? A simple question, but a loaded one—with two possible interpretations: how far one would go in subverting rules and the spirit of fair play, or how far was one willing to push oneself—through pain, injury, and psychological stress—to exhibit honor in the quest to win? Two questions seeking a single answer. Two notions—victory and honor—so entwined in American culture—that it has seemed at times impossible to pull at the loose threads of either without unraveling the whole cloth.

In the case of Aurelian Springs the search for an answer begins at the intersection of large and unavoidable vectors—time, place, and national ethos—with distinctions of region, profession, and psychology. It was an incident whose cumulative influences—southern peculiarities, the demands of the coaching profession, and mid-century American trends—produced a moment wholly unexpected and yet, in the end, not terribly surprising. Let us begin with the influence of the South.

The connection between loss and honor runs deep in the South. The memory and legacy of the Civil War still courses through southern life, though a mask of refinement and hospitality often hide the accompanying pain from outsiders. At times, the mask of cordiality has been cast aside in favor of a meanness that surfaced all across the region in the forms of dueling, lynching, and football. Though dueling was a spectacular and efficient means for avenging perceived slights and lynching was an abominable means for enforcing segregation, both were public relations disasters and had by necessity to yield to extinction. Football, on the other hand, seized lasting attention, becoming a public rite of exorcism that allowed for the brutish display of southern strength in a more honorable and acceptable way. As such, it became a crucial and visible touchstone for southern victory.

When Claude Moore arose with his bad throat on November 7, he pulled from the bed with him the tired bones but unflagging spirit of his cultural hero, Robert E. Lee, who had implanted in Moore's mind the idea that loss was one of life's tangible symbols of noble causes. Moore had become the principal of Aurelian Springs two years before the Franklinton game and had immediately set about transforming the public school into a facsimile of a private academy: planting the grounds with flowers, pulling in notable speaking guests, and instilling discipline. In 1961, the centennial of the beginning of the Confederacy, Moore would occasionally arrive for the school day as Robert E. Lee. Dressing in a Confederate general's uniform that he'd ironically commissioned from a Yankee tailor, Moore would apply gentility, dignity, and grey flannel honor to what he perceived as the South's eternal wound. Addressing his small but captive audience of students and faculty on the life and values of Lee, Moore had a treasure trove of quotes and thoughts with which to work. Asked how he expected to win a war that appeared so unequal, Lee had replied, "My reliance is in the help of God." In an assertion that Moore could have used verbatim in speaking to his young coach before the game with Franklinton, Lee had continued, "At present I am not concerned with results. God's will ought to be our aim, and I am quite contented that His designs should be accomplished and not mine."

The problem was that Lee had never seen a football game, and internalizing the general's outlook left Moore outside the circle of southerners who had learned that victory on the field was not only an effective balm for their own inferiority but also a direct strike at the haughty superiority of northerners. Football is a game southerners have to win. It was not difficult to spot differences in regional outlooks on the game even in the early sixties. They can be observed retrospectively in the approaches of and regard for two coaching legends, Alabama's Bear Bryant and Penn State's Joe Paterno. The two were friends, both committed to winning, but Bryant's legacy amplified the South's embrace of the rough-and-tumble backwoodsman who clawed his way to victory—the ends justifying whatever savage means were needed to get there. On the one hand, while he stood marginally as an example of the Southern gentleman—his voice all honeyed drawl, his mannerisms slow and casual, his philosophy spare homily and wit—he was more widely understood as the poor Arkansan who'd acquired his nickname and reputation from a rasslin bout with a bear. His brutish training camps at both Texas A&M and then Alabama were the font of tales in which tough young men were so undone by Bryant's demands that they slunk off into the night rather than return for another day of punishing football. His critics derided his overwhelmingly white team compositions, his preoccupation with national rankings, and the way he tapped into a good old boy network to commandeer talented players (he got Joe Namath when coaches at Maryland notified him that the quarterback would not meet their admissions criteria).

Paterno was Bryant's perceptual opposite—a quick-witted, fast-talking Brooklynite with an Ivy League degree, a fondness for Shakespeare, a public penchant for emphasizing education and the scholar-athlete, and pronouncements about the importance of excellence and the need to distinguish it from mere victory—he was, at least publicly, all about the journey, not the destination. A northerner through and through, Paterno, until his demise in the wake of the 2011 Jerry Sandusky scandal, was widely admired nearly everywhere except the South as the epitome of a football coach who had his priorities in order and his players' pursuits in balance.

It is hard to know in what ways the Aurelian Springs coach may have been tugged between the modern South's need to win and the Confederate need to diminish loss by conflating it with honor. Had he decided on the latter, he might even have been able to explain his decision to insert himself at halfback with a reference of his own to General Lee, who offered the following observation in the aftermath of a lost battle: "I can not tell you my regret and mortification at the untoward events that caused the failure of the plan. I had taken every precaution to ensure success and counted on it. But the rules of the Universe willed otherwise and sent a storm to disconcert a well-laid plan, and to destroy my hopes." We know that in fact the first impulse won out, the school's young coach having little use for some defeated general's blatherings about dignity, honor, and loss.

After his firing, the coach returned to his rural hometown in Maryland, and while that makes him technically a northerner, it does so only nominally. After all, Maryland was a slave state until the end of the Civil War, and its state song sported, until the thirties, the lyrics, "Huzzah, huzzah, she spurns the Northern scum." Maryland is also the burial site of John Wilkes Booth, the place where Abraham Lincoln's train was attacked, and a state that vigorously maintained segregation into the sixties. And, even if you prefer to argue for the state's Union sympathies against its Southern customs, the pull of the latter was strong enough to lure the Aurelian Springs coach to spend his undergraduate years at the University of North Carolina, which surely gave him a grounding in the attitudes surrounding southern football (though archival rosters show that he never played for the university team).

Even if nothing more than a thin veneer in this case, the Dixie varnish was one more complicating factor laid across the top of the dense and impenetrable mystique that was and is "The Coach" in America. Only "President of the United States of America" has matched "Coach" in the application of such a monolithic title to such a varied set of men and women performing such a broad range of responsibilities and encompassing such a wide range of images. "Coach" is the same word used to describe those whose executive apparel and miens serve as advertising for their micromanagement of eighteen-year-old basketball players; to describe men in their sixties who still wear baggy-pantsed baseball uniforms; to describe disfigured warriors who get down on mats and wrestle with their own charges; to describe stats freaks who spend hours poring over charts and game film; and to describe old men who can stand fifty feet away in suit and tie and somehow coax fourteen-year-old girls to leap in skates, spin in midair, and return to the ice safely.

For years I have been conscious that of all the historians who have delved into sports in America, not one has ever explored the roots and development of coaching. I considered the undertaking at various times, but was always deflected by the daunting complexity of the subject. How do you distinguish between hands-on tutors with one pupil and those who oversee squads of a hundred? How do you take into account the age differences inherent in coaching gymnasts and a team of mature men playing in the Ryder Cup? How do you explain the similar results that one coach attains by hardening runners in the elements of nature and those of a coach who tries to eliminate the vicissitudes of nature through appeals to science? How do you draw parallels between impelling the full-body conditioning of football players and monitoring biofeedback that allows an archer to release an arrow from the bow between heartbeats?

Even more challenging, how do you write a history of the coach without society-wide consensus on what constitute the duties and responsibilities of the profession? Are coaches primarily teachers, public-relations specialists, talent gatherers, strategists, big brothers and sisters, disciplinarians, chief executive officers, mediators, philosophers, evangelists, or con men? Maybe it is for some future historian to tell us in what measure and in what ages some of those things loomed larger than the others. Still, with all the variety and uncertainty that are apparent when we look closely at even just two coaches in the same realm of sport, one thing seems certain—even when we make allowances for differences in region, gender, temperament, age, and a myriad other variables, Americans spend little time worrying about those complexities and distinctions. To most, "Coach" is a readily understood, prestigious title, one bestowing enough power to make it, in some cases, as close as you can come in many communities to attaining the privileges of royalty—greater, in fact, because with the title comes the implication that somehow or other it has been earned.

Though my evidence in such matters is strictly anecdotal, my own experiences—first as a player in Little League, then in high school and college, then as a coach myself, and finally as an academic trying to teach a class called "The Principles of Coaching"—have led me to certain observations and generalizations that might be useful in trying to figure out the ways in which the profession itself inspired that young coach to enter the lineup.

As with most kids of my generation, my first contact with the idea of a coach came in Little League, where coaches were parents who had a little more time than the others, a little more interest in sports, and sometimes a little more understanding of their fundamentals. My dad was my first coach. Every practice was about learning, so I came to think of coaches as teachers. It never dawned on me that a good deal of what he was trying to teach could only be learned in my own experimental way. True, a few suggestions might speed the learning process (step with the opposite foot, don't stab at the ball, and other basics), but as David Epstein's *The Sports Gene* notes, the kind of deliberate practice that produces expertise is often the product of solitary rehearsal, and skills flourish when they can be executed "without thinking," without, that is, the sideline chirping and verbal reminders that coaches often confuse with teaching. Nonetheless, the parents who coached youth sports in the fifties and sixties were usually adamant about their roles as teachers. As such, they also felt compelled in the forties and fifties to dispense lessons about fair play and sportsmanship. They may have wanted to win, and they may have hoped their sons became high school stars, but that could only be a happy by-product, not the primary goal.

This attitude still prevailed when I played in junior and senior high school, where the coaches were quite literally teachers. In that atmosphere it was impossible—even in the case of zealous win-oriented coaches—to forget that you were always under education's umbrella. Particularly in the less-prestigious sports, like cross country, field hockey, or wrestling, coaches were often teachers without any background in those sports, people who could nonetheless raise their salaries by a few hundred dollars and their stature a few degrees by virtue of becoming "Coach." In the school setting, then, the coaches existed for the good of others; they appeared as servants of the athletes even when they were red-faced in raging abuse of them (or substituting for them on the field of play). This was the undoing of the Aurelian Springs coach. He was lashed to education, a calling that exposed his unseemly path to victory as doubly debilitating. What deadly lessons would have been passed along for life to his innocent players had his team's lone win been allowed to stand without penalty?

This is an unanswerable question, since we don't know if players generally take a coach's example on behavioral matters. We don't even know how the behavior of coaches and athletes leaks into our culture generally. I was appalled a few years ago when Yankee shortstop Derek Jeter convinced an umpire that he had been hit by a pitch that actually missed him. It is one thing to try to help an umpire get a call right when you think they've missed it; it is another thing to try to help them get the call wrong. Further, he exploited his own good reputation to dupe the ump. When I asked college athletes and coaches about this, however, they unanimously approved of the tactic as craftiness and "just part of the game." That is, Jeter was not role modeling new behavior; he was just reflecting an attitude already out there. As students tell me constantly, sometimes with pride, "if you're not cheating, you're not trying." They're getting this from somewhere, and if not from the encouragement of their coaches, then not from their dissuasion of them either. When coaches let this persist actively or passively, it is one more step toward a world in which the capacity of sports to produce excellence is being thrown aside, much as when I hear people yelling at refs to "let them play." What does that mean? Stop calling fouls and penalties? Just let them play with disregard for the rules that make sport challenging? Let them hold and grab and shove rather than move their feet and do their jobs? And, lest you confuse this kind of cheating with tactics, don't. Teaching players to hold the wrist of an opponent when going up for a rebound (which many of my students say they were taught to do) is not the same as calling for the old fumblerooski.

I seem to stand nearly alone in my belief that cheating in sports is a greater offense to life than cheating outside the lines. Sports are voluntary. If you're willing to cheat there, why wouldn't you cheat in real life, where real consequences attach to ethical decisions? If you're going to roll a golf ball to a better lie when no one is looking, why wouldn't you cheat on your taxes? But when I polled the same athletes and coaches about the Aurelian Springs coach, they were outraged. That, they said, was clearly going too far. Not one, however, could explain why, other than to say they were "totally" different things. They weren't, of course. Both were willful decisions to subvert the artificial challenge of sports—the only thing that really makes them worthwhile.

At any rate, the view of the coach as a beneficent educator would be forever altered in the sixties when a heightened emphasis on winning (caused by a complex set of unique occurrences, including the rise of wire service polls, the coming of television, the specialization of educational roles, the prominence of professional football and basketball, and the perceptions of elite sport as a winner-take-all market), already becoming evident in the fifties, was abetted by both a morally self-righteous countercultural backlash against competitive environments and a wider mainstream moral ambiguity that undermined traditional perceptions of sports as character builders (which included the possibility of victory with honor). It was as if the era's confusion served as a giant centrifuge, the laboratory instrument whose high-speed whirling separates substances of different densities. The centrifuge of the sixties revealed an essential truth about American sport not always clear in calmer times: that winning had moved to and would remain at its core, long after any of the peripheral ingredients — fair play, manliness, self-discipline, self-discovery — had been spun out to the margins.

This meant new things for the coaching profession. The coaching ranks — particularly in football — have never been short of those with a win-at-all-costs mentality, from Pop Warner to Knute Rockne to Vince Lombardi to Nick Saban. After the sixties, however, coaches no longer needed the masks of educators or the masquerade of character building to confirm the importance of winning. Because victory was suddenly alone as the most vital outcome of any contest (I've written about this in the 2001 book *SportsWars: Athletes in the Age of Aquarius*, and Randy Roberts and James Olson similarly noted it in *Winning Is the Only Thing: Sports in America Since 1945*), those who knew how to win — not how to impart life lessons — became more highly valued. This development produced a new alternative to the coach as parent or the coach as educator: the coach as business professional.

Whenever a calling becomes institutionalized, and, more important, professionalized, look for it to suffer from stagnation of the creative impulse; look for it to succumb to groupthink, insider jargon, an inflated sense of self-importance, and an overwhelming need to conform to the tenets of the system. From the time when Frederick Wentworth Taylor, America's noted turn-of-the-century "efficiency expert" proposed the idea of "scientific management," coaches — and football coaches, most notably — were quick to see themselves as leaders akin to those in the business world: executives whose cunning could mold many disparate parts into one smoothly functioning machine. It was a subtext that chugged along in the sports world, hidden beneath the encomiums of service, character, and education for many decades before exploding into unapologetic openness in the post-Vietnam years, and it may have contributed to the recognition by the Aurelian Springs coach that what he needed to do for success was simply to replace a few defective parts.

Coaches in the seventies, eighties, and beyond began to openly take up places not as the curators of good character in adolescents but as businessmen with the insider's perceived keys to success. (They are, sadly, only perceived, and it is unfortunate that so many of the country's institutions, including universities, have bought into the equation between business and credibility. What, after all, fails at a greater rate in this nation than business?) The degree to which sports as business has trumped the idea of sport as character-builder, sport as self-discovery, or sport as anything-other-than-business, is now self-evident. I teach in a program that produces sport management majors, all hoping for jobs in organized sport. When I arrived at my current position in 1995, there was no such major and there would have been few openings for graduates had there been one. My university's intercollegiate program administration comprised the athletic director, his secretary, two sports information directors, an academic counselor, and a handful of athletic trainers. Today, the department issues paychecks to at least fifty salaried management professionals, not counting the coaches, and not including a slew of unpaid interns from sport management programs.

At any rate, the failure of the sixties counterculture to displace the business culture (perhaps because they never formulated any real alternatives to it), left business riding higher than ever in the following decades. The more coaches appeared to tap into this mutually admiring world, the more assured—and rigid—it seems they became. This seems a bit of an oddity because it was in the decades between the twenties and the sixties that coaches gained their reputations for inflexibility, the "my way or the highway" philosophies that led many to leave the profession when questioning baby boomers relentlessly and mercilessly challenged them. For all practical purposes, however, what the coaching profession did in the face of this assault was to regroup and then arm itself with better means for deflecting future assaults. The means came from the business world, a place where published doctrine, seven-point prescription plans, and hours worked substituted for compassion, humor, and common sense.

Instances of business-think abound in contemporary sports. In baseball, many take the reliance of managers on new statistical data to be a sign of this; actually, in most cases, it isn't. That is just numbers extrapolated into common sense: if somebody hits a pitcher at a .130 clip, it makes sense to know that and use it at an appropriate time. What I am thinking of is managers who watch their setup man breeze through a seven-pitch eighth inning only to be lifted for the ninth inning closer who has just blown two consecutive save opportunities. The reason is pure management bunk: this is the closer's job; this is the division of labor according to policy. And, it has the added benefit known to all middle management of placing blame elsewhere in the event of failure. If the manager sticks with the setup man and loses, it is the manager's fault. If he brings in the closer, however, and loses, well, that is the closer's fault.

I got my own chance to coach during a period that trapped me between old and new. Schooled in the fifties and sixties to believe in the notion of the coach as moral guide (inflexible or not) but looking to secure a path to both satisfaction and financial stability in post-Vietnam America, I found myself at Arizona State in the late seventies, enrolled in a graduate program of physical education that I hoped would connect me someday in some way to sports. When I saw a flyer posted for a part-time position as an assistant wrestling coach at Gerard Catholic High School in Phoenix, I jumped at the opportunity. Though I'd been a largely unsuccessful high school wrestler, I had studied the sport assiduously; I knew a lot and thought I could help others avoid the crippling psychic pitfalls that had done me in. I got the job and quickly found that my background in Pennsylvania qualified me as something of an elitist in Arizona. Though I weighed 135 pounds, I found that there weren't any wrestlers on the squad that I couldn't handle easily, including the undefeated 165-pounder (bear in mind that I was twenty-seven years old in a roomful of high schoolers). My confidence running much higher than it had during my own days on the mat, I was intoxicated by my newfound abilities and the power that came from being referred to by everyone on the school grounds as "Coach" (one of my most cherished possessions remains a Christmas stocking that the wrestling cheerleaders made for me, with "Coach Zang" at the top in lovely glittering script).

As the season started to unspool, however, I found that I was at the mercy of the head coach, a man just a year older than me whose brain was the place where ideas went to die. His primary concern, particularly when I had the chance to see him mingling with other coaches at tournaments, seemed to be his standing among those other coaches. In that crowd, he spoke only of winning. We had a mediocre team, but he was constantly juggling the lineup in the hope of squeezing out a few more points. In wrestling, juggling means that an already-overmatched wrestler might be thrown higher into an even more difficult weight class so that

someone else can prosper below. I had no problem with maximizing team
prospects, but we seldom won anyway, and over the course of the season
the individual losses became dispiriting to a number of the wrestlers.
The head coach regarded this the way a businessman views depreciating
assets—some things need to be shed for the greater good; everything
that is not productive becomes disposable. In this case, what was being
cavalierly disposed of was the esteem and confidence of fifteen-year-old
boys already engaged in a series of ruthless Darwinian contests.

I further noticed from hanging around the coaches' lounge at tournaments and attending weekend clinics that nearly all of the coaches operated in the same way. I began to think I'd deluded myself about my own
importance and my ability to convince the wrestlers that they were on a
long journey to find out what worked for them and what didn't, to comfort them after their sacrificial losses with assurances that they weren't
disposable, and to assure them that they might find themselves, as I had,
to be good wrestlers years later than they expected. In my view, good
coaching was an art, but the others saw it as a paint-by-numbers exercise
in which they just had to pick out the colors prescribed by the instructions
and apply them to the designated spots to successfully complete a scene,
even if it was the same scene being painted by all the others, and even if
it lacked imagination and beauty.

In the decades since, working in a building where I've made acquaintances with scores of coaches and had the chance to watch them at close
range, I've found this paint-by-numbers approach becoming more preva-
lent than I could have imagined while growing up in the fifties. Often elusive and unspecifiable, its origins and means of spreading are nonetheless
evident. The coaching profession is more than ever a flock of sheep. The
flock's reverence for clichés and organizing planners passes for gospel.
Bromides that were once at least personal, if nonetheless overworked
and trite—"there is no 'I' in team." "perfect practice makes perfect," "quit-
ters never win and winners never quit"—are now mere supplements to the
overmanaged and depersonalized stratagems drawn from the business
world, where everybody is going to outwork everybody else; where nobody goes home until a play is run perfectly; where depth charts, weight
training schedules, and plans of study permit little deviation; and where
only the bottom line has any real meaning. Modern coaches may claim

innovation—they may even be trumpeted for it—but beneath nearly all of their methodology lurks the conservative pack mentality of a "who moved my cheese" world. That world, of course, says that you must not think deeply about change and its consequences, must not challenge change, just prepare for it and be ready to ride its currents.

In 1999 and 2000 I saw the effects of this mentality up close when I spent two seasons as a volunteer baseball coach for Towson University. During my first game on the bench, I noticed that the catcher was looking to the dugout after every delivery. I wondered why. I quickly came to realize that he was getting the sign for every pitch from the pitching coach. A former catcher, I was shocked—calling pitches was one of the true joys of the position. I asked the head coach why management was calling the shots. He told me he would show me at the end of the half inning. When pitcher and catcher trotted in following the third out, the coach asked the pitcher what he'd thrown to a hitter who'd just homered. "Hanging curve," came the reply. He then asked the catcher what the home run pitch had been. "Fastball up," he said. Only a few minutes had passed since the pitch had been knocked out of the park. Eyebrows raised, the coach turned to me and said, "You think I'm going to risk my job on the memories of two guys like that?" I saw his point, and I saw as the season progressed that not a single opposing catcher in even one of our fifty-four games called pitches. I realized that it would do no good to point out that the reason the pitcher and catcher did not remember the details of what was thrown was because they no longer had an incentive to do so. The cheese had moved, and I was the only one looking for it in its old spot.

When I teach "The Principles of Coaching," I find that nearly all of my students—sports lovers all—have been under the sway of this mindset for so long already that they cannot conceive of coaching as anything other than a business calling with its own set of buzzwords and acquirable techniques. They do not like to think about alternative approaches. They want to be told the exact ways in which a squad should be selected, a schedule composed, a practice plan devised, a problem dealt with. They like lists and policies that can be consulted for instant solutions. When I mention the techniques of some of the most successful and convention-defying coaches of all time—John Wooden, for instance, who seldom called a timeout as basketball coach at UCLA, preferring that his players learn for themselves when one was needed—they point to Wooden's formulaic "pyramid for success" as what they believe must have been the real key to his many NCAA titles. When I point out that John Gagliardi, the winningest football coach of all time, eschews overcomplicated playbooks, weight training, and too much practice time in pads, the students dismiss him as a lucky coach who wins only because he coaches in Division III. In short, they cannot envision a world where anything other than conformity has much merit.

Some of this is just a consequence of age. When I coached wrestling, I too was anxious to take part in the rituals and behaviors that I'd seen from my own coaches. It was especially intoxicating to walk the sidelines during matches in a jacket and tie. I imagined the envy of spectators when I walked up to a wrestler and gave him a sharp two-handed smack on the face before he ran onto the mat. My high school coach had done this with the intent of "waking us up." I realize now that it was just for show. The wrestlers I smacked were—just as I had been—too absorbed in the trial ahead to be woken up. There is nothing that can be done to clear the fog of fear just before combat, but I still see young coaches slapping away.

In some senses, then, the coach at Aurelian Springs might be applauded, if only for the part of his act that bounded with creative absurdity and not for the part that exhibited dishonorable subversion of excellence. But while the coach may have had at least a subconscious sense of the larger parts of the culture that were influencing him—the place of football in the South, the growing tilt of the coaching profession toward Lombardian claims that "winning is not everything, it is the only thing" (attributed to the late Packers coach, but not actually original to him: the line comes from the 1953 John Wayne film *Trouble Along the Way*)—they probably played a lesser part in his decision to play in the Franklinton game than his own need to remain in the action itself. Whatever vagaries of region and profession were pushing the coach, he was caught in what may have been the most influential tide rolling over the sports world at the time: the sudden overpopulation of the player pool caused by the baby boom.

I can still recall as a kid leafing through my mother's 1946 high school yearbook. It seemed that nearly every senior boy pictured played some sport or another. Many were three-sport athletes. Why? Was there that much talent walking the halls? No, it was because many of them liked playing sports, and there was room for them on nearly every squad. Uniforms might be old and mismatched, playing time might not be guaranteed, but the stigma of getting cut was absent. In the fifties, and evident particularly in the early sixties, the demographics of the baby boom changed that. *New York Times* writer Robert Lipsyte referred to the new phenomenon as the "Varsity Syndrome." I was a victim of it myself, getting cut from the junior high basketball team in 1963 because I was competing not with one or two others as might have been the case a few decades earlier but with dozens of others in a school district that had thousands of boys but still just fifteen basketball uniforms.

The Aurelian Springs coach had doubtless played in high school, but, unable or unwilling to test himself against his cohort at the University of North Carolina, he had not yet had his fill of glory. As would be expected with nearly any twenty-year-old trying to accommodate to a lesser role, he was not ready for the transfer from player to coach. As Claude Moore observed, "He told me he wanted to win so badly he didn't realize all the implications. He's so young." In other words, he had not yet lived enough life to understand that he was now an educator and not an athlete. It is, in fact, likely that one of the reasons he became a coach was because he wanted to stay close to sports and hadn't yet figured out that becoming a coach actually reduces one's opportunities for play. A coach still might get the rush that comes from sport's immediacy and its triumphs, but it doesn't hit you in the same spots as it does a player.

To be fair, or at least sympathetic, maybe none of us old jocks ever willingly forget the days when we moved more quickly, lifted more easily, and dreamed of conquest rewarded by medals and trophies. In fact, since the eighties, when baby boomers began to fade into the background of sport, Hollywood has produced a number of films (*The Best of Times*, *Little Giants*, *Second String*) in which grown men seek answers to their midlife crises in sports.

The current batch of young coaching aspirants reflects a slight variation of this. Having given up on playing sports earlier than athletes of older generations, they still seek attachment to sport and its elixir of glory and importance, but they are less concerned with playing again. They live in a world in which the more omnipresent and esteemed sports become, the more potential there is for a coach to catch its coattails and ride into the realm of celebrity as well.

The Aurelian Springs coach is now in his seventies, and I have wondered at times what he would make of all this and what he thinks about when glimmers of that long ago day and that long-lost touchdown run flicker through his mind. I'd like to know whether the exhilaration that must have pulsed through him as he made his way to the end zone was worth it. Was the spark hot enough to burn off the doubts, or would he—all things being equal—be more willing now to trudge off toward his own Appomattox with the spiritual guidance of good old Robert E. Lee? I decided not to ask him for several reasons: first, because it seems insensitive. How would you like someone to come up and ask you about your most egregious mistake fifty years after you thought it was buried? I mean, it's not like he got away with something and kept it hidden for a half century. He did lose his job, after all. Second, as a skeptic who has found through years of interviews that people are neither particularly self-aware nor publicly candid, I don't really believe that I'd get genuine or useful answers.

In the end, no one was immune to the coming surge of the naked need to win, not in the South, and not in America. Not even Claude Moore was oblivious to the coming deluge. The day after the Franklinton game, he told the local press that "it's been an unfortunate, embarrassing incident for the school and the community, but that's in the past now and we are ready to play basketball." As his hero, Lee, put it, "The gentleman . . . cannot only forgive, he can forget; and he strives for that nobleness of self and mildness of character which impart sufficient strength to let the past be but the past."

A LONG RUN TOWARD MEDIOCRITY

The first time I ran under the tyranny of a stopwatch was in 1963, when my seventh-grade class undertook the battery of challenges that made up the presidential physical fitness test. Until then, I associated running with speed and the exhilaration that came with a recess dash across the schoolyard in a new pair of Red Ball Jets or the sixty-foot bursts of high anxiety that came with laying down a bunt in Little League. Now a new component had been added: searing pain in the lungs and legs, a discrete unpleasantness that set in about halfway through the mandated 600-yard run and grew with each stride. Unfortunately, the buildup of lactic acid was only the beginning of distress; an equally unsettling discovery revealed itself when Mr. Pribula called out my finishing time of "one minute and forty-seven seconds." Alas, I was pretty good at this.

Armed with that knowledge and wishing to avoid future bouts of searing pain, I began avoiding running any distance not associated with a game: 180 feet at a time in baseball (I was incapable of hitting balls far enough to slither into the gaps where triples lay and far too powerless to hit the ball deep enough for a leisurely 360-foot home run trot); 90 feet up and down a basketball court; dashes of 20 or 30 yards on the soccer

Crossing the finish line of my long run toward mediocrity.
Photo collection of author

field. Of course, twice a year I was compelled by pride to repeat my best efforts in the 600-yard presidential fitness test, and I was required during the opening weeks of wrestling season to take three-mile pre-practice runs with my teammates, training that I short-changed by loping effortlessly ahead of the heavyweights and smokers but well behind those who busted a gut to be first back to the gym and out onto the mats.

By the time I went off to college at the close of the sixties the system of aerobic training espoused by Dr. Kenneth Cooper was beginning to make a dent in the lives of a number of middle-class Americans, including my father, and I became aware of timed endurance runs as yardsticks of one's fitness. For the next few years, I would occasionally test myself on my college track (an odd, five-laps-to-the-mile oval that cut across the corners of both football end zones) with solo runs of twelve minutes, running hard enough to assure that I could cover enough ground to remain in Cooper's category of "excellent."

Quite simply, I did not consider mere running, detached from a game, to be athletic enough to seduce me into daily confrontation with unnecessary pain. When I looked at my high school's cross-country runners I did not see anyone I considered to be an athlete. In fact, some of the team's best runners seemed to me to be ungainly, ungifted, and undeserving of varsity letters. My hierarchy of athletic achievement ranked putting one foot in front of the other right up there with male cheerleading.

By the time I returned to West Chester from college, however, things had begun to change. The great throng of baby boomers had swelled the competitive pools of sports, reducing chances to play on school teams. And the countercultural ethos of the Vietnam era had compounded the reduction in opportunities by its rejection of organized, adult-supervised sports. As the baby boomers reached their twenties and thirties many opted for the self-satisfying realm of individual endeavors. For some, it meant becoming part of the seventies tennis boom, but for many more it meant the therapeutic allure of the new running boom. Nudged to the starting line by Cooper's linking of endurance conditioning with improved quality of life and spurred a bit more by American Frank Shorter's marathon win in the 1972 Munich Olympics, the interest in running exploded with the 1977 publication of Jim Fixx's bestselling *The Complete Book of Running* (Fixx would die of a heart attack while running at age fifty-two, but the running community continues to hold that his end would have come even sooner without his dedication to daily runs). Millions of Americans who, like me, had always associated running with the mundane and often detestable effort required to play sports suddenly saw solitary miles on the road as an end unto themselves. Newly popular magazines like *Runner's World* expanded the science of Cooper and Fixx into more ethereal realms.

Running long, slow distances (LSD) was purported by some of the magazine's contributors and consumers to have the same transformative—though far milder and safer—power as hallucinogenic drugs. Hit just the right speed for just the right distance and a "runner's high" would supplant the discomfort of the pounding with a euphoric state that would make you want to run on into infinity. (The great marathoner Dick Beardsley lent a twisted perspective on what a real high is. His leg crushed and mangled by a John Deere tractor on his farm, Beardsley became addicted to the painkiller Demerol. Asked to hypothetically choose between never having had his body ruined by the tractor and never taking Demerol, he did not hesitate. He said he'd choose the Demerol.) Though I was not seeking a high—in fact, I have never experienced one while running—I was without the competitive outlets that had come easily while I was attached to educational institutions. I liked tennis and the newly risen racquetball, but these took time to schedule, and a mismatch in either meant too much time chasing errant shots or delivering half-hearted performances meant to keep things close against outmatched opponents, and so I soon allowed myself to be sucked into the road-running cult. Running, after all, called for nothing more than an ability I thought I already possessed—and the right shoes.

Ah yes, those shoes. Long before Mars Blackmon (Spike Lee) looked at Michael Jordan and exclaimed in a Nike ad that "it's gotta be the shoes," American youth knew the magical promise of new sneakers. Keds, PF Flyers, Red Ball Jets, and then, for the serious athlete, Converse Chuck Taylors, were wings for the feet, the source of irrefutable playground speed. (When I made the junior high basketball team my father took me to the local sporting goods store for my first pair of Converses; alas, he asked for tennis shoes, which is how many of the previous generation referred generically to sneakers. The prick of an owner, though I'm certain he knew they were not going to be worn on a tennis court, sold my father smooth-soled tennis shoes, leaving me a full season to slide up and down the hardwood as if on skates.) Long, slow distance running did not call for speed. It demanded not magic but new scientific attributes in shoes: cushioning, dispersion, stability, pared ounces.

To this day I don't know whether Nike anticipated the running boom or helped to start it. Certainly, they happily fed one another. I know that when I got my first pair of Nike Cortezes for Christmas in 1973, they were unlike any athletic shoe I'd ever owned. They were meant for running the roads, and that was what I used them for.

Within a year I had bought my first pair of Nike Waffle Trainers. Their very appearance startled me. Beyond the wide, flat, nub-riddled sole (the fruit of Oregon track coach Bill Bowerman's experimentation with a waffle iron), was the fact of their color. Medium blue with a yellow swoosh on the sides, they were the first pair of athletic shoes I owned that were not white or black. A year later, my waffle trainers were bright yellow with a red swoosh and made of a mesh that "breathed." By the time Nike started pumping air into the soles, I was deep into the mythology of shoes as technology, every nuance of their construction as critical to my health, psyche, and performance as a well-crafted shell was to a rower.

The shoes became the crown jewels. I found I also needed rain gear and lightweight shirts and shorts made especially to wick away distance-sapping moisture; I needed proper socks to keep my feet from blistering; and I needed hats, gloves, and cold-weather fabrics to layer for warmth and comfort in winter. In addition, I needed an annual subscription to *Runner's World* so I would know where my notions of training and racing fit amid the complexity that now attended the simple act of putting one foot in front of the other. And, of course, I needed to keep logs of the number of miles run (down to the hundredth), a tedious daily record that would eventually include the day's weather, my pace, my running heart rate, my recovery heart rate, my weight, my weekly and monthly subtotals, my interval ratios, and nearly anything else that one of the magazine's gurus might find germane to the right to call oneself a runner—something never to be confused with a jogger. To this day, the word "jogging," if applied to me, draws a reflexive rebuke. The term implies a lack of athleticism that I cannot abide. Joggers were housewives doing twelve-minute miles; they were gym class independents who circled the track slowly while the rest of us played games. I was never a jogger; I was a runner.

I entered my first 10K (6.2-miles) road race in 1979. A new graduate student at Penn State, I was startled to see the mixed population at the start line: there were other grad assistants from the kinesiology department—people like me—former athletes without a team to play for anymore, but also many joggers and participants whose black socks or clunky knee braces let me know that they'd never before ridden a team bus. These were people I would need to outrun, which meant that every race was going to be my junior high school 600-yard dash all over again. And, just as I feared, my first race confirmed that I was pretty good at running fast with my legs and lungs on fire. I averaged 6:09 per mile for over six miles up and down the hills of central Pennsylvania. When I ran through the finishing chute, I looked around to see whose company I was keeping. I was not pleased. Yes, there were guys like me, but also one or two women along with a gaggle of rail-thin nerds, some of them wearing the black socks.

The racing led me to some tough questions: Why was I doing this? Where was the scoreboard—was it my Casio wristwatch that could keep track of training splits, or was it the large digital clock at the finish line? If I beat half the field was I half a winner; if I finished was I never a loser? Were the T-shirts and bib numbers that I hung on a ribbon that ran from floor to ceiling in my office certifying my standing as an athlete or as something else?

Somehow, the whole racing community felt unnatural to me—no locker room, no daily banter and razzing, and worst of all, no sense of athleticism, at least not the kind I valued: skills requiring hand-eye coordination, one-on-one competition that called for cunning as well as muscle. I was becoming the buffoonish figure I'd ridiculed in high school, the cross-country runner, only worse, since I had no team, no uniform, and no coach beyond the training guidance of books and magazines. I was becoming what the onetime commissioner of baseball, Bart Giamatti, considered a social bane—the solitary jogger. "I know," he wrote, "one can jog or run with others," but "jogging . . . aspires to the paradise within . . . it is not civic or communal."

True, but, as I reminded myself, I was not a jogger, and I was pretty good at this. And, as the distance opened up between the athlete I'd been and the chance to ever be that again, I wanted to find a reason to keep running. Nike began supplying them.

There has never been another company like Nike, so intent on and capable of seducing so many diverse segments of the world's population. It began as a shoe company for track and cross-country runners before expanding to outfit everyone—young and old, jock and nerd, black and white, talented and talentless, active and inert—from head to foot. During the time I was running regularly, Nike had begun a series of ad campaigns that were often contradictory in message—some featuring elite athletes with genetic advantages over all but themselves, some appealing to the hyper-competitive ("Eat our dust" and "You don't win silver. You lose gold," and I could swear they also ran a short-lived ad that declared something along the lines of "If you reached the finish line and you were still conscious, you could have run faster"), some to the timid ("Yes to not being afraid to fail") and powerless ("If you let me play sports, I'll be less likely to stay with a man who beats me"), all under the wonderfully ambiguous and brilliant slogan of "Just Do It."

As could be expected, Nike aimed many of the campaigns at the baby boomers, a prosperous demographic raised as an undifferentiated pack and now greatly in need of a sense of specialness. Nike asked them to "Find Your Greatness," a task made less difficult by the company's assurance in an ad, "Somehow we've come to believe that greatness is only for the chosen few, for the superstars. The truth is, greatness is for us all. This is not about lowering expectations; it's about raising them for every last one of us. Greatness is not in one special place, and it's not in one special person. Greatness is wherever somebody is trying to find it."

Could there have been a more welcome balm to a generation raised on the mythology of the athlete as hero and the realization that time was running out on their own prospects for achieving that status? In its lengthy print ads, Nike was doing much more than they've been accused of—selling attitude—they were selling a ready-made philosophy to those unable to devise one on their own.

Adopting this solipsistic philosophy allowed you, in fact, to pretend that becoming a member of the amorphous Nike community would allow you to do everything on your own. Who needed coaches, teammates, uniforms, and a marching band? After all, "Everything you need is already inside," one ad promised. Thus was born the validity, credibility, and even nobility of the baby boomers' rubber crutch: the personal record, or P.R.

By the early eighties I was at a crossroads. My training runs had gotten longer and more regular. My interest in racing had produced a drawerful of 10K race T-shirts. I had begun scrawling my times on the race numbers hanging in the office. I had stopped taking stock of the other runners at the start and finish lines and begun measuring myself against myself. I now had P.R.'s for 5Ks, 10Ks, and ten miles. I had also begun to confuse Nike mantras like "there is no finish line," (a particularly insidious campaign that assured everyone that they were unlike everyone else—serious runners "addicted to what running gives you"), "everybody is a star," and "just do it" with athleticism, which means, of course, that I had essentially consigned my former sense of athleticism to the past and had begun thinking of putting one foot in front of the other as heroic. The new outlook did not sit well with my previous sense of sports, but I'd fallen for Nike's siren song of mediocrity.

Of course, Nike alone was not at fault. The whole movement from team sports to personal quests had swept beyond the baby boomers to infect their sons and daughters. When I first enrolled in a doctoral program at the University of Maryland in the mid-eighties, I was part of a cohort of graduate assistants that dominated intramural play on campus. I still remember the looks on the faces of the physics graduate students when they realized that today's football game was against kinesiology and that the department title was just the new code for physical education. By the time I left four years later, we could not even field a football team or softball team. Our ranks had been infiltrated and then taken over by runners, aerobic dancers, weightlifters, and other forms of "body fascists." Football was as alien to them as to those physics students. I had no trouble finding someone to run with; someone to play catch with was another matter.

I no longer wanted to be part of a movement that lacked, in my estimation, the capacity for movement excellence. I wanted the ways I moved to still mean something beyond one step at a time. And, thanks to a psychology of sports professor at Maryland, I was still able to see the difference. Don Steel was a generation older than me and loved playing more than any person I've ever met. He was a wonderful classroom teacher, but his main concern upon arriving on campus each morning was making sure that he had a full roster of players lined up for a noon-hour bout of basketball, tennis, or badminton. I was in his good graces and also within the fold of faculty figures who'd grown up playing rather than exercising. I was, then, always on Steel's list. Score was always kept. Violating the boundaries of fair play (not calling fouls on oneself in basketball, for example) led to banishment. It was the time of my life, and while I didn't give up running, I stopped entering races. Time on the road became again training for play.

Still, I couldn't shake the feeling that my views on the matter were unsettled and hypocritical. A final experience brought me a revelation. Just as I'd made a distinction between jogging and running, so too, I realized, there was a difference between running and racing. Apart from my first 10K, when I'd looked around to see who I'd beaten, I'd been running, not racing. I never entered a race thinking about winning or even what place I might come in. I was running against my own P.R., something that would always be there for the breaking if I found myself uninspired or uncomfortable on any given race day.

Occasionally, I'd become aware of other runners, but seldom did I try to beat them. An exception occurred during a ten-mile race that comprised two five-mile loops around the hilly Penn State campus. During the second loop I couldn't miss a much older man (I thought he was eighty; in all likelihood, he was in his sixties) who would go clomping by me during the downhills, his feet slapping the pavement with a sound like a horse from a TV western. Heading uphill—one of my strengths—I would in turn blow by him. When he passed me for a third or fourth time on a downhill, I began to get annoyed. The final stretch, however, was a brutal quarter-mile straight uphill, so I had no doubts about who would be finishing ahead of whom. Sure enough, coming home, I blew right by him and forgot he ever existed—until with about one hundred yards to go I heard the faint clopping sound approaching. As it got louder, its rhythm changed as well. I could not bear to look at him as he sailed by me and into the finishing chute. The odd thing was that I don't think he was even aware of me, much less trying to beat me; he was just running at his own pace—no doubt chasing some long-cherished P.R.

Running races that were peopled by thousands of runners, not racers, left me cold. There were too many happy faces at the finish lines. I remembered the high school track meets I'd attended with my father. The exhaustion on the faces of the half-milers, the jostling of the milers, the frantic crunch of cinders, and the exhortations down the home stretch from teammates reminded me that races were sports. The television coverage of Frank Shorter's Olympic marathon win in 1972 and the battle between Alberto Salazar and Dick Beardsley in their famous stride-for-stride 1982 Boston Marathon had managed to keep the 26.2 mile distance on the side of respectability in my ledger of acceptable sports events. As marathon finishes became, however, the grail of many roadrunners and surviving them became a badge of praiseworthy sacrificial effort, I began to turn against them as well. Looking at fellow graduate assistants who were slender as cornstalks but could not throw a ball against a wall with any assurance that they'd catch the rebound, I grew contemptuous. (My wife, Joanie, tells me that contempt is just my public expression of private shame, and, though it took me many years to catch on, I see her point. I was shamed to have been part of the cult of the P.R.) These wisps did not play noon-hour hoops; they ran marathons, and there were times when, in my presence, I shot verbal arrows at their arrogance, deriding a one-hundredth place finish as next to meaningless. One day, I backed myself into a corner, proclaiming that nearly anyone could finish a marathon. Within a week, challenged to back my claim, I was registered to run the 1984 Marine Corps Marathon in Washington, D.C.

A games-playing comrade in the grad office volunteered to do it with me. We went into training. We had just two months to get ready. My main concern was to stay uninjured. My friend decided we should at least set a goal that would require us to run the whole race rather than walk portions. We settled on four hours, which would require a pace of about nine minutes per mile. This, I reasoned, I could do in my sleep. To be on the safe side, we followed a conventional marathon training regimen. We would run six days a week, building our mileage for five weeks or so. We would then make one long run of twenty miles before tapering off during race week. The night before, we would carbohydrate load with spaghetti.

The training went well, though I began to resent the large bites of time it took out of my day. There were warmups and cooldowns, stretching, logging journal entries, and searching for new trails to fight the boredom. Still, in the final two weeks I began to look forward to the pageantry and excitement of it all. Joanie and a good friend, Syl, were going to take bikes into the city. Syl had plotted the race route and figured that they'd be able to catch me at at least six different points. A large contingent of faculty and other grad assistants were going to ride the Metro in to cheer us through the last few miles. I anticipated it as a great way to see the sights. The course would take us past most of the city's monuments and memorials, out to Hains Point, and would finish next to the Iwo Jima flag-raising statue, which I'd never visited.

The night before, we gathered with some other grad students for the carb-loading dinner. I decided on waffles rather than spaghetti and, against my better judgment, sought out one of the runners I'd needled into throwing down the gauntlet, and asked him if he had any advice for running the race. Bearded, slender, experienced, and often presenting himself as some sort of running sage, he floored me with his response. "When I'm out there," he said, "I repeat the mantra, 'I am a machine. I am a machine.'" I looked to see if he was kidding. His face betrayed only a serious sense of purpose. "The whole twenty-six miles?" I asked in disbelief. "Absolutely," he replied. To this day, I have never heard of a more robotic, soul-robbing routine. How would he take in the monuments? How would he acknowledge the applause of friends or the beauty of the day's clear skies? Who cared if a machine could complete a twenty-six mile race?

All the 10Ks had not prepared me for the circus that awaited my arrival in D.C. early on race morning. The field would be somewhere around twenty thousand runners, and the tag-alongs more than tripled the size of the gathering that milled around the starting line. The Marines were, naturally, efficient, so getting my number and instructions was no problem. We also got our commemorative T-shirts, and I noticed that a few of the runners put them on to wear in the race, which seemed to me like Terry Bradshaw wearing his Super Bowl ring in a game on the day he received it. Being in a contentious phase of my life, I had decided to wear a 1980 Moscow Olympics singlet I'd received from Soviet sprint medalist Valery Borzov. The Soviets had just boycotted our Los Angeles games, and I thought this a deliberate provocation. Not a single spectator or fellow runner would notice—so much for irony and provocation.

My friend and I were caught in the ethical dilemma of choosing a starting point. You were supposed to use an estimated finishing time to find your spot in the pack, it being unfair to those who would actually be running to win to be stuck at the outset behind those who intended only to improve upon their P.R.s of five hours and fourteen minutes. We decided to be honorable and moved to the middle of the field. It was a mistake.

The gun fired and we began running in place. Two or three minutes later we were still running in place. When we began moving, it became clear that a good part of the field had ignored the suggested starting points. When we actually reached the start line, the race leaders were already well out of sight. We were stuck doing a slow shuffle for what seemed like hours. Threading our way past the slower runners who had dishonestly started further ahead took a lot of concentration and energy. It was easy to step on the heels of those ahead, and our heels likewise were clipped repeatedly. No one apologized. Though it was against the rules, a fair number of frustrated runners took to the curbs and sidewalks, hoping to get some space. Some simply cut the corners off the routes, which certainly saved them many precious minutes because twelve miles into the race the course was still so congested that going around corners felt like being in a comedy sketch, those caught on the inside taking mincing steps in shoulder-to-shoulder traffic while those on the outside, thinking they could take longer strides, ended up shoving and stepping on those ahead.

In short, the race became a grind. We were unable to maintain any sort of steady pace, even a slow one. Forget the monuments. I ran by them all that day without even being conscious that I was in their vicinity. The one exception was when we hit windswept Hains Point a little past the halfway mark. There, trying to struggle free was an immense sculpture, *The Awakening* (it has since been bought and moved to a private spot up the Potomac River). An agonized, bearded giant's head had managed to poke through the earth. Next to his head, a grasping arm shot upward. Yards away, the fingers of his other hand had wriggled free. Some seventy feet distant, a bent leg struggled for freedom, while the giant's right toes popped through another twenty feet further. This was a monument I'd never seen, and it seemed that race directors might have plotted the course to ensure that the statue would abrade any false confidence that runners might still be harboring.

The effect on me was the opposite. I was feeling uninspired, true, but also untired. I'd already spotted and waved to Joanie and Syl a few times, and I was expecting to see them again shortly after I'd looped around Hains Point. As we left the small park that housed the sculpture, we heard an official calling out intermediate times. I started to extrapolate our likely finishing time and was shocked to realize that at our current pace we were going to come in at over four hours. I informed my partner of this and was met with a shrug. Well, that would be okay by him. I couldn't believe it. No, I said, I was not going to expose myself to ridicule in the grad assistant office by posting a time that any novice with just a few more months training than me would be proud of. I made the selfish decision to pick up the pace and leave him behind.

Within a hundred yards of ditching my training partner, I ran into an old neighbor that I had not seen in seventeen years. A year older than me, Mike Miller had been the best high school athlete in the county in his senior year, a gifted baseball and basketball player and an all-state soccer player. I was surprised to see him in a marathon. It was his first also, and we agreed to run the last ten miles of the race together.

The pack had finally thinned a bit and we hit a comfortable rhythm. Catching up on news of old acquaintances and swapping training stories with Mike, I lost track of the race itself. We had run past the eighteen mile marker without any effects from hitting the proverbial "wall," an invisible and dreaded barrier that in marathon lore locked up the legs of runners somewhere between eighteen and twenty-two miles. I had privately feared the wall might be my embarrassing undoing. While I didn't find any signs of the wall, I became aware that I also hadn't seen any sign of Joanie or Syl for the last six miles. I assured Mike that they'd be up ahead with some Gatorade and water.

When we got within five miles of the finish, I began to hear my name from encouraging spectators. These were the faculty and grad assistants from the University of Maryland who had come out to offer support. Many of them were former female college athletes, large and rugged enough to put a scare into most of the students—male and female—they taught. As we passed, Mike asked which one was my wife. I was relieved to tell him that I was married to none of them, but I was concerned that Joanie and Syl were still missing. With just a few miles to go, I decided that they had likely had trouble negotiating the large crowds with their bikes; I would just have to look for them as I crossed the finish.

The end was anticlimactic. I didn't seize up; I didn't throw up; I didn't feel much of anything. As we neared the Iwo Jima Memorial, I did misjudge the finish line by about two hundred yards, but even that was not distressing. Mike and I finished in about three hours and fifty-three minutes, and in the chaos of the moment, I wished him well before quickly losing sight of him. As I walked through the roped off chute, I was looking left and right and listening for Joanie's voice. It never came. When I exited the chute, a race volunteer pulled a large foil bag over my head to keep me warm. I wandered aimlessly for a few minutes, giving Joanie and Syl a chance to find me. About ten minutes later, I noticed that there were areas marked off for "lost" runners, so I wore my new foil suit over and sat down with a few others under the sign marked "T–Z."

I'd been there about a half hour when I became aware of three things: only a few lost runners remained under their alphabetical signposts; I was very hungry, and my legs were beginning to cramp up. I saw lingering runners eating bananas and was told there was a stand handing them out. Unfortunately, the stand was at the bottom of a grassy slope. Getting down was little problem—I half rolled and half slid, my foil baggie acting as a slippery sled. After claiming my banana, however, I found that my legs would not get me back up the slope. While many watched, I worked my way up by crawling sideways, like a wounded crab that had been dropped on the rocks by a seagull. It felt as if it took an hour. I have to admit now that had I been one of the onlookers, it was precisely the type of agony I would have been laughing at. Finally, I arrived back at my "T–Z" station and noticed that I was now the only lost runner left.

The race was over except for those runners who would finish with times in excess of five hours. Presumably, they'd be easy for their loved ones to spot and would not require services for the "lost." Volunteers began breaking down the area. None asked me why I hadn't been found. It was clear that Joanie and Syl were not going to claim me. On legs as stiff as concrete pillars, I managed to stand and then began an endless trek toward a Metro station. It took me as long to get there as it had taken me to run the marathon. When I got there, I had no money. I bummed enough for a one-way weekend fare and boarded the train in my foil bag, the car's only Pop Tart passenger. I honestly don't remember how I got back to our College Park apartment from the station. I know that when I arrived, Joanie and Syl had also just arrived, frantically trying to figure out what had happened to me. To me? What, I asked, had happened to them? Where were they at eighteen miles and twenty miles and twenty-four miles and the finish line?

Well, when they had somehow missed me at fourteen miles, they figured I'd dropped out. They had begun a wearying effort to backtrack, stopping at every aid station along the way, searching for their friend and husband—the quitter. Had they ever considered, I asked, going ahead to the finish line under the assumption that perhaps I was still ambulatory?

The answer really didn't matter. I had my sub-four-hour finish to rub in the faces of my fellow grad students. I had my Marine Corps Marathon T-shirt to wear to summer happy hours. And I had a ton of questions to think about surrounding the meaning of not just this one marathon, but the whole marathon boom, and the solitary practice of running taken up by millions of Americans, and what we accomplish when we keep putting one foot in front of another.

The answers have come to me slowly, in dribs and drabs, across the last thirty years. Good thing it's been thirty years; it's taken all of them to get to a point where my consideration is not so often illogical, not so habitually self-righteous, and, for the first time, not so unnecessarily harsh. In all likelihood the disdain was yet again shame, this time for having been so thoroughly seduced by the one-foot-in-front-of-the-other crowd. But the greater shame now is that I would be ashamed by this. So much of my identity has rested all my life in the notion of what constitutes athleticism and the belief that I had more of it than most. In fact my athleticism is nothing more than a set of things that I prefer when I play or watch sports: coordination, grace, power, and strategy. For me, endurance had just been a component in service of those. I needed movement exhilaration or excellence, and I couldn't find any in the agony of simply enduring.

Of course, I was fooling myself, defending my own views, because no one, after all, wants to think they've lived a foolish life. What need is it of mine to diminish whatever aspects of movement others value? Only those who reach the top echelons of sport through measured competition find true excellence; the rest of us are all chasing the dreaded P.R. nearly every time we step on a track, field, or court.

That is about as far as I can go with my compassionate intellectualizing. While I lost my affinity for road racing, I have remained under Nike's spell, buying shoes I don't need (McDougall's terrific *Born to Run* tells us our feet would be better left unshod), doing my part to help the swoosh remain the giant of the running industry. And I wonder more and more about that ill-fated ad from the nineties, the one that said, "If you reached the finish line and you were conscious, you could have run faster." Along with most, I first considered it cruelly absurd; but now I'm not so sure. Maybe if I'd run with that as my goal, particularly on those days when everything had synced up for me physiologically, rather than shaving a few seconds off my P.R. here and there, I'd have approached excellence. I don't know what the finish line felt like to all those others smashing through the barriers of their own P.R.s—maybe movement exhilaration, maybe excellence—but for me it will always feel lacking. It's just not in me to value too highly the achievement of something I already knew I could do. If the others did not know beforehand that they could complete the race, then I suppose finishing meant something to them. My lack of satisfaction was not the fault of the sport, of the other runners, or even of Nike.

Ten years after the marathon, out of grad school and badly missing regular sports participation, I took up the decathlon. Though quite undersized and bringing only novice technique to the discus, shot put, and high hurdles, I finally had what I'd been after: standards that transcended the P.R. The points book for the decathlon had taken decades and tens of thousands of recorded, compiled, and sorted performances to arrive at a scale of excellence. You could claim a P.R., but you couldn't hide from your final point total, an outcome that compared you not to yourself but to every other decathlete who'd ever competed. Though all the hurdling, vaulting, and jumping would one day lead to a hip replacement, my two age-group All-American awards, capped by a bronze in the Nike World Masters Games, underlined what should have been clear to me the morning I sat in my foil baggie as a lost soul: I needed to run away from mediocrity much more quickly than the years I'd spent running slowly toward it.

WISHFUL THINKING

> What decides why one thing gets picked to be the way
> it will be? Accident? Fate? Some weakness in ourselves?
> Forget your harps, your tin-foil angels—the only heaven
> worth having would be the heaven of answers.
>
> *Mark Slouka*

A MILLION ANSWERS SHORT OF HEAVEN

The core of this essay first appeared under the title "American Brigadoon: Joe Paterno's Happy Valley," in a 2013 University of Illinois Press collection of original essays on sport and community titled Rooting for the Home Team. *Written in May 2011, my essay quickly became outdated in the wake of the November 2011 Jerry Sandusky scandal that sent Happy Valley into a tailspin. I have added an epilogue here but left the essay in its original form because it is more provocative, instructive, and humbling to read sentences like "Joe has done far more good for the game and for Penn State than he can possibly undo in his fading years." I was wrong about that and other things as well. It seems that the values associated with Penn State were just as unsustainable and illusory there as elsewhere, and the riots that took place after Paterno's dismissal seem to confirm a great deal of what I wrote about our impulse to defend our voluntary associations to the death rather than entertain the possibility that we've lived a foolish life.*

(D.Z., December 2014)

It's October, and as I've done on nearly every autumn Saturday for four decades, I've settled in front of a television. As a panoramic shot captures a gorgeous landscape of distant mountains and rolling foothills, ESPN's

Winning helped make Happy Valley happy—and as haughty as a lion.
Penn State University Archives, Pennsylvania State University Libraries

announcers reveal that we are "live from Happy Valley." Scanning the more than one hundred thousand spectators in Penn State's Beaver Stadium, a camera comes to rest on a manic student who is gesticulating wildly, as contemporary fans tend to do when they realize their three seconds of fame have arrived. This one is wearing a full-headed rubber mask that caricatures the bulbous nose and black pompadour of Penn State football coach Joe Paterno, and I can think of only two things—first, I want one of those masks, and, second, if my father had lived to see it, he would not only have owned one, he'd have actually worn it.

And who could blame him? My father didn't like himself all that much, but he was happy around Penn State football, specifically Penn State football under Joe Paterno. Raised near the State College campus, my dad grew up playing tackle football with his brothers in the shadows of the school's sheep barns. My grandfather was an itinerant preacher, and his travels took my dad in his teens to the suburbs of Philadelphia. Dad remained there until the mid-seventies when, nearly fifty, he decided to chuck his pension and twenty-seven years of seniority at a local chemical plant to return to Happy Valley. He bought a run-down biker bar at the top of Mt. Nittany and operated it as a restaurant for over twenty years. (One night in the eighties, "JoePa" stopped in for dinner. The staff did not think—or bother—to summon my father from his home fifty paces across the parking lot.) All the while his love for the area expanded several-fold, revolving around and boosted by Nittany Lion football.

Maybe I'm just guessing at some of this, but I think his passion for Penn State—and that of many others—grew from an illusion that Happy Valley, particularly and uniquely under Paterno, was as much a mindset as a place. I know you could argue the same about any number of campus locales, Tuscaloosa being just a mental way station for those in search of the lost, mythic South, for example. But even there, fans are acutely aware of being Alabamans (or, in other areas, Nebraskans, Iowans, Ohioans, Kansans, and on and on) in a way that Penn State fans are not connected, for the most part, to a sense of being Pennsylvanians. Indeed, many natives hate Penn State; Philadelphians and Pittsburghers, in particular, are anchored to different realities and identities. That's not to say that there aren't shiploads of alums and fans in those metropolitan areas, but when I envision the prototypical Penn State fan, he is from a geographical band that begins around Johnstown, runs northeast through Scranton, and stops in Allentown near the Jersey line. Life in those areas, though transforming from the days when they supported coal and steel industries, is still decidedly slower and more loyal to the state's blue-collar ethos.

Deeply invested in a sense of tradition, these Penn State fans draw their sense of community from the shared belief that Happy Valley is not only a mythic place but a singularly righteous one as well. Further, they are adamant that the righteousness is deserved, springing as it did from the success that Paterno seemed to fashion from values outdated and unsustainable elsewhere. In short, many, myself included, see Happy Valley as a fantastical American Brigadoon that will vanish forever when Paterno is gone. There. I've said it. Now stop rolling your eyes at the pompous academic and listen up.

The State College area acquired the "Happy Valley" nickname because of its seeming immunity to the economic misery of the Great Depression. In the decades thereafter, most industry—other than Penn State—largely withered away. Still, because the university grew into a prominent research institution (on the back, some believe, of Paterno's football successes), many inhabitants are confident that the area remains recession-proof. Years ago *Psychology Today* declared it one of the least stressful places in America to live, and one publication or another in the decades since has trumpeted its livability. Penn State's enrollment has grown to nearly forty-five thousand, and the campus, large enough that when I taught there in 1980 I had to jog briskly to get to classes on time, is truly monstrous. The town has spread a bit, but it still feels quaint, even charming by some measures. The Tavern (Paterno's favorite), the Corner Room Restaurant, and the Rathskeller have scarcely changed in over sixty years, and there is nothing chichi about the businesses or the town's aspirations. Still, to travelers not in the mood for shopping for a hundred thousand different articles stamped with "Penn State" or its stylized mountain lion's head logo, and resistant to the nonstop efforts of travel agents to pump up the place, the area can seem a bit anachronistic—which is just how the mythmakers like it.

Paterno came to State College as an assistant coach in 1950. Four years later, *Brigadoon* debuted in American movie theaters. It was the tale of an enchanted village that appeared once every hundred years; by covenant, if anyone left, the village would disappear forever. Though set in Scotland, it served as a metaphor for threatened ways of life everywhere, one more twist on the notion of not being able to go home again. Brigadoon is more about time than space; more precisely, it is about the inextricable linkage of the two. Lose contact with one or the other and you risk losing both. Passing years or abandoned spaces lead to irretrievable loss, a surety underscored in *Brigadoon* when one of the show's leads asks, "Why do people have to lose things to find out what they really mean?" Paterno's wife, Sue, alluded to the same sense of paradise lost while addressing a homecoming crowd a few years back: "Welcome back to the home where your heart was," she told alums, "and always will be."

Like Brigadoon, the lore of State College began with physical inaccessibility. The town is isolated in the center of the state, so for the better part of the twentieth century visiting teams had to make their way first to Harrisburg, from which point, according to a New York sportswriter, "you swung the final ninety miles through the trees." Paterno's legendary first assessment: "It was a cemetery." It was a perfect place, in another words, for Paterno to conduct, shortly after becoming head coach in 1966, what he called the "grand experiment," a slippery concept alluding to the possibility that Penn State could become virtually the first football program in American history to reconcile the gap that existed between intercollegiate ideals and the reality of how college sport was conducted. It meant that he would—in the face of ramped-up expectations, new money from television, ascending influence from wire-service polls, and a generation of students poised to blot out the traditions and values of all preceding generations—hold Penn State to a character-based standard. It was a giant gamble, because the standard he had in mind was pretty much passé by the mid-fifties and had never gained a foothold in the actual behavior of college football players.

Identified pejoratively by young athletes today as "old school," Paterno's experiment was to fulfill the tenets of sport's character-building ideology, or as *Philadelphia Inquirer* sportswriter and astute Paterno chronicler Frank Fitzpatrick wrote, "He seemed single-handedly to be defending loyalty, simplicity, and virtue against the disturbing forces that were just beginning to shake sports and the wider world." And it worked, owing to two time-honored truisms: "location, location, location" and "timing is everything."

Paterno had the privacy (which many claim grew into unseemly secrecy across the years) and the timely blossoming of his team's on-field success to make the experiment look like reality. So assured did the program and its backers become over the next two decades that Paterno was able to define his standards in language that seemed to belittle every win-at-all-costs coach (basically nearly everyone else): "What really matters is reaching a level of internal excellence. It does not matter whether one is thought of as being successful, that is, a winner. It does not matter, simply because too often we make the serious mistake of equating excellence with success, and they are not the same thing." Try taking that and a 1–9 record to your athletic director and see what it gets you.

Penn State had frightening success. Within two years of his hiring, Paterno posted back-to-back perfect seasons. He rolled into the early nineties with so much weight and public confidence behind him that people began to think that he was, as his actions hinted, really more than a winning football coach. In the shadows of the ever-expanding battleship of a stadium (original capacity 46,284, now 107,282), Paterno gave generously: millions to endow faculty positions, to the Mt. Nittany Medical Center, and to the main campus library that now bears his name. Bill Lyons of the *Philadelphia Inquirer* wrote: "Even though he is enormously successful at it, from the perspective of meaningful contributions to society, the least important thing Joe Paterno does is coach football." The clincher, according to Fitzpatrick, had come in 1972, when Paterno's rejection of the New England Patriots' lucrative overtures lent him unquestionable moral authority. All well and good, and nary a cynic ever suggested that the coach's generosity was not both valuable and sincere. But what did all this goodness add up to in terms of community?

This is the point where I hoped to have a few words from Paterno himself. I sent him correspondence requesting a brief meeting, but I guess, as John Updike observed, the gods really don't answer letters. Just as well. It would have been unfair to ask Joe what I was going to ask him. I wanted to ask him how he managed to create something beyond Bear Bryant's Alabama or Woody Hayes's Ohio State, but more than that, I wanted to find out how much of it he thought was real and how much was public relations hocus pocus. Anyway, there is no way he could have answered honestly and maintained any sense of humility, and, who knows, maybe he's never really thought about any of this stuff anyway. Lord knows there is already enough horrific academic theory and jargon floating around to turn any normal person off, much less a busy emperor. One professor, for example, has posited that Joe's white shirt and dark tie suggest status and power and that the plain Penn State uniforms symbolize values like hard work and teamwork. Well, when Joe wakes up on game day, how many choices of clothes do you really think he has? Do you think he asks his wife, "Now where did I put that outfit that summons perceptions of low self-esteem and social timidity?"

If clothing and apparent symbols like a mascot in a "fuzzy costume" that "suggests the fun and lightheartedness associated with the collegiate ideal" are too facile—if not nonsensical—as contributions to Penn State's exceptionalism, they have nonetheless become part of the accepted landscape surrounding the school's sports. Let me try something every bit as ordinary, but, I think, less nonsensical and more persuasive: there are two keys to our membership in voluntary associations (and, if you ask me, to all human behavior). The first is that we all need to spend some time being someone other than who we are (or think we are); and second, nobody wants to think they've lived a foolish life. The first creates a grounding for the communities we choose to belong to; the second compels us to defend those communities to the death.

The post–World War II proliferation of self-help books urging us to find ourselves and then be true to what we find is powerful testament to the fact that we are more than a tad afraid of what we think is there. Every time I hear former defensive end Michael Strahan say, "I love me some me," I think, "Probably not so much." If self-esteem were as attainable as pop culture hints, self-help gurus wouldn't have to keep clubbing us over the head with the claim that it was within our reach.

Like religion, community is the hope that something bigger than us can save us from ourselves. To indulge in community is to refute isolation. Being alone can be a fearful condition because most of us are not comfortable with ourselves. A writer whose name eludes me ventured (I'm paraphrasing) that the worst place to be is alone with yourself driving on a rainy night, because, with nothing for company but the slapping of windshield wipers, that is when you are most inescapably who you are. Philosophers, of course, have always known this (except for the windshield wiper part), and in the once-upon-a-time of the Middle Ages, all segments of society knew it. The festivals in which the world turned upside down allowed peasants and rich lords alike to don masks and invert the social order for a day.

Two aspects of modern life still offer vestiges of this possibility. There are the secular celebrations like Halloween and Mardi Gras in which we indulge in the fantasy of becoming something other than what we are, and there are sports. Sports lend themselves readily to the medieval conceit; in fact, contests that allowed the common class to publicly exhibit the veiled threat of their physical prowess were often part of the festival celebrations.

In sport, the power of the crowd creates both the possibilities for doing the right thing and, for the less noble, a mob mentality. The character-building ideology sides with the first, holding that we are something different—better—when connected to uniforms. We subsume ourselves in team, work hard when we don't have to, and make believe that the lowest of us can, on any given day, rise to the top of the heap. The uniforms themselves make for fine masks: Michael Vick, dog slayer, for instance, costumed in pads and helmet masquerades as a role model and leader. My father had a fondness for costumes and public occasions when he could holler out loud without penalty. Feeling always outstripped by his brothers, he desperately sought the esteem bestowed by an official association with sports. In a photograph of his second-grade class, he is the one wearing a full baseball uniform.

In our time, even the facsimile of a uniform can be enough to claim membership in a community. I was at an outlet mall recently and saw a twenty-something wearing a T-shirt emblazoned "Abercrombie Track." Since I know that the trendy clothier has lots of money invested in ad campaigns featuring nearly nude models, but none in athletics per se, this at first struck me as odd and more than a bit off-putting. On second thought, however, I realized that Abercrombie & Fitch has as much right as any other commercial entity, including, say, a university, to tap into our need for artificial, virtual, and even nonexistent communities.

Though I'm guessing that strangers in Abercrombie Track shirts do not seek out one another, belonging to Abercrombie Nation is as telling as membership in Red Sox Nation. Both signal the post–World War II rise of atomism that has meant the loss of American communities—including civic clubs, bowling leagues, and faculty dining rooms, as detailed in Robert Putnam's *Bowling Alone* (2000)—that were once rooted in interwoven vectors of time and space.

In choosing our voluntary associations with one community and not another we have been freed from the requirements of proximity. Once, we identified with whatever was at hand—if you got stuck with Al Davis, the Phillies, or Rice University, so be it. When those things were in opposition to what we thought ourselves to be, whether elitist, thuggish, or undeserving, we wore the mask anyway. In other words, we didn't so much turn the world upside down as have it flipped over on us. But now, bound as we are only by the axiom that no one wants to think they've lived a foolish life, victory has surpassed geography in claiming our allegiances. Little else explains the recent unattractive explosion of Red Sox Nation than the increasingly status-hungry need to be a winner. Has anyone heard from Pirate Nation?

While technology has made it easy to jump onto any bandwagon that rolls down the information highway, and while I would never claim that Penn State football could have grown in the absence of great win-loss success, for many the program's real appeal is that it combined the best of all worlds, that is, it won "the right way," an idea last articulated for public consideration in the dying days of Paterno's old stomping grounds, the Ivy League of the late forties and early fifties. There, it was claimed by its athletic directors, they could "hate enough to beat each other, but trust enough to schedule each other." A website has adopted this same exclusive attitude as its banner: "We are not normal. We are legends. We are Penn State."

Nearly alone in the world of big-time college football, Paterno's Penn State was an independent until the early nineties, freed from conference dictates and also free to construct its own identity. With a schedule that critics derided for decades as too soft, Paterno was able to be selective in recruiting athletes who furthered his declarations about the possibility of truly joining the dichotomous aspects of sport and the academy, blending them to make the term "scholar-athlete" something other than oxymoronic. When Heisman winner John Cappelletti's heroic support of his dying brother became the subject of a prime-time television special in

1977, the nation began to think that maybe the air around central Pennsylvania was indeed rarified.

More remarkable, perhaps, than the insistence on principles out of step with the Woodstock generation—the same insistence that would drive a number of head coaches to the unemployment lines—was Penn State's ability to win big while quietly integrating a handful of black athletes. Elsewhere, coaches were heavily recruiting blacks, and, though the coaches struggled to reconcile the differing sensibilities that mixed teams invited, there was tacit agreement, even in the Ivy League, that teams that excluded African Americans would be settling at the bottom of conference standings.

Penn State, in no small part because of its geographic and cultural distance from black communities, was and remains a difficult sell to black recruits. The State College area, even in the twenty-first century, is eighty-five percent white and less than four percent black. But Paterno has been able to continue a tradition begun with standout running back Lenny Moore and defensive lineman Roosevelt Grier in the fifties, convincing a few quality blacks to come to his Brigadoon and stay. In the seventies and eighties my father was nearly as proud of this—noticeable in the cases, for example, of Lydell Mitchell, Franco Harris, and Curt Warner—as he was about any other facet of the program. Part of the nostalgia for Main Street America, particularly during the Vietnam era, was that there once had been a time when blacks were able to adapt to their second-class status and live happily in mainstream white America. Penn State appears to embody this pseudo-assertion.

Some might say that this is all fine when you talk about Penn State in the sixties, seventies, and even the eighties, but the notion that Paterno and the values of a pre-sixties America are still a part of Penn State is laughable in 2010. Some will say that this essay comes at least ten years too late, that the throwback luster Penn State once had was wiped out when the new millennium delivered a series of public arrests of football players involved in campus altercations, embarrassing Big Ten losses by the truckload, and a team that struggled to beat even the non-conference foes once brought to Beaver Stadium for early season sacrifice to the Lions.

There is no doubt that losing seasons in 2000, 2001, 2003, and 2004 disenchanted older fans and positively alienated the younger generation, which increasingly sees athletes as commodities (witness the rise of fantasy sport leagues), teams as entertainment troupes, and rules as impediments to overcome in the name of victory. The crowd in Beaver Stadium has turned more demanding, and, at times, ugly. Paterno has drawn some boos, and in one of those losing seasons, I watched a young, untested quarterback leave the field at halftime to a scathing and obscene stream of vitriol from an entire section of fans seated near the players' tunnel to the locker room.

The spate of JoePa masks that flood Happy Valley in the fall became as much mockery as tribute during the losing seasons. When Paterno righted the ship, however, in the last few years, the fan base reached renewed consensus that things were both OK and still distinctly unique in Happy Valley (because, remember, no one wants to believe they've lived a foolish life). In 2005, *Sports Illustrated* stamped its approval, calling game day in Happy Valley "the greatest show in college sports." And when Paterno told the *Philadelphia Inquirer* on the cusp of a new season, "Right now I have no plans whatsoever as far as whether I'm going to go another year, two years, five years, or what have you," the loyal agreed that he has earned the right to go at a time of his choosing.

Still, it's impossible to argue that things are as they were before. If Brigadoon did not disappear, it certainly began a slow fade. Little by little, whenever Paterno and Penn State fall short, the community will be changed, settling for less of the old as they cede to the standards of the new. For the older crowd, it will be as if the Amish decided that the new way to get around would be on Harley-Davidsons.

To a dwindling number, including me, the losses will be minor compared to the glimpses we've had of JoePa when he has let the mask slip. The unpleasant sight puts me much more in mind of *The Wizard of Oz* than *Brigadoon*. First, there was his nomination of George H. W. Bush at the 1988 Republican National Convention. Though Paterno's politics are still tough to pin down, his journey from Sports World to the Real World betrayed the apolitical nature of all American dreamscapes, Brigadoon included. On a college campus, even tweed-and-pipe profs can nurture a secret love of football so long as the reactionary forces running it don't make an issue of politics.

More rankling still were the contradictions that Joe's behavior offered against his claims about internal excellence. In defeat, he often became whiny and petulant. In 2002, after a loss to the University of Iowa, Joe ran off the field in angry pursuit of a referee. The next day he failed to apologize, rationalizing that what we witnessed had been blown out of proportion by the press. In an unsporting gesture to victory's importance, in 2004 Paterno repeatedly waved his arms on the sideline, exhorting the home crowd to make enough noise to drown out Purdue's ability to hear its own signals.

Most disturbing of all, and in contrast to the lack of ego that Paterno often proclaims, was the 2006 placement outside Beaver Stadium of a seven-foot tall bronze statue of the coach. To me, the statue smacks of the same lack of humility we see in Duke's arrogantly named basketball floor, "Coach K Court." In both cases, the coach is the most powerful employee at the institution (and, at least in Paterno's instance, the highest paid). Would it be too much to ask them to simply say, "I'm flattered that you want to memorialize me. If you can't wait for me to die, could you at least hold off until I retire?"

Still, because I too don't wish to believe I've lived a foolish life, I've maintained my membership in the Penn State community, forgiving Paterno at every turn, choosing to remember his cheerful but innocuous greetings at 6:30 each morning, our paths momentarily crossing as I walked from the graduate building to Rec Hall. I forgive him, too, because focusing on his shortcomings is as much a collective failure as his—the willful ignoring of the care to be taken against idealizing any human being. In truth, Joe has done far more good for the game and for Penn State than he can possibly undo in his fading years. It is we, the media and fans, who created Happy Valley, and we who fear it to be a college version of Brigadoon. If Paterno or Penn State didn't take great pains to discourage our illusion, why would or should we expect them to? This coach is a man in search of victories, each one carrying him one more week, one more month, and one more season in a life of his own choosing and one that many of us envy.

I forgive also because of a personal failing. To try to state outright my fondness for what Joe brought to my life would push me too close to a blubbery sentiment that would in turn expose me as being soft and vulnerable. In this, I am much like my father. At my sister's wedding, when my grandfather, the officiating preacher, asked, "Who gives this girl's hand in marriage?", my father intended to say, "Her mother and I do." What emerged instead was a great, ghastly sob that left most guests awkwardly stunned and me thinking, "There but for the grace of God go I."

What I most wanted to tell Coach Paterno if he had granted me an interview was how much he meant to my father. If he needed to wear a mask to do it, well, I would have needed one to address him on such intimate matters. It's what we all do now and then, isn't it?

When my father died in 1995 (in a hospital where a nurse inexplicably referred to him as "Mr. Zerbe" and just as inexplicably turned off the radio broadcast of a Penn State women's basketball playoff game, possibly the last sounds my father ever heard), the only item I wanted, other than family photos, was the Penn State jacket he wore to athletic events. With embroidered letters and logo it was—by necessity—slightly more tricked out than the famed plain jerseys. Some years later, having been unable to bring myself to wear it, I tossed it into a bag of clothing headed for the Salvation Army. I wish I had it back. Somewhere there is a man walking the streets of Baltimore wearing a piece of my life and one of the few tangible remembrances I had of my dad. He is also wearing a symbol of homage to an illusion extinct for sixty years outside of Happy Valley.

Epilogue

For Joe Paterno, Penn State football was not a passion; it was his life, and not many were surprised when his life ran out shortly after his football career ended. Now that he is gone, what makes me think that it is for me to search for and defend or attack the record of another human being? That is just one more question in an unending string of them left in the scandal's wake: In the end, did Joe consider whether his grand experiment had been a success? Had it met his definition of excellence? Was Jerry Sandusky his responsibility? Was a football player brawling at a frat party the failing of Joe Paterno, sport's character-building claims, or just one of a thousand uncontrollable aberrations? Did age or hubris rob Paterno in later years of good judgment? Did Joe ever wonder if he'd lived a foolish life?

I recently viewed the documentary film on the scandal, Happy Valley, and a few weeks ago I gave an invited presentation at Penn State on the grand experiment. The reactions of those interviewed in the film and those at my talk confirm that State College is not short of true believers. Ignoring or incapable of heeding the dictum about a foolish life, they have begun parsing the Freeh Report that held Paterno and others accountable, hoping that a flawed process might erase the fact that some really bad stuff had happened. I've wondered often whether my father would have been one of those parsing and rationalizing. I'd like to think he would have felt like so many of us other Penn State fans: unspeakably sad.

While I was in State College, I also became aware that there is a growing movement demanding that Paterno's statue—torn down behind screens that kept the public from watching the "desecration"—be brought out of storage and placed again on campus. Perhaps the fate of this movement will be the best indicator of time's ability to make us forget. If the statue, this remnant of an extinct epoch in college football, does make a comeback, the living of foolish lives can begin anew. But neither the statue, public relations campaigns, nor time can hide the fact that we can't answer the most basic queries: why Jerry Sandusky did what he did, why one boy and not another, why Joe did what he did, and why he wished he'd done more. When science or someone is able to supply answers to those, perhaps we'll be more content. Until then, I have about a million more questions, which leaves me a million answers short of heaven.

> Things you did. Things you never did. Things you
> dreamed. After a long time they run together.
>
> *Richard Ford*

IMPOSSIBLE DREAMS

In 1984 I was one of five delegates the U.S. Olympic Committee sent to Olympia, Greece, for the International Olympic Academy, an educational forum on Olympic issues. On the eve of the conference's final day I was out of time in which to explore the ancient stadium at Olympia free of the clamorous and despoiling effects of tourist hordes. I decided that daybreak might be my best chance to see it alone. When I arrived at 6 A.M., utter silence and a rising mist created a setting that would have thrilled a filmmaker. It thrilled me, and I had just curled my bare toes into grooves carved into a flat stone sill—the ancients' version of starting blocks—preliminary to my dash down the 120 meter field when I got a feeling that I was being watched. Stepping back, I looked up and saw a figure at the far end of the stadium. "Damn," I thought, "tourists—even at sunrise." I was doubly put off when I noticed that the intruder was walking through a stone arch gateway—the entry point reserved exclusively for athletes in antiquity. As the only historian selected by the USOC, I was aware of and annoyed at this unknowing gesture of disrespect. As the interloper walked toward me, I considered whether to mention the transgression. When he was within forty yards, however, I saw that he had used the right entry. It

1972 Olympic gold medalist Valery Borzov prepares to race the author, 1984.
Photo collection of author

was Valery Borzov, the 100 and 200 meter Soviet gold medalist from the 1972 Games in Munich.

I was startled not only that Borzov—one of the Soviet delegates—was up so early, but that he'd managed to slip the dogged attention of an intimidating handler who had shadowed all the Soviet delegates for ten days, and who most of the international delegates had begun referring to more confidently each day as "Mr. KGB." He had kept me—and all others—away from the Soviet athletes during the conference's events. Now Borzov approached and asked what I was doing in bare feet. His English was halting, but good enough to get beyond a handshake and mere gesturing at one another. I did my best to explain the use of the grooves to

The ancient entrance for athletes at the stadium in Olympia, Greece.
Photo collection of author

begin a race in ancient times. He seemed skeptical, but we settled none-theless into starting stances. I tried to convince him that the Greek runners had stood upright, but I could not dissuade him from crouching—and not into his conventional sprinter's stance, but awkwardly into a three-point stance used by American football linemen. A sideways glance confirmed that he was humoring me and had no intention of actually racing me. We rose and began talking. He had a reputation for iciness, and he did not smile. I sensed both his desire to talk to me as well as a wish that I was not there at all. Clearly he'd come to be alone, too. As the conversation stalled, he politely tried to keep up his end by asking me my favorite sport. I answered honestly: baseball, a reply that turned him contemptuous and ruined the moment.

Later that night, however, as the conference's last meeting ended, he sought me out and gave me two gifts: a singlet with the emblem of the 1980 Moscow Games (which I would wear several months later while running the Marine Corps marathon) and an Olympic athlete's participa-tion medal (after the Western boycott of the 1980 Games, more than a thousand of these never made it into the hands of actual Olympic ath-letes). Strangely, it was the gift of the medal, now obviously intended as a souvenir for a mere ballplayer, that ended a delusion that I'd entertained for over a decade: the possibility that I might one day find my way into the Olympics as an athlete.

British scientist Richard Dawkins, in his bestseller *The God Delusion*, expressed great frustration with the inability of most humans to acknowl-edge what seemed obvious to him: the great improbability that there is a God. In doing so he failed, I think, to give enough credence to what seems obvious to me: gods aside, we do not arrive at our conclusions about su-pernatural or any other phenomena through ignorance. We know when we're being duped and deluded—it's just that we enjoy it, or at least find it necessary. We crave delusion to build and sustain otherwise unlivable lives.

Because much of my life rests on a specific relationship I've built with sports, the consummation and culmination of which comes every four years during the Olympics, I've been unable as an academic to delve into the particulars of bribery, steroids, politics, economics, murder, showmanship, or even symbolism that are the foundation of scholarly critique of the Games in modern society. I am more given over to the feel of the Games—a collection of subjective whims and deeply felt currents that leave me not only poorly equipped for critique but also constricted by the zeitgeist of the Games in my own lifetime, at least as I've experienced them.

Of all the Games that have left an imprint on me, the deepest marks come from the 1972 Games in Munich. Of course, you might say. Those seventeen days stood out in so many ways that we could defensibly claim them as pivotal in turning the Olympic movement in a dozen directions: they were the high-water mark in the rivalry between the U.S. and the USSR; the explosive success of the East Germans foretold open confrontation with the steroids issue; the Cuban boxers foreshadowed the ability of Third World nations to claim credible world status based on Olympic performance; Olga Korbut lit the television stage for petite pixies in a way that would commandeer future American television time and dollars; the only hippie Olympian in history died in a car crash a month after winning a silver medal; and the Israeli massacre, of course, exposed us all to the long reach of terror.

In short, in '72 the Olympics were so animated by the era's tumult that it was tough to get a fix on whether one influencing breeze was blowing harder than the others. However, as a political writer had observed in the aftermath of World War II with regard to Washington politics, "Every now and then a wind starts blowing and suddenly all the little weathervanes point one way." Over the course of several retrospective decades, I realized that amid all the turbulence in Munich, one vane had indeed spun and come to rest 180 degrees from where it had begun seventy-six years earlier. That vane in 1972 was pointing toward a new Olympics—one divorced from my experience, ideals, and wishes—in which athleticism would become, at least to the public, increasingly specialized, technologized, commercialized, and remote. A new wind was blowing away the illusion of accessibility. No longer could Everyman find a spot on an Olympic roster, much less an Olympic victory podium.

This loss of accessibility is linked to the idea of amateurism. The very word, of course, is so shrouded in ancient misperceptions, rigid classism, and blatant deceit that it was bound to seduce millions worldwide. I, however, am not delusional about amateurism. Along with most Olympic scholars, I understand that it is an archaic invention of exclusivity defending and defended by money and class. I also recognize that it provides a

paradoxical rebuke to Olympic founder Pierre de Coubertin's wish that
the Games not be anchored in the crassness of victory but in the glorious
ideal of taking part, since he didn't mean just old anybody could take part.

Coubertin had little use for Africans, Asians, exotic islanders, or Latinos. Had he made the trip from France to St. Louis for the 1904 Games, he would have prevented, or at the least been repulsed by, the marathon entries of Lentauw and Yamasani, two South African blacks who'd been brought to the World's Fair (which bled into the Olympic Games) to help reenact battles of the Boer War for upper-class visitors. He was far more enthralled by the likes of Baltimorean Robert Garrett, an upper crust scion of the B&O Railroad family, who arrived at the first Games in Athens from Princeton, picked up a discus for the first time, won gold by ingeniously creating a crouch-and-spin technique, then never threw one in earnest again. Now, that, in Coubertin's estimation, was an amateur worthy of his Games.

However problematic it may have been to match the elitist aims of amateurism with real outcomes, it was nonetheless a concept that took a savage hold on America and thus on the Olympics. Because the United States was eclipsing England—the other bastion of amateurism—in world power at precisely the same time as the Olympics were taking wing, it meant that if the United States espoused amateurism as a necessary part of the Games, the rest of the world would need likewise to pretend that it was important. Because of an American need to provide a rationale for our burgeoning and already uncontrollable turn-of-the-century intercollegiate athletics system, we embraced amateurism and all of its character-building mythology in a way that came naturally to a nation whose founding documents are idealist menus for perfection but whose institutions reward practical deviance: that is, we wrapped our arms around both amateurism and its hypocritical manifestations. To use a common aphorism, we came to believe in having our cake and eating it too.

The American public's definition of amateurism came to lean not on dollars or class—though certainly the upper-crust administrators who guided our Olympic efforts were not in on this secret—but on vague interpretations of an athlete's intentions. Two possibilities were clear: you could play sport for money or some other commercially linked incentive—bad; or you could take part in sport because it was the path to admirable character, to life lessons that made one a well-rounded, responsible citizen of the world (at least the part of the world that mattered)—good. The two motives seem to share little and appear, in fact, to be at polar opposites: crass motives versus noble ambitions.

The opposition is illusionary—both money and good character are extrinsic motivations—two sides of the same coin. But because they appear to be so different and because one seems so appealing, most observers have not needed to search past the obvious to justify our culture's interest in sports. Thank heavens, because the real source of our interest—the third possible motive for engaging in sport—is alien to us, and, in a lifetime spent around sports, I've spoken with no other American who has claimed it: we play simply because it is a deeply rooted part of human existence and growth.

Classical composer Ned Rorem once wrote incredulously about other composers who, in their assessments of modern music, "denigrate the *liking* of music, the *bodily* liking of it." We seem incapable of admitting that too many connected to sport are apologetic about what should come naturally—the "bodily liking of sports"—and search instead for something that seems more defensible. This bodily liking that we feel deep in our bones but are ashamed to reveal was heralded unabashedly by England's Sir Roger Bannister. "The runner does not know how or why he runs," he has written, "he only knows that he must run, and in so doing he expresses himself as he can in no other way." Running and playing, then, is not a noble pursuit; it is merely a fulfillment of human instincts. It becomes noble only when the urge to run combines with the spirit needed to do it well. Surely, it was this that drove Bannister down the final straightaway as he broke the four-minute mile in 1954: "I felt that the moment of a lifetime had come," he says. "It was my chance to do one thing supremely well. I drove on, impelled by a combination of fear and pride." Having breasted the tape and collapsed, he lay "in the most passive state without being quite unconscious. Blood surged from my muscles and seemed to fell me." So close to death he was that the pain became exultation.

That is all I require of an Olympic performance—a marriage between the acceptable adult urge to play and the exaltation of human life through it. For me, no qualities of character, good citizenship, commercial viability, or entertainment value need be attached. I am often alone in this—indeed

I work among kinesiologists, many of whom are too embarrassed by play to take pride in the simple love of sport and physical education that once drew them to the discipline.

To my eye, this level of liking and its revelation through outstanding performance was once accessible to Everyman; if I allow myself a normal dose of skepticism, I might say it was accessible *only* to Everyman. That is, it seemed possible to believe that the best Olympic athletes were compelled more by the bodily liking of sport than the extrinsic regard for what their talents could bring them. Perhaps this is indeed an Olympic delusion. It's hard to know definitively because the nature of sport and the Games obscures our ability to identify spirit and motive.

Exposed for just seventeen days every four years, the Olympics are largely immune to the scrutiny and analyses that entice scholars to track other social phenomena, e.g., pop explosions like the one the Beatles ignited. The Games are, instead, an evolving spectacle whose glacial progressions and regressions are mostly hidden from public view; their eruption every four years becomes overshadowed by the host's display narrative, the obvious political issues of the moment, and commercial complications. But the core of the spectacle—the athleticism—lies pretty much unexplored. Yes, we know something of remarkable performances, but we do not track them or their causes across time. In fact, we tend to be drawn to them as touchstones because of other reasons: Jim Thorpe's wondrous decathlon performance because of our later repulsion to Avery Brundage's mean-spiritedness in taking away his medals; Jesse Owens because of his color; Mildred "Babe" Didrikson because of what her physique said about sexuality; the East Germans because of their blatant exposure of a millennia-old problem, performance enhancement. And on and on. The guiding assumption when assessing Olympic performance is simply that it will get better across time—the idea of progress that blinds us to much of life's intricacies and to deeper thoughts of them.

Athletes, not surprisingly, buy into this. Each generation assumes it should and will outstrip its predecessors. And the false consciousness of athletes about why they play—confusing mere victory with excellence, as demanded by the culture that raised them (a Nike billboard in 1996 above the highway leading to Atlanta proclaimed, "You Don't Win Silver; You Lose Gold") leaves them unequipped to think honestly about, much less articulately speak about, abstractions like motives and spirit.

This is all a long run-up to my claim that the spirit that valued the bodily liking of sport began to observably fade in athletes after the 1972 Games in Munich. "Everyman" bid us farewell. What drove him out? There are a number of possibilities for why athletes began to tend toward a professional spirit (which leaves one questioning whether there is a "liking" of sport at all). First, television exposure inflated and amplified all the extrinsic value attaching to participation, whether it was a U.S. victory against a dirty commie, the hope for financial recompense, or a future coaching job. During the Cold War, Soviet athletes were essentially professionals, and their dour expressions gave little evidence that they enjoyed anything associated with their play.

Second, as the character-building ideology took a sound beating from the American counterculture in the years leading up to Munich, victory as a bald outcome not needing any rationale became accepted. Winning provided its own self-evident meaning. To match those joyless Soviet pros, Americans poured a dose of Dream Team on the world. The first of these basketball teams went to Barcelona for only one purpose. The members stayed in a luxury hotel away from the Olympic Village and acted boorishly during competition, and several topped off the experience by cynically draping an American flag over their uniforms' Reebok emblems while accepting their gold medals. They were, after all, not American athletes, but Nike athletes.

Third, the ability of science and technology to enhance the possibilities for victory became more widely known and accepted. When the East German women's swim team arrived in Montreal in 1976 with cannonball shoulders and broad backs that tapered dramatically to tiny waists, nearly everyone knew something was up. The something was, of course, steroids, administered through a systematic doping system begun sometime around the Munich Games. Since then, suspicion about pharmaceutical supplementation has shadowed and tainted some of the greatest performances in history—by Ben Johnson, Florence Joyner-Griffith, Marian Jones, and Carl Lewis, among others. How much room could there possibly be for "bodily liking" in a syringe full of synthetic muscle?

Fourth, as an outcome of the "athletic revolution" that toppled character building during the Vietnam era, more athletes believed that their athletic lives should entail not just freedom to train and compete as they wished, but that they should be rewarded by money and other commercial enticements as evidence of this freedom. When financial reward skyrocketed via entertainment value, athletes began to take seriously their roles as personalities. I cannot imagine Jesse Owens pulling up after his 100 meter win in Berlin and shooting an imaginary bolt, à la Usain, in the Führer's direction.

Finally, the professional spirit has been advanced at the Olympics by the inclusion of events for which the Olympics do not represent their sport's pinnacle, such as tennis, baseball, soccer, basketball, and ice hockey. Soccer's World Cup, hockey's Stanley Cup, the Opens in both golf and tennis, the World Series—all are more alluring targets for their participants than the Olympics.

If the Olympics are, by virtue of these developments, no longer accommodating to Everyman, 1972 was a crucial moment in his disappearance. While my evidence for this may be substantially anecdotal and emotional, it is rooted in the same thinking that led Milan Kundera to observe that because French historians deal with something that will not return, the "bloody years of the Revolution have turned into mere words, theories, and discussions, have become lighter than feathers, frightening no one." Thus historical perspective and the illusion of objectivity can sweep out emotion; in so doing, it may sweep out its essence as well, and for me Everyman's role in the Olympics was both emotional and essential.

As Martin Luther wrote, "Sin boldly, but believe boldly." Herewith, three short tales of athletes that seem indicative of both Everyman's presence in the 1972 Games and his disappearance thereafter. Tale number one: Aesop's "The Cricket and the Ant," in which a cricket spent his time singing, while down below an ant struggled to harvest his grain; and when winter came, the cricket went hungry, while the ant had food. A cautionary tale for all times, but one that had specific currency in Munich, when both a cricket and an ant showed up as members of the same American wrestling team.

The ant was Dan Gable, an Iowan whose college record was 180–0 entering his final match for a third national championship. When he lost, his appetite for hard work, already legendary in the sport's circles, redoubled. He began a workout schedule of seven hours per day, seven days per week, that left the Soviets searching their provinces for someone who could beat him and left his body, in the words of novelist John Irving, "no more pretty than an axhead, ... no more elaborate than a hammer." His professed goal was to be unable to get to his feet following a workout. "A couple of times, I was so exhausted that I would start crawling toward the door. But then I'd be good enough to get my feet." Gable arrived in Germany more renowned than any wrestler in history.

The cricket was Rick Sanders, a 125-pound bantam from Oregon. He had lost his first collegiate match at Portland State, reeled off 103 consecutive victories, and then, like Gable, dropped his finale. According to critics, he lost because he'd spent the previous night out drinking. Sporting long hair, a beard, and a necklace of hand-carved wooden beads featuring a hash pipe, he arrived in Munich in Gable's shadow.

Gable went through the Games not only unbeaten but unscored upon. He won gold and, in the decades afterward, coached the University of Iowa to twenty-five consecutive Big Ten championships. Coaches and wrestlers adopted his manic dedication to year-round workouts as the surest route to success on the mat. It is the ideal still in place.

Sanders sailed a different tack. Proclaimed the wrestling hippie by the press, Sanders became a lightning rod for controversy. On his way to the Olympic tryouts, Pennsylvania state troopers picked him up hitchhiking along the turnpike. He was naked. Placed in the back of the squad car, Sanders crawled over the seat, got behind the wheel, and began to drive away. He told the police that someone had put LSD in his coffee. In Munich, Sanders spent his days and nights with large gatherings of new friends, smoking dope and drinking. When an assistant coach entered Sanders's room in the Olympic Village, he found empty beer bottles littering the floor and Sanders in bed with two women. "Don't cross me on this," the coach said. "I want those two women out of here now." When he returned the next day, he found that Sanders had followed orders to a tee. "If I hadn't seen it, I don't know if I'd believe it," the coach told me. "He was in bed with two more."

When he arrived at the Ringerhalle, Sanders was the center of attention for a different reason. Spectators scrambled for seats near his mat as soon as his name was announced. He wore his necklace of beads to mat's edge, removing them only upon the referee's demand and only long enough to wrestle. His performance was nothing short of breathtaking.

He had a need for constant movement, for fearless experimentation, for reckless creativity. In short, Sanders's act was one of a kind and all that wrestling was ordinarily not—scintillating, entertaining, fun, . . . playful.

Against an Italian named Maggiolo, Sanders—as I've noted elsewhere— worked "a spectacular cow-catcher cradle, inching almost imperceptibly from a position of disadvantage beneath Maggiolo to purchase an instant of possibility. Then, impossibly to the untrained eye, he levered Maggiolo suddenly and irreversibly to his back, folding his opponent's head and rear end together until they nearly touched, the Italian's body rendered as motionless as if it had been dipped in quick-drying cement."

Two matches later, Sanders lost to the eventual gold medalist from Japan. He finished with the silver medal and, sure enough, people began making unflattering comparisons to Gable. The ant's sacrifice rewarded, the cricket's dissipation punished. Sanders died in a car crash a month later while touring Europe, sealing his hippie legacy forever as a remnant of a slacker hippie culture. I see it differently: to me, it was the play instinct—sport as joy—that took a beating. Gable, no doubt, had a physical liking for wrestling. Indeed, Irving also once wrote that "when Dan Gable lays his hands on you, you are in touch with grace." But what all comments about Gable then and to this day circle back to are his ceaseless work and his outsized need to win. In the years since Munich, I've known no Olympic wrestlers who didn't feel that the path they needed to follow was Gable's—a professional approach that makes the outcome of a match the only worthy measuring stick. Asked about the value of what he accomplished, Gable talks of values: discipline, hard work, indomitability. Rick Sanders was singing the cricket's song—and in elevating play above work wouldn't it be a joy to hear it sung? Don't strain yourself listening— Olympic wrestlers have no use for it. They follow Gable's example, a regimen that a sportswriter for Portland's *Oregonian* once likened to "row[ing] stroke on a slave galley," a regimen surely bereft of bodily liking.

Tale number two: "Nature Boy" and "Enhancement Man." I made up these sobriquets—though Aesop surely would have understood the timeless parable they represent. American Dave Wottle, running the 800 meters in the first Games following the famous black power salute in Mexico City in 1968, became well known for his appearance on the Olympic victory podium, where he forgot during the playing of his national anthem to remove the lucky golf cap he had run in, creating a stir among millions of Americans, but even more among the nation's journalists who saw in the inadvertent act an opening line for a few days' worth of sensational gossip.

Known to this day for being the guy who ran to gold and then forgot to take off his hat, Wottle's greater meaning lies unnoticed. I call him "nature boy" because he reminds me of a character from my hometown: an old man who could be seen running year round in what appeared to be a diaper. It was not uncommon to be out for a family ride and come across him many miles from town on rural roads. All the locals called him "nature boy," in part because of the partial nudity but also in part because he seemed to be born to do nothing other than run—he was a natural. The running itself seemed to be enough—in fact must have been enough because I don't ever recall seeing him do anything else. The same seemed true for Wottle. He seemed to be running simply because that is what he did. The notion that the podium hat-wearing was part of an agenda is ridiculous in that it was apparent that his only agenda was running.

In comparison with what would come later—the calculated flamboyance of Carl Lewis, the personal animus of the Steve Ovett–Sebastian Coe rivalry, the hype that followed Michael Johnson, the expectation that burdened Hicham El-Guerrouj—Wottle genuinely seemed to have come from nowhere, to run as if he had no notion of where he was, and to settle, gold medal in pocket, into a relatively obscure corner of the Olympic world. In fairness, this is, of course, only the public dimension of his story. I don't want to convey the mistaken impression that Wottle had no ambition, no cares, or no respect for where he was.

In fact, though he surprised a good number of people when he won the 800 meter gold medal, he was not an unknown in track circles. He was an NCAA champion at 1,500 meters, and at the U.S. trials for Munich he had equaled the world record for 800 meters. But how did he train for his events and become a world record holder? By eating junk food, drinking lots of soda, and being chronically injured through a "modified marathon" training regimen of 70 to 120 miles per week. The distances were set, however, not by his choice, but through the schedule imposed by his coach at Bowling Green State University. Wottle believed in lots of off-season rest, but his schedule in the seventies was geared toward dual and tri-meets, meets that tested his allegiance to the college that had paid for his schooling. I spoke with Wottle by phone, and he told me that, unlike the trend that began after Munich in which athletes commit as individuals to specialty meets held around the country, in his day college meets had priority. At those meets, for the honor of dear old Bowling Green, he might run three or four different races in the course of a few hours, demands that left him hobbled on three different occasions in the year before the Olympics. The races were not optional—his duty was to meet all demands made by his coach.

In international races Wottle became noted for falling to the back of the pack and then surging during the final 100 meters, a tactic that earned him the nickname, "the Head Waiter." In the Olympic final, he stayed true to form, dropping to last place, then passing runners one by one down the final stretch, winning the gold by a step. His post-race demeanor seemed to be shaped by joy, but no hubris. He seemed naïve but not ignorant. Like Sanders, he seemed to have enjoyed what he had done. He seemed, in short, to be Everyman. He told me recently that he never looked at his Olympic performance, before or after, as something that would be life-changing. He ran, he says, to simply prove that American runners were—that he was—among the world's best at that time. Though he had a sense that the sport's throwers were using some sort of performance enhancers, he said that he never saw enhancers and knows that the runners, including sprinters, were not yet using them. This assertion led me to ask him about Lasse Viren, "Enhancement Man."

Viren paralleled Wottle in many ways. The Finnish police officer did not debut in international competition until 1971 and arrived in Munich as a dark horse for medals at 5,000 and 10,000 meters. Like Wottle, he had put in many weekly miles in training. And, like Wottle, he fell behind in his Olympic 10,000 meter final, though involuntarily, having fallen after an accidental entanglement with Wottle's roommate, eventual marathon champion Frank Shorter. Having lost nearly 100 meters, Viren picked himself up, made up some ground gradually, and then began an unprecedented 600 meter kick that carried him to victory. His second win at 5,000 meters made him a national hero in Finland, and he became an icon when he repeated his double at the 1976 Games in Montreal. Like Wottle, who went on to become the dean of admissions at prestigious Rhodes College in

Memphis, Viren, too, left sport, becoming an elected member of the Finnish parliament.

Despite the parallels, however, Viren became Gable to Wottle's Rick Sanders, a man who seemed to foreshadow the way in which the future would break with the past. After Viren's wins in Montreal, rumors began to circulate that he had increased his aerobic capacity through blood doping, that is, freezing some of his own blood, then returning it to his body later to boost the richness of oxygen. Indeed, Viren had been so remarkable in Montreal that eighteen hours after his 5,000 meter final, he ran and finished fifth in the marathon. His Montreal victories, followed by the rumors, immediately cast suspicion on his Munich races as well. A few important notes about his case: first, blood doping was not illegal then. Second, runners, including Wottle, upon hearing of the technique, were not convinced of its worth in actually improving performance. And third, to this day, Viren has never acknowledged that he participated in blood doping. In fact, he was once offered a million dollars by a magazine to reveal his secrets. When he said the truth was that he'd never doped, the magazine withdrew the offer.

Yet the rumors about Viren have never subsided, and his name remains linked to blood doping. In the Games that followed his medal-winning races, the idea of elite athletes using performance enhancers has become a commonplace assumption among the public and competitors alike. Further, Viren's grueling training schedule came not from allegiance to a college team but to the single-minded goal of peaking at the Olympics. This is certainly not an unworthy or villainous goal, but it is one that calls into question his physical liking of what he was doing and hints at ambitions that went beyond the Everyman test for human excellence: what could a body do well for the sheer sake of doing it well?

I have no nickname for my final representative athlete in tale number three. She was simply the highest-flying athlete on the planet until Michael Jordan came along. I have no one to compare her to, either, because the Soviet gymnast Olga Korbut was both the past and the future; she was Everywoman and she was Exceptional Woman.

When Korbut arrived in Munich, the favorites in female gymnastics were her teammate, the stoic veteran Ludmila Tourischeva (who would later become Valery Borzov's wife), and East Germany's Karin Janz. Korbut was the lowest-ranked member of her team and was there only because of an injury to another Soviet. But Korbut, at 4'11" and eighty-four pounds, a seventeen-year-old with pigtails and a toothy smile, was the athlete whose breathtaking and original routines would make her the darling of television and lead her to three gold medals and one silver. To this day, experts argue about the extent to which Korbut's infectious joy and tele-genicity caused judges to overmark her routines; many claim Tourischeva was technically better and more deserving. Still, whether Korbut was bet-ter technically has no bearing on the indisputability of her meaning. She quite literally changed the character of gymnastics.

Her influence as Everywoman is undeniable. Across the world, waves of young girls immediately took up gymnastics. If Olga could do it, why not me? What she did looked like fun. And how could anyone question her physical liking of her body's phenomenal twists and turns in space? As she herself proclaimed in an interview, "Medals and titles don't do anything for me. I don't need them."

Her next sentence, however, betrayed the other part of Olga, the one that has left women's gymnastics as one of the most hyped and com-mercialized dramas in the Olympics. What did she need if not medals? "I need the love of the public," she said, "and I fight for it." She needed, that is, the spotlight, the red light of the television camera, the adoration.

Four years later in Montreal, Korbut's impact became immediately evident. Nadia Comaneci became the first "perfect" gymnast, her routines as fraught with difficulty and flourish as Korbut's. She, too, was a smiling pixie, but her smile looked forced, as rehearsed as any of the flawless toe-pointing that forced judges to reward her with the first set of 10's in Olympic history. The line of clones since has been a succession of over-coached, overworked, overrehearsed, and oversexualized yet undersensu-alized girls. Their "joy" is joyless, the bouts of anorexia always just around the corner, the taped body parts, fixed smiles, and limps ceaseless. How can one know if a fifteen-year-old girl, immersed in a sport year-round for hours a day since the age of four or five, has a physical liking for her sport? How would they themselves know it? The degree to which I wanted to believe in Korbut's pleasure is the degree to which I am certain that I don't see it in the Olympic gymnasts who have followed. I ask myself at each viewing, do they want to be out there? For this, the motives and motivation, the "wanting to be there" are the keys to Everyman and his disappearance from the Olympics.

If we wish to be specific about the dates for the demise of amateurism, in its narrowly defined terms, we need only look to the international sports governing bodies and trace the dates at which they deemed professionals to be acceptable. By 1988 it is certainly evident that professionals no longer carried any sort of public stigma at the Games. But if we wish to pinpoint the time at which a spirit of bodily liking gave way to our suspicion about the influence of extrinsic incentives, perhaps these sorts of examples are the best that I can do. With enough time and energy I could expand the search to examine sets of athletes beyond those I've cited in '72 as before and after snapshots. Take, for example, Bob Mathias compared with Bruce Jenner in the decathlon—a relatively modest high school phenom in 1948 versus a calculated, attention-seeking driven flag-waver in 1976 (Wottle cites the penchant of Carl Lewis and other track medalists to grab their flags for a victory lap as little more than a tactic for insuring more television face time). You could look at the wave of athletes television has promoted over the past twenty years as exemplars of the Everyman spirit—Eddie the Eagle, a British ski jumper whose efforts were sixty meters short of the leaders; an African swimmer who trained in a motel pool and struggled to complete his 100 meter heat; an Egyptian luger who dragged his feet at the top of the run in hopes of slowing himself down because his only training had been forty days spent in a cave at the will of his father; the Nike-sponsored Kenyan cross-country skier who finished dead last—and see that these athletes were, in fact, not Everyman but caricatures of Everyman, ludicrous to the point that the Jamaican bobsled team became more Hollywood comedy than real inspiration.

Ultimately, my own Olympic dream was more a fancy than a real delusion. I was already twenty-two when I began thinking of Olympic participation, and I already had, deep down, too many doubts about myself to think I could sustain the kind of training that would transform a 135-pound wisp into something even as substantial as Dave Wottle. As Paul Weiss wrote in *Sport: A Philosophic Inquiry*, "Sometimes men speak of desiring something, though they do nothing to realize what they say they desire. Above all things, they say, they desire to become great athletes, but they do not train, do not practice, or do not watch their diet. The harsh truth is that they do not in fact desire to be great athletes. They only *wish* to be so." I'd already seen some Olympic wishfuls fail close-up. One graduate teaching assistant from my days at the University of Maryland fell short of the Olympic luge team. Another, a muscular one-time decathlete, made the Olympic bobsled team as a pusher. However, on his team's first run down the course, they flipped over at the top and took the entire ride on the tops of their helmets. My friend said the heat was so intense that it felt as if his head were melting. Unable to cross the line from wish to real desire, he turned in his helmet that day.

My dream was more substantially undercut by the attendance at the 1984 International Olympic Academy of Israeli delegate Esther Roth (now Esther Roth-Shachamorov), a sprinter, hurdler, and pentathlete. During her stay, she was virtually unapproachable, not because of any security issues, but because she was withdrawn, sullen, and bitter. Esther had been a member of the small Israeli Olympic squad in 1972. Most of her team-mates had been murdered in Munich, and she could not, understandably, bring herself to share in the bonhomie of this international gathering so intent on spreading the Olympic message of peace through competition. She was a stark reminder that some dreams turn to nightmare. In this case, the intrusion of forces stronger than those of "bodily liking" had robbed her of the inspiration necessary to go on—she left Munich before the semifinal heat of the hurdles.

And inspiration is what was ultimately lost with the disappearance of Everyman. Everyman inspires us not just to say "I can do that," but more important, to say, "I want to do that." Around 1972 Richard Bach wrote, "The world needs models, people living interesting lives, learning things, changing the music of our time. What do people do with their lives who are not struck down with poverty, crime, war? We need to know people who have made choices that we can make, too, to turn us into human beings." If the Olympics are ever to achieve their full potential, we need to sense again that its athletes are models of nothing less than human excellence, that they are human beings who compel us to nothing short of our true natures; something, that is, that even a delusionary athlete can dream about for a lifetime.

We do not stop playing because we grow old, we grow old because we stop playing.

Variously attributed to Benjamin Franklin,
Karl Groos, Oliver Wendell Holmes, Herbert Spencer,
and George Bernard Shaw

WHY CAL RIPKEN TOUCHED US

In the provincial, defensive enclave that calls itself Baltimore, watching for signs that Cal Ripken Jr.'s career might be nearing an end had become, by September 1995, something like waiting for the Vatican smoke signals, a not altogether ludicrous parallel. During that month, Baltimore hosted two mega-events that showcased first the Pope and then Ripken as the saving seraphs of Catholicism and Baseball, respectively. It is instructive that tickets for—and blessings from—the Holy One riding in his Pope-mobile were free; on the other hand, you needed lots of luck or lots of bucks to glimpse Ripken and have him anoint you during his passing–Lou Gehrig extravaganza.

I was neither lucky nor loaded, so I found myself a few miles away from Camden Yards that night, watching on television. As Ripken began the midgame stadium trot that capped the celebration sanctifying his 2,131st consecutive baseball game, my first reaction was knee-jerk bitter: the monied folks who had paid as much as five thousand dollars for their seats in special, temporary on-field bleachers were once again going to reap rewards unavailable to the masses. But as the Oriole shortstop moved beyond the reach of the conspicuously rich and made his way

Vir Ferreus Ludens—"Cal the Player"—breaks an unbreakable record for play, 1995.
Courtesy of Baltimore Orioles

toward the outfield bleachers, some of whose occupants were willing to fall out of their lower-rent seats to touch Cal or have Cal touch something of theirs—a hat or glove or baby—my reaction turned to wonder. Wonder in its literal "awestruck" meaning and wonder in its "inquisitive" terms. I wondered at and about these people who had to touch this man and wondered why my own eyes were misted over by the time he reached the left-field stands. How and why had the public animosity toward six-million-dollar men evaporated so quickly, leaving behind this star-flecked residue?

It may be that an answer is beside the point. Maybe the simple act of a large community gathering to celebrate is itself reason enough to celebrate. But the fact is that everyone involved with the event sought to elaborate on its appeal and meaning. As Ripken closed his days in the sun in 2001, having voluntarily ended the streak during the 1998 season at 2,632 games, and then inched his way to 400 homers and 3,000 hits, his legacy became even stiffer than his ailing back, a hagiography encased in the cement that passes for some sports commentators' brains. Much of it was well-intended—yet wrong.

Judgments of Ripken came in several hues: first, in the bright colors of the clichéd portrayal of the athlete as immortal, evinced by such as ESPN's Chris Berman, who proclaimed Ripken on the record-breaking night to be "superhuman." This word has emotional spark, but it fails to hold our attention beyond the moment of the thunderbolt home run—or beyond the first hint of mortality. The impossible skills of youth always cede to age, as they did with Wayne Gretzky on the eve of his retirement, or they cede to our culture of unrelenting scrutiny, as they did during Michael Jordan's attempt at playing professional baseball. Sure enough, after a brief grace period, muttered carping began anew in Baltimore about Ripken's mortality, and indeed about his ability and even his right to be in the Oriole lineup every day.

In only slightly quieter tones came the yearning of middle-class parents to find meaning in—and excuse for fawning over—an athlete who is decent and says things appropriate for their children to hear—a role model in an age of perceived incivility and dubious character. Not bad, particularly inasmuch as Ripken, the milk spokesman, broke Gehrig's record at the very same time that O. J. Simpson was being tried for murder. Certainly it is nice when our public figures turn out to be good people; but we don't really know much about Cal's private life, and even his reputation at the ballpark was subject to the sniping and innuendo that strangle all of our celebrities. Again, it is a hope, but one threatened endlessly by the sharp hatchets of cynicism, envy, and revelation.

Finally, there was the explanation of greatest currency, one that subsumed the others, one that sounded so naturally right that it was hard to recognize it as the least defensible: that what appealed most to us about the consecutive games streak and Cal Ripken's career were their monumental tributes to the work ethic.

It was understandable to hear Ripken lauded for working hard. In an age in which many adults—and now a fair number of teens—complain about the bone-wearying pace of daily life and their loss of time, where the average work week climbs rather than shrinks as we were once promised it would, it was moderately satisfying to look at Ripken and think that he too had to work hard. Indeed, much of the public ill will directed at million-dollar ballplayers stems from a distaste for those who seem to make too much for doing too little. The distaste turns to pure venom when we think that they are not even doing that little bit earnestly—that they're pondering their financial portfolios instead of running out ground balls, worrying about protecting long-term contracts by begging out of games when injuries seem slight or imagined, and turning up their noses at part-time roles, autograph-seeking kids, or potential trades. So, perhaps we do want to see more effort, but were we really cheering so unabashedly for Cal as "Workbucket Joe"?

I don't think so. I propose that we loved Ripken and applauded his streak for a reason so deeply buried that when given a voice it sounds radical, nearly heretical: we honored this man not because he was devoted to work, but because he delighted in play. This is not an easy concept to embrace. Play fits awkwardly into a modern life. Many regard surviving the hardships of daily routines as an admirable and noteworthy feat in itself. And though surviving isn't necessarily the same as living the high life, the attitude that regards them as the same thing has permeated much of popular culture, including sports. Too many of the participants who trudge, pedal, and stroke through the apposite sport of the post-Vietnam era, the triathlon, aren't looking to win, or even excel—they're seeking to survive a prolonged bout of misery and pain. Well, the bumper stickers tell us that "life's a bitch and then you die," right?

Not for Cal Ripken. Ripken's streak and his play weren't about survival. They were about—as he tried to tell us a number of times—the joy of play, not about the rigors of work, even if a measure of that certainly was required to amplify the degree of joy. Why, then, didn't we take him at his word? For several reasons.

Clearly Ripken's connection to Baltimore is one reason. Residents like to think of the city as blue collar and down to earth, a place far removed from the glitz and hype of New York or Los Angeles. This is a city that incorporated a warehouse into its stadium design and then, for good measure, pretended that this made it a haven for working stiffs. When Camden Yards opened in 1992, pitcher Mike Flanagan told *Sports Illustrated* (presumably with a straight face), "It's a working class park in a working class town." At some point, apparently, the working class acquired access to and a taste for brie and wine coolers. At any rate, Ripken's saintliness followed nicely in the Baltimore tradition set by the city's other twin tower, John Unitas. Superficially at least, the pair were made of the same stuff. Unitas—quiet, strong, independent, a winner, a western-Pennsylvania boy who made himself a home in Charm City; Ripken—tough, resilient, a winner, a native of nearby Aberdeen, Maryland, who wandered the minor leagues with his dad before making himself a home in Baltimore. The public perception of both was and remains blue-collar.

The nature of Ripken's career amplifies this illusion. Though his approach mirrored that of both Gretzky and Jordan, athletes who were also forgiven their large salaries for skills immeasurably beyond those of even the most deluded of ex-high-school jocks, Ripken's career traveled a different arc. Despite his MVP seasons and wondrous skills, Ripken's history was largely devoid of the spectacular flashpoints that mark our remembrance of the other two—Jordan forever hanging as the midair silhouette that advertised his shoes, Gretzky creating a sliver of space for an impossible pass. Ripken's numbers—the ones that put him in the Hall of Fame—came through longevity and consistency, through a ceaseless march of games that seemed to echo the assembly line production of the city's, and the nation's, working class.

A deeper and socially broader reason underlying the embrace of the Ripken work ethic rests in the no-nonsense mentality that has prevailed for the last four decades—a long stretch in which the nation has had time to reflect upon the costs of play. Conventional wisdom among repentant baby boomers is that the hippies and freaks of the sixties explored that whole "fun and playing around" thing and left us with the legacies of defeat in Vietnam, drugs as brain toys, abdication of personal responsibility, and trifling activities like frisbee. The reduction of the decade to a time of misdirected energy was highlighted when Crosby, Stills, and Nash offered regrets for the entire Woodstock nation, confessing in a 1982 hit to time "Wasted on the Way."

With regard to sport, the benefits of hard work have been perpetuated and massaged for public consumption by the mainstream media, much of which is constituted of the tradition-bound early baby boomers as well as nose-to-the-grindstoners spawned in the post-sixties backlash against fun. Howard Cosell was just the loudest and oldest member of a cohort willing to subvert the playful side of athletics to an exploration of what he thought were the deeper (and usually darker) sides. A critic once observed that Cosell treated the world of fun and games like the Nuremberg trials. His example provided an avenue of legitimacy for nearly all who followed.

Today many sports journalists, though they decry sport's loss of innocence and long for the days when players supposedly played for the love of the game and the thrill of the grass, have immersed themselves in the economic, legal, and sociological aspects of elite sport. Knowledge of salaries, for example, accompanied by slow-motion instant replay that turns the spectacular into the mundane (and vice versa) by a sixth viewing, has led many members of the media—and in turn the public—to assess athletes as mere commodities, their worth seemingly as knowable as the price of a can of corn on the grocer's shelf.

The commodification of performance, in turn, has promoted the belief that athletes are slaves to economic self-interest. It is understandable that many in the media would take this tack. As people of words, it is their job to turn the thoughts and banter of athletes, some of whose intellect can seemingly be plumbed in fifteen seconds, into entertaining and enlightening reading. How ably would professional athletes be able to articulate their deep emotional engagement with sport? Knowing the answer, why bother to ask? The business of sport is more solid ground to stand on—or write of or talk about. Still, when journalists insist that modern sport is about labor—work—they tamper with a crucial reality: heroes seldom materialize out of the tedium of work. Work is too often how we answer the cries and needs of others, and only infrequently do those needs call for real heroism, as they did on 9/11. In the aftermath of 9/11, journalists, including notable sports writers, quickly abandoned or ridiculed the notion of athletes as heroes, seeming to take real pleasure in their demotion to mere players and acting as if heroism were a finite treasure to be grudgingly meted out.

In short, focusing on sport as business obscures an important point that nearly all North Americans—save its elite athletes—have either forgotten, don't believe, or wish to obscure: that play is an acceptable adult urge. Thus, underneath our cynicism about pro athletes lurks the envy and dislike of outsiders—or those picked last for the school yard recess games. The expression of it may be relatively new, but the sentiment is not. For many, the playful sixties were just a brief aberration; fear, resentment, and trivialization of fun constitute a long-running neurosis in American history.

The Puritans may not have been quite as joyless as the history books tell us, but face it, any group of people who jumped back in abhorrence from Morris dancing had a touch of grim in them. Why we have selected them as our cultural touchstones, rather than the gambling, carousing, sporting folks of the other colonies, however, is what's instructive. As a society we appear frightened of the play impulse, afraid that time we spend at play robs us of time that could be spent in the serious pursuit of—what exactly? This, in turn, has, I believe, affected the work of historians, and specifically sport historians. It is one thing for journalists, other academics, and the public at large to be deluded about the value of the so-called "real world" and to be envious and cynical about the world of play; it is another thing for us to follow suit.

Perhaps, then, the largest reason that the idea of play was left out of the public discourse on Ripken was this: scarcely—if at all—in the discussion did we hear the voice of sport historians. Not only was our voice noticeably missing, it had to be missing owing, in part, to our own devices. For we, in sharing the nation's defensiveness about play—indeed, in fear of being seen by the public as playful ourselves, have, in the course of our studies, immersed our world of games in the same vat of "real world" significance that every Al, Bob, and Bryant swims in. We too often, I think, choose power relations and their foundations in gender, class, and race differentials as our starting point for examining sport. We assume, I suppose, that a play instinct is universal, some sort of pure, unchanging essence that makes the game played in Mayan ball courts in 1100 just a skip pass across the centuries to the NBA. The particulars of this essence we leave to the philosophers. That is, we look at the entanglements of this play impulse in our economy, politics, social life, and perceptions of national character and vigor, but we do not do the opposite. We do not often see the ways in which the impulse is itself transformed by time and events or the ways in which the impulse transforms time and events—this we leave to the anthropologists, who can scarcely be bothered. Anthropologists might think they do this—in the famous examination of Balinese cockfighting, for example—but are they looking at the physical sensation or its cultural ramifications? Is our thrill at watching a basketball make a net ripple rooted in the same physical impulses that caused the Mayans to struggle with and then behead one another? Football and boxing are often cited in our literature as reflections of both a cultural point in time and an aggressive nature encouraged and reinforced by a capitalist economy. But in what ways do our economy and times reflect and become shaped by our urges to fight and brutalize others?

Why we lean away from exploring these questions is understandable. Collectively, sport historians still do not have an accepted and secure place in academia. The resulting need to fit in causes them, I believe, to always fit their explanations to the view of the academy rather than to the view of the athlete. Take this example from page one of my biography of Moses Fleetwood Walker: "Though he once was a good student, Walker has begun skipping classes on a regular basis, forgoing the classroom for the baseball diamond." One hundred fifty pages of fine print stocked with racial theory, courtroom drama, and childhood meanderings later, I have still not written a single word more on Walker's urge to play—the very fact of feeling that had not only led to his involvement with all those other things but was the sole thing responsible for leading historians to him in the first place. I have, in short, abandoned the idea of Walker as athlete in favor of the idea that Walker sometimes played the role of an athlete that had some bearing on his views on race which in turn made for an interesting—and more important, a significant—life. In fact, if I revisit that first page I find preceding my dismissal of Walker the athlete my favorite sentence and perhaps the most revealing: "Walker has been at Oberlin for nearly three years, his lean, muscled body refining the possibilities for hitting a baseball long distances, his flair for the dramatic fueling his determination to do the impossible." Revealing, but at the time I wrote it, following that thread further seemed dangerous. I moved quickly to more secure ground. Indeed, how often do we hear that most athletes are unworthy of biography because their lives are uninteresting away from the field—that they are "only athletes"?

Maybe there is something to be said for this (as much as I love the Phillies, I'm not dying to read *The Chooch Ruiz Story* any time soon), but maybe there is more to be said about the difficulty of capturing the feeling of being an athlete, much less describing its nuances across time. A columnist in the *New York Times Book Review* asked why it is so hard to stay in a committed relationship. Consider, she wrote, all the intellectual ramifications of personal relationships: "Bookshelves filled with advice for the lovelorn; public policy analysts fretting about declining marriage rates; evolutionary psychologists positing genetic motives for philandering; biologists, historians, economists, and anthropologists all contributing their two cents—and none of them who can help us understand love as we experience it personally." Substitute the word "sport" for "love" and you have, perhaps, our dilemma: a population in quest of something elusive and desirable—and we, the experts, are unable to help them understand, much less celebrate, the feeling as they experience it. But that doesn't mean we shouldn't try. Because—the difficulty of the task notwithstanding—we are the people best positioned to try. We are uniquely equipped for the task, first, because most of us came to sport history because our loves for sport and history are intertwined and inseparable. And second, and almost assuredly not a coincidence, because history is itself play.

We play at our work, not necessarily with the facts, but with the meaning and significance of those facts. Often at conferences people have approached me to tell me they enjoyed my presentation, only to ask a moment later, "What were you getting at?"—to which I have often had to answer, "I'm not sure." What my presentation topics have always been are echoes of my own play life—a process dedicated to process. I am playing, at times unable to muster enthusiasm for the outcome because there is a more pressing need: to keep the game alive, to thrill to new discoveries (having MFW clippings passed along—waiting for someone to call to tell me they've found his diary and I can begin all over again), and, in truth, to hide from my mortal self. Almost every day that I work on a project I hear in my head historian Dick Crepeau's lecture in which he riled up an academic audience before they even got beyond his title, "History: In the End You Can Never Prove a Thing." Some were offended; I was exhilarated at the revelation. Despite my embrace of his warning, when I sit down to write I still find myself pulled toward the need to prove something—a human sickness, doubly lethal when allowed to infect our reckoning with games.

Henry Adams warned famously that order is the dream of man; chaos the reality of nature; but why, I wonder, have we as historians, with the license to consider the whole scope of human existence, led such a relentless search for order? Why is a structured, rational gravitas rather than the freedom of play our collective dream? History, in giving prominence to the institutions of economy, politics, military, education, and religion promotes a version of humans as the sum total of an imposed order rather than as the chaotic playing out of unfathomable, unreasoned, often indescribable behaviors of a primal, often primitive, sometimes even playful, nature. It has to do, of course, with our fear of meaninglessness. As Philip Slater observed some decades ago in *The Pursuit of Loneliness*, no one wants to believe they have lived a foolish life.

Feeling the weight of that truism, I have lashed out at those who ask me at cocktail parties how one gets a PhD in "gym": "Bounce the ball higher?" Once ashamed, I would stutter in red-faced and angry defense. Now I answer: "Why, yes, of course I do." But in truth, my interest in bouncing the ball higher has diminished, and in the desire's lessening, I see as well a final reason for our backhanded treatment of play: we are the products of G. Stanley Hall's recapitulation theory that we have all cited so often. Actually, we are more extension than product since recapitulation theory stopped at the point where the complexity of organized sport mirrored the moment of our entry into young adulthood. He stopped short of saying how play would manifest in individual humans living in an aging, civilized world in which sport had lost its simplicity and become entwined with all manner of serious undertakings and implicated in all manner of social regression. Have we as adults and historians echoed this in our own lives by moving beyond or forgetting the play impulse that initially drew us to sport? If so, it is a cruel thing to have happen at the very same time that our perspective—and thus our breadth as historians—grows sharper. As my own body and soul lose touch with the impulse to play, so does my sense of how to approach it, and with that so too goes my ability to stay in touch with students on the topic of sport. We in sport history are caught in a paradox: though the American public seems to be dying to find a rationale to justify our love of sports and our adoration of athletes, it fails to have much interest in interpretive sport history.

How many of us, in our years of self-important and self-consciously serious scholarly endeavor, came to disdain the organization of elite sport with its hypocrisy, racism, drugs, big money, and overexposure? And how many of us, in trying to pass on these simple but crucial discoveries to our students, found them, too often, disinterested or disbelieving. When we discuss the Nazi Olympics, they listen attentively and with mild interest about the uses to which Hitler bent the Games, but they "ooh" and "aah" when they see on film Jesse Owens pulling away from the pack as if being reeled to the finish line by a winch anchored in the heavens. They find the tale of Jack Johnson's flight from the law somewhat absorbing, but they nearly come out of their seats when they see Papa Jack, stunned by a knockdown, leap to his feet and hit Stanley Ketchel so hard that both men spill to the canvas.

This attention to the moments in sport that border on the sublime and indescribable is why, I suspect, halls of fame pack them in, yet there is little public attention to academic sport history. It is also, perhaps, why no sport historian wrote *Seabiscuit*, and why only a few of us, as does Randy Roberts with his books on Jack Johnson and Joe Louis, have even examined what athletes look like at play or sport, how they move, and how those things link themselves to and alienate themselves from culture.

We as historians ought to be looking at the particulars. I did not look closely enough at Ripken during all the years he played in front of me—I was too busy taking note of his salary, his statistics, and the conventions of iconography to take in all that I should have—and much of what I would have when I was an aspiring ballplayer at the age of twelve, nurturing a love of sport so deep I never would have dared to reduce it to words. Nonetheless, when I look at Ripken now through the play lens and think about his meaning as an athlete, this is what I see: that what we have squeezed out of our daily routines are the clockless rhythms in which hunger, seedlings, and sunshine dictated when we had to work, and, thus, when we might play. Even children are allowed to move their bodies with kinesthetic abandon for precious few years before adults bunch them into groups and tame them with uniforms, drills, and expectations. If we allow people to play beyond their Little League years, we demand that they either get paid, get famous, get regenerated for more work, get fortified against eventual stroke or incontinence, or learn character lessons that will supposedly yield good things in the more important "real" world (these are all the things, incidentally, that provide the fodder for our study of sport). There is, in short, little time to accommodate play on its own terms anymore, and those who have been able by virtue of talent and guts to make the world of play their world of "work" rather than a stolen moment of leisure simultaneously attract and repulse us.

One of the surefire ways that the public and press blister high-salaried professionals is with the dismissive observation that they are playing children's games. Well, yes and no. Baseball, in particular, is a complex and demanding game, played best by adults with some years of experience behind them. Kids are terrible at baseball. George Will made this clear in his book on the game's intricacies. But an essential truth of sport slipped by Will: that though the undertaking is deadly serious, childlike joy marks the players' best moments (have you ever seen twenty-five stockbrokers pile ecstatically on one another in the middle of the trading floor?), Will regrettably but predictably called his bestseller *Men at Work*. And guess who he selected for his chapter on the prototypical workmanlike short-stop? Right.

For most of the minutes he was afield, Ripken's countenance seemed to be an affirmation of our accepted bias against playing beyond one's ado-lescence—his attention to details was indeed workmanlike, his demeanor in public coolly professional (unlike that of, say, Magic Johnson, who may have been the most explicitly playful athlete of the last few decades but whose diagnosis with HIV caused many to again take an accounting of what a life of play costs). Indeed, the appeal of Ripken, Gretzky, and Jordan to adults rested at least in part on their ability to present themselves as composed and dignified men, an image that clashed with the childish pranks of Shaquille O'Neal, which, as a *New Yorker* article pointed out, go over big with the segment of the market—teenage boys—that commands so much of pop culture's attention. Adults reject athletes who appear to be boys and girls because, after all, we're incapable of a biological reversal. Recognizing a play instinct in an adult, however, conjures, subconsciously at least, the possibility of a partial and meaningful reclamation of our youth.

The grin that wouldn't leave Ripken during the streak ceremony was more than happiness at getting relief, a new rock for his front lawn, and a pickup truck. Cal Ripken, by all accounts, had an insatiable appetite for play. He raced other Orioles onto the field. He out-trampolined his children and tried to snuff his wife in one-on-one basketball games. On his record-setting night the idea of a man playing games endlessly into adulthood was rewarded. Ripken's speech lacked the dour moralizing of Oriole owner Peter Angelos, a labor attorney who harped again on the work ethic theme. The word "work" was absent from Ripken's address. He told the crowd, "You are challenged by the game of baseball to do your very best day in and day out. And that's all I ever tried to do." He told President Clinton, "All I did was show up everyday and do something I enjoy."

Circumstances and a long history may have been conspiring for centuries against play, but it doesn't mean we don't miss it deep in our bones. We nearly all work in service of our shortcomings, laboring to shore up the mistrust we have of one another. We have lawyers because we need advocates, an army so others won't attack us, business because we must make sure that our material stockpile will suffice against an uncertain future. When we accept sport as just one more institution like all the others—laden with the paranoia of the real world—we become jaded, railing at players with briefcases and aloof attitudes. Yet when we find someone who, beneath this facade of sport as real life, actually likes to *play*, what do we do? We scramble in our envy and jealousy to accord him the mundane gifts and speeches we use to honor our fellow workers.

Cal might have worked, but he reported to the ballpark to play. He recognized baseball as an artificial challenge, one that needs to be met on its own fantasy terms. The rules in his "otherworldly" place demand that if you want to put someone "out" you touch second base while you have the ball, even if you're in a hurry to turn a double play. If you watched closely across the seasons, you noticed that Cal usually did it, seldom exploiting an "in the neighborhood" retreat from oncoming runners, though surely he had earned from umpires the right to cheat a bit if so inclined.

The fact that he didn't, that he seemed to compete night and day without personal animosity toward the opposition, but rather with a rare understanding of just what it was he was battling, made 2,131 special for another reason. It marked one of the few moments in America's long love affair with triumph in which the exhilaration could be shared as one, without the foil's burden of loss that is unavoidable in most sports moments. The thrill of Mariner playoff victories later that fall, for example, came at Seattle's (and much of the country's) delight in the agony of New York's loss. The Mets' '86 win that sent New Yorkers into hysteria put goat horns on Bill Buckner forever. Did anyone really want to see McGwire and Sosa deadlocked at the end of the '98 season? Somebody had to lose that race. Ripken's run down the home stretch was unlike these. You would be hard pressed to find even a New Yorker who, perhaps disgruntled at the eclipse of a Yankee, could build a case that the gracious Gehrig would have been upset when his record fell. In fact, when Ripken's achievement was announced in Yankee Stadium at the end of the sixth inning, the crowd there rose to applaud. It was a night not of victory *over*, but victory *with*. At Camden Yards, the California Angels blended seamlessly into the celebration, transformed from opponents into baseball confreres.

Somewhere in our souls we know that what Ripken did—play—was and is an extraordinary thing. And so, on September 6, 1995, we turned back the hands of time. Not to a time when sport seemed to yield simpler truths and better people like Gehrig, but to a time perhaps beyond the consciousness of any of us. In *Father Stories*, former all-Ivy basketball player John Edgar Wideman wrote

> One day . . . the people gathered on a high ridge, . . . [and] began speaking one by one, telling the story of a life, everything seen, heard, and felt by each soul. As the voices dreamed, a vast, bluish mist enveloped the land and seas below them. Nothing was visible. It was as if the solid earth had evaporated. Now there was nothing but the voices and the stories and the cloud of mist and the people were afraid to stop the storytelling and afraid not to stop because no one knew where the earth had gone.
>
> Finally, when only a few storytellers remained, someone shouted: Stop. Enough, enough of this talk . . . We must find the earth again.
>
> Suddenly the mist cleared. Below the people the earth had changed. It had grown into the shape of the stories they'd told, a shape wondrous and new, . . . but a world also unfinished because all the stories had not been told.
>
> Some say death and evil entered the world because some of the people had no chance to speak.

In the case of Cal Ripken, all the stories were not told, but it is not because we had no chance to speak. It is because we are still staring at the blanket of mist. Evolutionary psychologists blame our harried, anxious, depressed times on the gap between the primal environment we evolved in and the high-tech society in which we're now forced to survive. If true, the gap has compelled us to leave behind our more primal, playful nature, or has too often left us unable to fit it into our stories. Cal Ripken Jr. was a throwback not to bygone decades but to bygone eons. Cal returned us not to a sense of who we were, but to who we still fundamentally are dying to be. To touch him was to connect with a part of ourselves that knows there is meaning in something as arbitrary as the bounces of a little white ball and in a thirty-eight-year-old man still bouncing on a trampoline. And we in sport history ought to have known this all along: that Ripken's streak—and career—were celebrations of life, of stories untold, and testaments to *vir ferreus ludens*: Cal the Player.

Now you will not swell the rout
Of lads that wore their honours out,
Runners whom renown outran
And the name died before the man.

A. E. Housman

TO AN ATHLETE DYING . . .

A few days ago a friend and colleague went out for a jog and dropped dead of a heart attack. Viewings are not my cup of tea, but I went anyway, both repelled by and drawn toward the waxen figure resting in the open casket, a figure that, of course, bore little resemblance to the fit, trim, active friend, a former member of the University of Maryland track team and longtime physical education teacher in the public schools. His shocking end reminded me again that former Catholic priest Michael Novak had it right when he claimed that "the underlying metaphysic of sports entails overcoming the fear of death."

I first read those words when I was in my thirties and instantly said, "Of course." It was so obvious: we are never more alive than when we are deeply engaged in play. We never come closer to metaphoric extinction than when we fail in a sporting contest—it's not called "sudden death" for nothing. Still, they were just words—an expression of academic observation—until they were reified for me by the stillness in the coffin. A man whose liveliness—whose very living—depended on the vibrancy of play, had succumbed to permanent stasis. I could not help but think he'd stayed in constant movement for so many years to stave off the underlying certainty that death was always right around the corner, kept at bay

Monk Howard and Buzz Shank as juniors on Pennsylvania's best team, 1967.
Photo collection of author

only by his immersion in sports, and then ironically summoned by his overexertions in them.

By Novack's reckoning, my own life of play must bespeak a terrible fear of death, as must my stony dismissal of and scant grief over the deaths of many of those close to me—I still have not shed a tear over my own mother's passing. Further evidence of the fear may be found in my strange relationship to cemeteries, those pastoral landscapes of eternal nonbeing. On the one hand, I am deathly afraid of them; on the other, I am fascinated by what they contain, for they are not "resting places," they are death's silos. In quiet cemeteries I can summon great emotion for those I never met but whose style of living influenced my own. To stand over the grave of a deceased athletic "hero" is to come face to face with the contrast between remembrance of what he was and the reality of what he now is—both to the hyper-electric "aliveness" that once compelled greatness, and, more often than not, the degree to which the inevitable march of time decays the memory of that greatness even more surely than decrepit appearances at old-timers games.

As the remains reduce first to bone and then debris, athletes, finally no different from the rest of us, slip into anonymous mortality. Indeed, graveyards hold tens of thousands of former professional athletes, in- distinguishable from the commoners surrounding them. To find a stone designating a former great can be a demanding task. To find Bill Tilden, for example, perhaps the greatest tennis player who ever lived, you need the help of a Philadelphia cemetery caretaker and some patience to find his marker, nearly flush with the ground and unvisited for long stretches at a time. When I found it, fear shook its way up through my legs until I was able to move away only in stiff, tiny increments.

I am not sure what inspires my morbid curiosity about athletes once they are gone, but there are a fair number who continue to stick in my mind year after year, in part because I never considered any possibility for them other than alive and athletic. I actually witnessed one former athlete who died doing what he loved best. Sitting in the stands at Farrell Stadium, I saw West Chester State College's football coach, Jim Bonder, die in 1965 on the sidelines in the midst of a victory over Millersville, bring- ing an end to an all-too-brief 39–9 career. I never visited his grave, but I have visited some of those listed here, hoping that there might be a clue

there to unlock the mystery of my continuing absorption. I haven't found
anything specific yet, but that notwithstanding, herewith is a collection
of those whose passing meant something to me.

With reference and gratitude to Housman's famous poem, this is to an
athlete dying …

As a "King of a Man"

At first it was always "BuzzyandMonk," one name for two cousins who
lived next door to one another just in front of their family-owned auto
salvage yard—inseparable; as one. Actually, they shared the same first
name: both were Tom. Other than a few teachers, however, everyone used
their nicknames. In fact, in the baseball team photo in their senior year,
seated next to one another, they are identified as M. Howard and B. Shank.
In later years it occasionally became Buzz, Monk, and Ira. At one point in
the late nineties it became Buzz and Ira; following Ira's death in 2001 it
was again Buzz … and … Monk, now with a degree of separation. Now
there is just Monk. I attended the memorial service for Buzz last week, a
sad and mystifying occasion if ever there was one.

I met Buzz Shank when we were both 60-pound Little Leaguers. I was
wary of him at first because my father identified his one-armed father,
Buzz Shank Sr., as one of the toughest SOBs alive. A crane in the salvage
yard had severed his arm near the shoulder. As local lore had it, Buzz Sr.,
holding the dangling limb, drove himself to the hospital, patiently waited
his turn in the emergency room, then had the arm amputated. Before he
died decades later, he also lost both his legs to blood clots.

Though "Little Buzz" would also turn out to be one of the toughest
SOBs alive, I quickly learned that I did not have to fear him. Indeed, as
Buzz grew to be a 200-pound halfback and star third baseman while I
remained small, I felt bigger by virtue of being his friend. When you weigh
ninety pounds in high school, one of the things you learn is to stay out
of trouble. It was an impossibility if you were one of Buzz's friends. He
was smart, kind, tough as nails, loyal, tender-hearted—and devoted to fun.
Because of Buzz, I thought I might never pass algebra and graduate. First
in ninth grade, when we joked our way through six marking periods that
ended with a final grade of F and six weeks of remedial summer school

for both of us, and then again in eleventh grade, when I made the mistake of sitting behind him in Algebra II, Buzz put quadratic equations at the bottom of his class-time priorities. When he discovered R&B that year, he would turn in his seat and serenade me with full-throated versions of songs like "Devil With the Blue Dress," oblivious to the teacher standing over him with grim face and crossed arms. Once alerted, he would smile at her and all would be set right. Even when he and Monk were tossing me naked into the hallway from the locker room, he never seemed a bully; quite the opposite, his attentions made me feel part of things. He was never confrontational, and his troubles nearly always ended in laughter.

He was the rare athlete who lifted weights back then, and that and the work in the yard made him solid. In our junior year, he was the third baseman for the state's best high school team and for the town's crack American Legion team. He was a starting halfback on the football team. Everyone in town knew Buzz and, because he was handsome and witty as well as athletic, girls by the score had crushes on him. At home, he used to read the dictionary, always looking for new words, and in later years he used to fill me in on the details of whatever program he'd just seen on the History Channel. In short, his future looked bright. Following graduation, I went off to college in Ohio and Buzz went to play football for the University of Delaware. When I came home for my first summer visit, however, I learned that Buzz was back in West Chester for good. He'd dropped out of Delaware and begun full time work at the family auto parts business, and Monk had gone off to serve the first of two tours in Vietnam.

When I finished college and returned to West Chester, I spent hours of good times with Buzz: drinking from a keg after he finished work, visiting strip joints in Jersey after Flyers games (where, in a stunning twist that was too cruel for me to even acknowledge at the time, the strippers would actually try to pick up Buzz), and playing tennis with him and Ira Nesbitt, Buzz's best friend apart from Monk. Buzz also played street hockey regularly with a group of jocks, and he played adult baseball in a very good town league. I filled in one night at second base on his team. After a base on balls, I drew a pickoff throw that got ten feet away from the first baseman. I took off for second and was thrown out by approximately forty feet. Buzz came over to me and shook his head in disbelief, then laughed and trotted out to third. On many fall nights in high school,

Buzz and Monk played full-court basketball at an elementary school with eight-foot baskets. Buzz and Ira also bought oversized boxing gloves and fought bouts in Ira's basement, hilarious affairs that never tempted me to do anything other than watch. In short, Buzz was always playing.

Once I moved to Baltimore in the early eighties, I saw Buzz about once a year; he was always in good cheer. Shortly before we turned fifty, Ira was diagnosed with colon cancer. He lost a leg to postsurgical infection. Obviously, the boxing and tennis matches stopped. While Buzz was still as witty as ever, particularly with Ira, something was changing. When we drove down to the University of Pennsylvania Hospital to see Ira, Buzz became reflective and revealing. I learned that he'd gotten himself into trouble at the University of Delaware, bringing his career and college days to an end. He developed a nervous tic in one eye that embarrassed him to the point of social withdrawal. On one drive to Philadelphia, the strangest thing happened—Buzz, the boy who'd grown up maneuvering cars through the auto yard with all variety of speed and derring-do, could not back his SUV into an on-street parking space. He put the car in park, got out, and asked me to please do it for him.

In the final year of Ira's life, Buzz was as loving and dedicated as any friend I ever saw; he'd drive sixty round-trip miles three and sometimes four days a week to sit and talk with Ira. Most often, they insulted each other the way that jocks do, each former misstep by the other being cause to retell it, reshape it here and there, and relive it one more time for laughs. When Monk and Jimmy MacFadden joined the gatherings in Ira's dying days, the mood could be as raucous as a locker room before practice.

After Ira's passing, Buzz seemed undone. As content as he'd always been in athletic settings, he was suddenly discomfited around others. Without the locker room and the friends he'd known there, he seemed lost. I saw him only once in his final ten years, when I attended the funeral of "Big Buzz." Little Buzz sat wearing sunglasses to hide both tears and his tic. He could not read his farewell to his father and had his younger brother do it. I spoke to him briefly, but he did not seem to be aware of who I was. In fairness, I didn't really recognize him, either. From what I learned later, not long after a crowd of friends (including me) and relatives had filled a VFW hall for a surprise fiftieth birthday celebration for him, a new Buzz had begun to emerge. This one ventured into drugs and by necessity the life that supporting them entailed. I thought it was not in his nature, but as Cyril Connolly wrote in *The Unquiet Grave*, "The craving for the drug proceeds from the brain-cells which revolt and overrule the will." Weakness is in all of our natures.

In an eerie replay of his father's and Ira's ailments, Buzz lost his colon to cancer and then a leg—in three stages of amputation—up to his groin. Doctors were battling to save his other leg when he died at age sixty-three from sepsis. I drove up to his service on an overcast day, fearing there might be just a small assemblage of mourners. But the room was filled with people who loved Buzz and delivered heartfelt tributes to him. In the vestibule, photos of a young, athletic, engaging Buzz Shank filled two large boards. His cousin spoke, so for one last aching moment there was a final union of BuzzandMonk. Buzz's teenaged son, aware of all his dad's troubles—legal, medical, and emotional—called him "a king of a man." I was a bit surprised at that, but as I sat too choked with emotion to get up and speak, I thought about how deep the pain and sorrow must have burrowed, hollowing out bits of Buzz's soul for decades. I'm just guessing, of course, but I don't think I'd have ever lost him if he'd found a way to stay connected to the world of sports. It was the place where he felt no shame or fear; it was the place where he was competent and alive; it was the place that had kept his demons at bay. Even adrift, however, he remained a father beloved by his son and daughter, and I know that his son got it just right: Buzz was a king of a man—and one of the best men who ever called me friend.

Bewildered

When I was a boy, coveting the life of an athlete, there weren't any sports that did not present themselves to me as worthy of attention. Boxing was still big in the late fifties and early sixties, and I found the pageantry of the "sweet science," as revealed to me in the drama of Gillette's "Friday Night Fights," to be seductive. It made me think that there was something appealing about hitting and being hit in the head. My father, a former Marine, was not afraid to fight and did get me a pair of boxing gloves one Christmas, but he seemed to take pains to not encourage me too much in that direction. In fact, though he occasionally allowed me to watch the fights with him, when my brothers and I were left in the care of a babysitter, the program was off limits. So it was without permission that I turned on the TV set in March 1962 — the babysitter being occupied elsewhere — and watched an athletic contest in which Emile Griffith revealed the murderous rage in all of us and changed my view of boxing forever.

The night marked the third time that middleweights Griffith and Bennie "The Kid" Paret had fought and, as revealed recently in the documentary *Ring of Fire,* there were two things unknown to the public that would influence the fight. The first was that Paret, the onetime world champion, had taken an unusually heavy beating in his last bout but was being urged to get back in the ring again by a manager hoping to squeeze another good payday from him. The second thing was that Paret, at the weigh-in, had taunted Griffith with the whisper of *maricon,* the Spanish version of "faggot." Maybe if they had fought in the new millennium, when the stigma attaching to gay life does not course as strongly through the athletic community, Griffith would have ignored it or laughed it away. In the ultramanly environ of the fight scene fifty years ago, that was not possible. And so, as I watched it live, at age twelve, when Griffith found Paret with his upper body and head partially caught in the top rope, he felt no mercy. He hit the defenseless Paret over and over, his right hand, in the words of ringside observer Norman Mailer, pummeling Paret's head to produce a sound resembling that of a "baseball bat smashing a pumpkin." Paret finally slumped to the floor unconscious, and the cameras stayed with him as he was carried from the ring on a stretcher. He would live a few more days in a coma, but for all intents and purposes, he died on the canvas. In all likelihood, he was bewildered by the rage in Griffith; after all, playing head games at the weigh-in was just a part of the fight scene. It was never meant to inspire murder.

I can't say that I was so repulsed that I never watched boxing again. I was as mesmerized as the rest of my generation during Muhammad Ali's reign. But I also heard the verses of Bob Dylan's "Who Killed Davy Moore?" and wondered if the possibility of death inherent in every fight (nobody has a punch that renders a man unconscious but guarantees he will wake up again — you hit your opponent just as hard as you can) made boxing the ultimate sport, that is, one that entailed real rather than metaphorical death or a spectacle whose deadly ambitions disqualified it as a measuring stick for human excellence.

I do know that I never got in a fight again. Actually, I never fought much to begin with—mostly scrums with my brother and shoving contests in grade school—but I went out of my way afterward to stay away from conflict. For many years, I mistook this as fear and cowardice—the possibility that the same "half-smile of regret" that crossed Paret's face would freeze me long enough to die at someone's hands. There have been many times in the past several decades, however, when I have felt the same murderous rage that overtook Griffith and can almost feel my fists hammering relentlessly into another's bone and flesh, and so I can imagine the harm I'd cause if I let it go just once; perhaps, then, the effort of pinning it inside testifies to at least a bit of civil courage.

In the end, the killing changed three lives—that of Paret's widow; her son, Bennie Paret Jr.; and Emile Griffith, who was never the same fighter or man and who, until his death in July, 2013, lived with uncertainty about why it all happened as it did and what it all meant in a society that pays gladiators to risk their lives and their sanity in the names of sport and entertainment.

Young

Before the age of specialization, every town had one, though no other town in Chester County, Pennsylvania, had one like Bobby Owens. The son of a West Chester State College physical education professor, he was part of my consciousness since the first time I realized I loved sports—hell, he was a part of why I loved them. I was ten when Bobby was the twelve-year-old catcher for the East Side Little League All-Stars; his return throws to the mound were clothesline straight, flicked from a wrist cocked behind his right ear—just like I'd seen in how-to illustrations. Every two or three pitches, he'd walk part way to the mound, giving the pitcher alternate doses of hell and encouragement (a practice he would continue into high school, where he badgered Jon Matlack, a first-round draft choice and eventual All-Star game MVP with the Mets).

First in junior high school, then in high school, Owens was the starting quarterback, the starting catcher, and the starting point guard on winning, sometimes great, teams. He was seldom the most athletic player on the field, but he was always the most dominant and indomitable. He could have been West Chester's Chip Hilton, except that he was two steps past Hilton in cockiness. Though I was on high school teams that brought me into occasional contact with him, and though he knew my father—a local umpire—well, he had no idea that I was alive. I did not take it personally; we were all beneath him. I was likely lucky that he took no notice of me, because he could at times be coarse, immature, and brutish to those less gifted. I've never again seen anyone whose swagger seemed no cause for smirks or jokes; it was as natural and unaffected as his talent.

As the late sixties conferred on young men the right to grow their hair as long as women, Bobby kept faith in his blond butch cut, always as square and perfect as that of Johnny Unitas. He was the acknowledged on-field leader in every season, and his unremitting need to be better than everyone else never took a break. A personal circumstance caused him to miss a few days of opening practice in his senior year of football. The coach, determined to treat the situation fairly, made Owens a fifth-team halfback. He responded by hitting everyone on the field so hard for two days that Buzz and Monk finally went to the coach and begged him to move Owens into his rightful starting position before he disabled them all.

He graduated in 1966 and was drafted by the Chicago Cubs in the third round. He immediately scorched his Rookie League opponents for a .331 average at Treasure Valley. In West Chester, we all believed it just a matter of time before Owens was with the big league club. But he hurt his shoulder, and during his next three minor-league seasons he failed to hit above .231. I don't know what kind of dreams he'd been nursing for twenty years, but just like that they were gone. Bobby Owens returned to West Chester and funneled his enormous competitive spirit into coaching and refereeing. They obviously weren't enough because the unspent energy also went into chain-smoking cigarettes.

The entire town was shocked when Owens, while officiating a basketball game, dropped dead in 1987 at the age of thirty-eight. The cause of death was a heart attack—what else could it have possibly been? He was little other than heart. The times had changed the town considerably since his high school days. Reverence for the character and feats of small-town legends had been crushed by the onslaught of money and television in the seventies, so while a generation of older citizens would remember him always, there was no swell of locals to bear his coffin through the streets as was the case with Housman's fallen star. Still, his alma mater, Henderson High, now plays its games at Bob Owens Memorial Field, and in 2012 he was finally inducted into the Chester County Sports Hall of Fame. At least until the last of my generation is extinguished, Bobby Owens will be West Chester's eternal boy—and a reminder of the eternal boy in all of us.

Overlooked

When ESPN compiled its list of the fifty greatest NBA players of the twentieth century, Pete Maravich came in at number 48, so how does that qualify as overlooked? Because, as new stars like LeBron James create a larger firmament of athlete-entertainers, Maravich will begin to slide down the list and beyond the anemic, ahistoric memories of the younger generations. Already he is being cited as much for his period of Christian redemption and his early death at age forty as he is for his matchless skills. This does him a disservice because Pete Maravich was both unselfconsciously ornate and deadly effective. Dedication to fundamentals came at a young age from his father's insistence and his desire to please the old man. But somewhere along the line the dedication expanded to include the most innovative and mind-boggling flamboyance ever seen in the game. Magic Johnson credits Maravich with opening up to him a whole new world of possible ways to get the ball into the hands of teammates.

If you were old school when Maravich was averaging 44.2 points and 5.1 assists at LSU from 1966 to 1970 (he is still the all-time Division I scoring leader, and in his first freshman game he scored 50 points and handed out 11 assists), and then 24.2 points and 5.4 assists with the Atlanta Hawks, New Orleans Jazz, and Boston Celtics from 1970 to 1980, it was a struggle to applaud him, just as it had been hard to embrace Namath over Unitas. All you could see was the showmanship—from the long, floppy haircut to the look that betrayed any possibility that Pistol Pete was trying hard—"look like you care, damn it." Still, there was something that just kept drawing me in, a quality that remained elusive until recent years when I found myself watching and rewatching the many Internet highlight clips posted of Maravich. True, these are highlights, so the many times he failed trying to do the impossible didn't make the cut, but what I see in every underhanded seventy-five-foot pass that falls into the hands of a teammate at full speed, every pass bounced between the legs of an opponent and into the hands of an unsuspecting big man, is the determination that this move, this surprise will result in points. Pete Maravich was not playing to look good; he was playing to win while finding ways to do it that looked like wretched excess but in fact was merely excellence. He had a thousand ways to score—and, since he was a good shooter from long range, his per-game stats would be off the charts had he played during the era of three-point shots. He was Cousy with the inventiveness factor raised several degrees, and he was Magic without the benefit of title rings. He was all that basketball ought to be.

Unforgiven

Rick Sanders was the Pete Maravich of the amateur wrestling world—amateur by necessity, because people do not part with money to watch real wrestlers—only those who engage in the theater of pro "rasslin." And only in the conservative world of real wrestling could a two-time Olympic silver medalist who changed the sport forever be regarded as an outcast.

I first became aware of Sanders in my junior year of high school wrestling when I saw him peering from the cover of the *NCAA Wrestling Guide*. He was at that time a 123-pound whirlwind, but he looked like a choirboy in tights, meaning he was someone who both puzzled and ultimately misled me. Most of the 95-pounders I was wrestling seemed to me to have the visages of old men perched atop the shortened and gnarly bodies of munchkins. But Sanders was elfin, like I imagined myself to be. More important, he was a terror on the mat, like I imagined maybe I could be if I could learn his secrets. He'd lost the first match of his college career at Portland State, then run off 103 consecutive victories before losing the last match, the finals of the NCAA national championship. Eventually, he won national AAU titles, the first world championship ever won by an American, and silver medals in both 1968 and 1972. He did it with the same flair and eye for results that Maravich had.

Sanders learned to put himself into precarious positions, seemingly for the thrill of seeing how to escape them. He concocted imaginative, unprovable theories. By the time he hit Munich in 1972 for his second Olympics, he'd become one of a kind and all that wrestling was ordinarily not—creative, entertaining . . . and fun, a trait that put him in disfavor with the sport's traditionalists. He sealed his fate among the cognoscenti when he became the only elite hippie athlete in American history, growing long hair and a beard, partaking in marijuana, LSD, and peyote. While he was living life in concert with the surging fun crusades of the counterculture, he was winning big and making it look deceptively easy. But wrestling is not an easy sport, and to those in charge, daring to make it look so was a cardinal sin. In my case, it made me think that I had the right ingredients for success—I, too, was interested in flair, trickery, and fun. Of course, beyond what we all could see was a Sanders driven by the need for victory and a hidden dedication beyond that of nearly everyone else. He may have been having fun, but he was also paying for it.

A few weeks after the Munich games ended, while touring Europe, Sanders died in an accident in Yugoslavia. He was carrying seven dollars, his silver medal, parts of his Olympic uniform, and a pocket chess set. I wrote a long profile of him for *Amateur Wrestling News*, and the research took me to Portland, Oregon, where his stepbrother gave me some of the hand-carved wooden beads and an unfinished hash pipe that Sanders strung into a necklace that he wore at the Munich Olympics, removing them only long enough to wrestle. It took weeks to get his body returned to Eagle Creek, Oregon, and none of his Olympic teammates attended his funeral. Even in his hometown of Portland he remains unforgiven by some for daring to be what he wanted to be. Wrestling has never produced another one like him—the sport's just desserts for remaining so narrow-minded.

Beloved

Richie Ashburn was synonymous with "Phillies" when I began following baseball in the fifties. Actually, Robin Roberts, Curt Simmons, and Harry Anderson (because he was from West Chester State) also conjured images of the team for me, but only Ashburn fully encompassed what I thought baseball was at its best. Roberts and Simmons, after all, were pitchers— the most restricted of sport specialists back then, and Anderson was gone after a few seasons. Ashburn played every day, routinely chasing down fly balls in Connie Mack Stadium's cavernous centerfield, where the wall, after being shortened up, was still 447 feet from home plate. He led off, which meant he came to the plate more than anyone else. He was fast, making him the only Phillie of the fifties that I regarded as a base-stealer and a threat to hit a triple. He lacked power, and boy, did I ever identify with that. He got on base by virtue of bunts, slap hits, walks, and balls slashed into the alleys. His ability to foul off pitches was renowned. In fact, one of the unlikeliest baseball stories of all time happened on August 17, 1957, when Ashburn lined a foul ball into the stands of Connie Mack Stadium, hitting a woman and knocking her out. Medical help arrived and put her on a stretcher. As they carried her from the ballpark, Ashburn lined another foul that hit her unconscious body on the stretcher. The best part—and what would be a real stretch for today's athlete—was that Ashburn went to visit her in the hospital that night. The two became friends and exchanged Christmas cards annually until her death.

Eventually Ashburn's play—lifetime .308 batting average, 2,574 hits, two batting titles, and seven of the top ten putout seasons ever by an outfielder—put him in the Hall of Fame. But to any Phillie fan born between 1955 and 1990, "Whitey" Ashburn was not the fiery-tempered star, but the laid back radio and television voice who, when paired with Harry Kalas, formed the warmest and most beloved broadcast team ever. In August 1997, I attended a game at Veterans Stadium in a seat behind home plate. During the seventh inning stretch, along with everybody else in the park, I turned to watch Ashburn leaning out of the booth and waving to the adoring crowd. A month later, Philadelphia got the shocking news that Ashburn had died of a heart attack at age seventy. He still seemed boyish, and the city gave him a hero's farewell. Eventually he got a statue as well, and the stadium's centerfield concourse is known as "Ashburn Alley."

Fulfilled

As a boy, there was a time when I stopped reading anything that didn't have to do with sports. I read Ted Williams's *My Turn at Bat*; *Bob Cousy: Magician of Pro Basketball*; *Heroes of Sport*; and *The Quality of Courage*, ostensibly written by Mickey Mantle. I thought Joe Garagiola's *Baseball Is a Funny Game* was the finest example of literature ever created—something that could hold its own against Huck Finn or Moby Dick. Then, in

1963, I bought a paperback copy of *Veeck as in Wreck* for the cover price of twenty-five cents. Not only could it actually hold its own with the great books of the time, it introduced me to the most fascinating man in the history of team ownership. Bill Veeck not only presided over pennant-winning teams and record-setting crowds as steward of the Cleveland Indians, St. Louis Browns, and Chicago White Sox (twice), he infamously sent a midget to bat (I once saw Eddie Gaedel's number "1/8" jersey on display at the Smithsonian), planted the ivy in Wrigley Field, concocted the fireworks-launching scoreboard at old Comiskey Park, pioneered the art of giveaways, and held the respect of nearly all of his players and managers. Years before Branch Rickey and Jackie Robinson integrated the game, Veeck had taken preliminary steps toward buying the Phillies with the thought of stocking it with players from the Negro Leagues.

Furthermore, he read books by the bushel while soaking the stump of a leg amputated after a World War II artillery mishap, thereby encouraging me to broaden my own reading list and legitimizing the acquisition of knowledge for its own sake. He became my only off-the-field sports hero, not only because he was intelligent, articulate, innovative, and contentious. I valued most the fact that he obviously saw involvement with sports as a great way to spend a life. No matter the unavoidable unpleasantries of business necessary to remain there, Veeck recognized that a life in baseball was important, fulfilling, and fun.

In the seventies, during his second go-round as owner of the White Sox, I sent him my copy of *Veeck as in Wreck*. I had read it so many times that the covers had dropped off. I wrapped the whole bundle with rubber bands and sent it off to Comiskey Park, requesting his signature. Maybe, I thought, he'll take pity and send a new copy. A week later I had my bundle back, complete with a warm inscription. I'm glad he didn't replace it—the worn copy is a reminder of the time I spent as a kid internalizing the philosophy of what Chicago sportswriter William Gleason called "one of the great jolly men who ever walked the earth."

At Odds

Mickey Mantle's image was on the baseball card that every kid wanted—except me. Because he was a Yankee, and my collection consisted primarily of Phillies—down to fourth and fifth replicates—I traded the only Mantle I ever found in a bubblegum pack for a Johnny Callison, even up. I don't think I even bothered to ask for another throw-in. The Phillies' right-fielder in the mid-sixties, to my young and biased mind, had the same assets as Mantle—power, speed, a throwing arm to match that of Clemente from the right field corner, the boyish good looks. Of course, I was deluding myself, because with the possible exception of Babe Ruth and Willie Mays, I don't think anyone ever had as many gifts as Mantle. What Mantle and Callison actually shared was puzzlement: from their moments of entry into the big leagues right up until their deaths. What puzzled them was the place of baseball in American society and everything that went along with it: the adoration and hatred of fans, the capricious interests and opinions of the press, the tag of "role model" that held them accountable to kids they'd never meet, and the notion that they were being paid to do what millions of Americans said they would do for free.

During his playing days Mantle handled it all horribly on most days. He disdained the unwelcome stardom, despised the press, and actually had to take a rankling pay cut from the Yankees one year when he'd fallen slightly short of his Triple Crown numbers. Only among rambunctious teammates, particularly while drinking, was he accommodating and fun to be around. He was always aware of his "hero" status, and the fact that he did not embrace all of its baggage led me for decades to think of him as ungrateful. When liver cancer brought him in the final years of his life to contrition and determination to undo some of the damage his boorishness had wrought, he became lionized one more time as the epitome of what an athlete was supposed to be.

While any personal fence-mending he did was fine by me, the attention on his private life led the public away from what remains his most outstanding accomplishment: that he played for nearly two decades on a crippled knee, anchoring Yankee teams that were the envy of both leagues. He was one of the greatest performers in the history of American sports, and that simple fact was what had brought him the worship of so many kids. They didn't want to act like Mickey Mantle—scarcely any of them had an iota of what went on in his off-field escapades; they just wanted to play like Mickey Mantle. Maybe someone should have pointed that out to him and saved him from a half century of unnecessary bitterness.

For many years after his career ended, Callison was bitter for the opposite reason. He didn't understand why he hadn't been judged a bigger star, why he never played for a winner, why in retirement he had to tend bar and sell cars to make ends meet (particularly in the years following free agency, when even ballplayers who were merely competent became millionaires). For years he lived in the suburbs north of Philadelphia. I was tempted several times to drive up and talk to him. I was dissuaded by the rumors of his unhappiness. If it would have been unseemly to approach him as a kid or as a teen, it seemed ridiculous to think he'd be anything short of contemptuous at the fawning of an adult. But Callison was the athlete I'd grown up wanting to be: a strong hitter, great right-fielder, excellent base runner. So what was it I wanted to see in the flesh? I'm not really sure, but I think I was curious to see what physical grace became once it left the field of play—in short, though I didn't think it consciously at the time, I wanted to see how a dying athlete looked. Eventually, Callison surrendered to cancer, and I learned that he was not nearly as unapproachable and angry as I'd been led to believe. He made no public proclamations, so he didn't get Mantle's redemptive public affection, but I'd like to think he made peace with the fact that, acclaimed by outsiders or not, he'd gotten a chance to pursue his talents in a measurable and glorious form, something that eludes millions of men all of their lives.

Too Full of Thoughts

I know that this list is a politically challenged selection of white men, but we are the products of our times and our upbringing. These are the people I identified with. And, speaking of that, who's had a bigger impact on me than me? That question is part of the problem I always had in sports. When the one great scorer comes to write against my name, I don't know what the hell he'll write other than "that Dave Zang sure did spend way too much time thinking about sports. Too bad he didn't get it all figured out when it could have done him some good."

Of course, I am the only one on this list who's not dead yet, but I'm getting there more quickly than I'd like. Each year makes it tougher for me to find play outlets that my body finds acceptable. In my mid-thirties, with two months' training, I ran the Marine Corps marathon. That should have cured me of my running affliction, but in my forties, I took up track and field and, despite having a physique ill-suited to it, made the decathlon my event. I finished second in the nation and third in the world in my age group. Aside from the pole vault, where I was limited to ten-foot heights by my fear of bending a fiberglass pole and turning upside down in mid-air, the events gave me new things to work at—and revel in. I retired when my body began to break down regularly (the jumping and landing events—particularly the high hurdles—brought me an artificial hip later on), and so I next learned how to row. I found the sport satisfying but the inhabitants of the Baltimore boathouse insufferable. In nearly every instance, they were people who'd never found their way onto a team bus, but now that they'd fallen across something they could do without fear of being cut or actually having to be good at (almost all of them rowed and practiced daily, but hardly any of them actually competed), they became snobs, scolding one's technique at carrying the shell to the dock, washing it down after a row, and a myriad other inconsequential details.

Throughout my forties and fifties I became a good badminton player, something not easily pursued in the United States, where the sport's reputation as a backyard patty-cake game makes good partners and facilities hard to find (not true elsewhere: badminton is one of the largest spectator sports in the world). I had the good fortune of teaching the sport at a university. Since I rarely encountered a student who had played before, I had little trouble with their constant challenges. During one semester, however, I kept hearing that Patrick Murphy, a physical education major, was seeking a showdown. One day, Patrick appeared after class. He was carrying a bag with eight three-hundred-dollar rackets in it. We began a game. A half hour later, I had not scored a single point. "You're really good," I said to him. "Were you ever ranked?" "Yes," he said, "I was ranked."

"Well, what were you ranked?"

"One," he said. "I was the U.S. hopeful for the Barcelona Olympics until I blew my knee out playing ice hockey."

From that point forward, Patrick began giving me lessons, drilling me on footwork (badminton players at the highest levels don't hit backhands—their footwork is precise enough to hit forehands from everywhere and still get back to center court), strategy, and the futility of hitting too many slams. But Patrick graduated and took with him my prospects for continuing to get better.

So, I'm running out of options. I refuse to enter the Senior Olympics, where there are entrants who have never tried an event before (I once endured a high jump competition that went for nearly seven hours, during which I jumped only four times because inexperienced men in their seventies took turns straddling a bar that began at 2' and two hours later had crawled its way up to 2'8"). I do not want to play senior baseball. I've watched games in that classification that more closely resembled slow-pitch softball than baseball. Don't get me started on slow-pitch softball; my complaints are too numerous and cranky to merit an airing. At the moment, I'm left with golf—the monkey island of sports inasmuch as too many of its participants seem to have little understanding—and absolutely no humor—about how they look to the outside observer. I enjoy it, but it's not quite the same as something requiring a broader mix of strength, flexibility, coordination, and endurance.

The less I play, the more I think about playing. I think I've figured out a lot about why we play and why we ought to play more, but maybe I too am simply wishing not to believe that I've lived a foolish life and so have begun clinging ever more feverishly to reasoning that seems irrefutable to me but merely zealous to others. I am increasingly aware that students have begun to regard me as something of an evangelist for qualities of sport that have little connection to their own associations. Well, too bad.

So, now that I'm done with this—a decades-long turn at thinking about and dissecting sport—I'm ready to return to the most elemental foundations of my first love. I'm playing catch again, determined if I'm ever asked to throw out a first pitch not to look like the decrepit fifty-somethings I see short-arming it in major league ballparks. And I'm shooting baskets again, because nothing is quite as pure as the nothing-but-net arc of a soft jumper. Who knows, I might even try a season of senior baseball just so that I can steal home one more time. I may be alone in thinking that sports are the greatest thing humans have ever had going for them, but that's my story and I'm sticking to it—even if it kills me.

NOTES

p. 2   "I'd like to borrow his body": Jim Murray, quoted in Robert Lipsyte, *SportsWorld: An American Dreamland* (New York: Quadrangle, 1975), p. 252.

p. 3   "too many conflicting emotional interests": William Maxwell, *So Long, See You Tomorrow* (New York: Vintage Books, 1980), p. 27.

p. 4   "all humans are out of their fucking minds": Albert Ellis, quoted by Adam Green, "Ageless, Guiltless," *New Yorker* (October 13, 2003).

p. 5   "that the act of writing allows": Don DeLillo, *Falling Man* (New York: Scribner, 2007), p. 30.

p. 17   "tissue of lies": John Updike, misquoted in Julie McCarthy, "Harry Crews on Writing," http://www.juliemcarthur.com/2014/07/harry-crews-on-writing.html; see Updike's original quote in http://www.nationalbook.org/nbaacceptspeech_jupdike.html#.VGDsp_nF_LM.

p. 72   "I had a moment of mixed joy and anguish": Roger Bannister, *The Four-Minute Mile* (New York: Lyons & Burford, 1955), pp. 213–14.

p. 76   "I looked it up once": Jackie Robinson's August 2, 1944, testimony in *The United States v. 2nd Lieutenant Jack R. Robinson, 0-10315861, Cavalry, Company C, 758th Tank Battalion*.

p. 78   "Starting to the plate in the first inning": Jackie Robinson, *I Never Had It Made*, pp. 71–72, as cited in Arnold Rampersad, *Jackie Robinson: A Biography* (New York: Knopf, 1997), p. 172.

p. 78   "Chapman mentioned everything from thick lips": Harold Parrott, *The Lords of Baseball* (New York: Taylor Trade Publishing), p. 194, quoted in Jules Tygiel, *Baseball's Great Experiment* (New York: Oxford Trade Books, 1938), p. 182.

p. 78   "stride over to that Phillies dugout": Robinson, *I Never Had It Made*, p. 184.

p. 79   "It is unthinkable that American Negroes would go to war": Paul Robeson, quoted in the *New York Times*, April 21, 1949, as cited in Rampersad, *Jackie Robinson*, p. 211.

p. 79   "I have grown wiser and closer to the painful truth": Robinson, *I Never Had It Made*, p. 24.

p. 80   "Malcolm has big audiences": Jackie Robinson, *New York Herald Tribune*, April 26, 1964, quoted in Rampersad, *Jackie Robinson*, p. 389.

p. 80   "I was surprised . . . by their indifference": Dick Young, Transcript of ceremony, Oct. 15, 1972, quoted in Rampersad, *Jackie Robinson*, p. 459.

p. 80   "Are ideals attainable?": Herman Hesse, *Steppenwolf* (New York: Holt, Rhinehart, and Winston, 1963), p. 118.

p. 80   "The word for Jackie Robinson is 'unconquerable'": Red Smith, *New York Times*, Oct. 25, 1972, quoted in Rampersad, *Jackie Robinson*, p. 460.

p. 81   "There was a time I deeply believed in America": Robinson, *I Never Had It Made*, p. 242, quoted in Tygiel, *Baseball's Great Experiment*, p. 340.

p. 91   "the Greeks were the first intellectualists": Edith Hamilton, *The Greek Way* (New York: W.W. Norton, 1942), p. 20.

p. 91   "the Greeks were the first people in the the world": Hamilton, *The Greek Way*, pp. 30–31.

p. 108   "little darkey": Cap Anson, *A Ball Player's Career* (Chicago: Era, 1900).

p. 114   "then some tiny fleck of it is attached to you": Heywood Hale Broun, in *Fields of Fire: Sports in the 60's* (New York: HBO Home Video, 1995).

p. 115   "people, places, and events far removed from ourselves": Devin McKinney, *Magic Circles: The Beatles in Dream and History* (Cambridge, MA: Harvard University Press, 2003), p. 24.

p. 119   "change your sense of time": Alexander Stille, *The Future of the Past* (New York: Picador, 2002), p. ix.

p. 124   "My reliance is in the help of God": Robert E. Lee, *Personal Reminiscences of General Robert E. Lee*, compiled by Rev. J. William Jones (1875; reprint, New York: Macmillan, 2004), p. 30.

p. 136   "the 'Varsity Syndrome'": Robert Lipsyte, "The Manly Art of Self-Delusion," *New York Times* (August 4, 1991).

p. 137   "it's been an unfortunate, embarrassing incident": Claude Moore, quoted in *Florence (South Carolina) Morning News*, November 21, 1961.

p. 137   "The gentleman . . . cannot only forgive": Robert E. Lee, *Personal Reminiscences*, p. 148.

p. 143   "one can jog or run with others": A. Bartlett Giamatti, *Take Time for Paradise: Americans and Their Games* (New York: Summit Books, 1989), p. 74.

p. 160   "you swung the final ninety miles": Stanley Woodward, quoted in Frank Fitzpatrick, *The Lion in Autumn: A Season with Joe Paterno and Penn State Football* (Penguin, 2005), p. 33.

p. 160   "It was a cemetery": Ibid.

p. 160   "He seemed single-handedly to be defending": Ibid., p. 93.

p. 161   "What really matters is reaching a level of internal excellence": Joe Paterno, quoted in Daniel Nathan, ed., *Rooting for the Home Team* (Urbana-Champaign: University of Illinois Press, 2013), p. 161.

p. 161   "Even though he is enormously successful": Bill Lyons, *Philadelphia Inquirer*, quoted in Nathan, *Rooting for the Home Team*, p. 161.

p. 162   "suggests the fun and lightheartedness": J. Douglas Toma, *Football U.: Spectator Sports in the Life of the American University* (University of Michigan Press, 2003), p. 52

p. 166   "the greatest show in college sports": "Sports Illustrated on Campus" (October 27, 2005), quoted in "Penn State football weekend tabbed 'Greatest Show in College Sports,'" Penn State News website, http://news.psu.edu/story/207434/2005/10/28/penn-state-football-weekend-tabbed-greatest-show-college-sports.

p. 176   "denigrate the *liking* of music": Ned Rorem, "The Music of the Beatles," *New York Review of Books*, January 18, 1968.

p. 176   "The runner does not know": Bannister, *The Four-Minute Mile*, p. 229.

p. 179   "bloody years of the Revolution": Milan Kundera, *The Unbearable Lightness of Being* (New York: Harper Perennial, 1999), p.4.

p. 180   "no more pretty than an axhead": John Irving, "Gorgeous Dan," *Esquire* 79 (April 1973): p. 109.

p. 180   "A couple of times . . . I was so exhausted": Dan Gable, quoted in Nolan Zavoral, *A Season on the Mat: Dan Gable and the Pursuit of Perfection* (Simon and Schuster, 2003), p. 10.

p. 181   "row[ing] stroke on a slave galley": Leo Davis, *Portland Oregonian*, 1972, quoted in David Zang, *SportsWars: Athletes in the Age of Aquarius* (Fayetteville: University of Arkansas Press, 2001) p. 27.

p. 186   "Sometimes men speak of desiring something": Paul Weiss, *Sport: A Philosophic Inquiry* (Southern Illinois University Press, 1969), p. 60.

p. 187   "The world needs models": Richard Bach, *The Bridge Across Forever* (New York: William Morrow, 1984), p. 87.

p. 192   "It's a working class park": Mike Flanagan, quoted in Tim Kurkjian, "A Splendid Nest," *Sports Illustrated* (April 13, 1992), p. 44.

p. 202   "One day . . . the people gathered": John Edgar Wideman, "Father Stories," *New Yorker* (August 1, 1994), p. 36.

p. 205   "the underlying metaphysic of sports": Michael Novak, *The Joy of Sports: End Zones, Bases, Baskets, Balls, and the Consecration of the American Spirit* (New York: Basic Books, 1976), p. 47.

BIBLIOGRAPHY

Bee, Clair. *Fence Busters*. New York: Grossett and Dunlap, 1953.

———. *Hoop Crazy*. New York: Grossett and Dunlap, 1950.

———. *Ten Seconds to Play!* New York: Grossett and Dunlap, 1955.

———. *Tournament Crisis*. New York: Grossett and Dunlap, 1957.

Connolly, Cyril. *The Unquiet Grave*. New York: Persea Books, 1981.

Dawkins, Richard. *The God Delusion*. Boston: Houghton Mifflin, 2006.

Fitzgerald, Ed. *Heroes of Sport*. New York: Bartholomew House, 1960.

Fixx, James F. *The Complete Book of Running*. New York: Random House, 1977.

Garagiola, Joe. *Baseball Is a Funny Game*. Philadelphia: Lippincott, 1960.

Gelman, Steve. *Bob Cousy: Magician of Pro Basketball*. Sports Magazine Library 12. New York: Bartholomew House, 1961.

Hillenbrand, Laura. *Seabiscuit: An American Legend*. New York: Random House, 2001.

McDougall, Christopher. *Born to Run: A Hidden Tribe, Superathletes, and the Greatest Race the World Has Never Seen*. New York: Alfred A. Knopf, 2009.

Mantle, Mickey. *The Quality of Courage*. Garden City, N.Y.: Doubleday, 1964.

Mead, Rebecca. "A Man-Child in Lotusland." *New Yorker*, May 20, 2002.

Novak, Michael. *The Joy of Sports: End Zones, Bases, Baskets, Balls, and the Consecration of the American Spirit*. New York: Basic Books, 1976.

Oriard, Michael. *Dreaming of Heroes: American Sports Fiction, 1868–1980*. Chicago: Nelson-Hall, 1982.

Putnam, Robert D. *Bowling Alone: The Collapse and Revival of American Community*. New York: Simon and Schuster, 2000.

Rampersad, Arnold. *Jackie Robinson: A Biography*. New York: Knopf, 1997.

Roberts, Randy. *Joe Louis: Hard Times Man*. New Haven, Conn.: Yale University Press, 2010.

———. *Papa Jack: Jack Johnson and the Era of White Hopes*. New York: Free Press, 1983.

———. and James S. Olson. *Winning Is the Only Thing: Sports in America Since 1945*. Baltimore: Johns Hopkins University Press, 1989.

Slater, Philip. *The Pursuit of Loneliness: American Culture at the Breaking Point.* Boston: Beacon, 1970.

Stewart, Susan. *On Longing: Narratives of the Miniature, the Gigantic, the Souvenir, the Collection.* Baltimore: Johns Hopkins University Press, 1984.

Stille, Alexander. *The Future of the Past.* New York: Farrar, Straus and Giroux, 2002.

Tygiel, Jules. *Baseball's Great Experiment: Jackie Robinson and His Legacy.* New York: Oxford University Press, 1983.

Veeck, Bill, with Ed Linn. *Veeck as in Wreck.* New York: Putnam, 1962.

Will, George F. *Men at Work: The Craft of Baseball.* New York: Macmillan, 1990.

Williams, Ted, with John Underwood. *My Turn at Bat: The Story of My Life.* New York: Simon and Schuster, 1969.

Zang, David W. *Sports Wars: Athletes in the Age of Aquarius.* Fayetteville: University of Arkansas Press, 2001.

David W. Zang is a professor in the Department of Kinesiology at Towson University. He is the author of *Fleet Walker's Divided Heart: The Life of Baseball's First Black Major Leaguer* and *SportsWars: Athletes in the Age of Aquarius*.

SPORT AND SOCIETY

The University of Illinois Press
is a founding member of the
Association of American University Presses.

Designed by Dustin J. Hubbart
Composed in 10/14 PT Sans
with Hawksmoor display
by Kirsten Dennison
at the University of Illinois Press
Manufactured by Sheridan Books, Inc.

University of Illinois Press
1325 South Oak Street
Champaign, IL 61820-6903
www.press.uillinois.edu